☆

WHO SPEAKS
for AMERICA?

Who Speaks for America?

WHY DEMOCRACY MATTERS IN FOREIGN POLICY

Eric Alterman

CORNELL UNIVERSITY PRESS

ITHACA AND LONDON

First published 1998 by Cornell University Press

Printed in the United States of America

Library of Congress Cataloging-in-Publication Data

Alterman, Eric.
    Who speaks for America? : Why democracy matters in foreign policy
/ Eric Alterman.
      p. cm.
    Includes bibliographical references and index.
    ISBN 0-8014-3574-9 (cloth : alk. paper)
    1. United States—Foreign relations—Decision making. 2. United
States—Foreign relations—Public opinion. 3. United States—
Foreign relations—1989– . 4. Democracy—United States. 5. Public
opinion—United States. I. Title.
E183.7.A45 1998
327.73—dc21   98-30148

Cornell University Press strives to use environmentally responsible suppliers and materials to the fullest extent possible in the publishing of its books. Such materials include vegetable-based, low-VOC inks and acid-free papers that are recycled, totally chlorine-free, or partly composed of nonwood fibers.

Cloth printing   10 9 8 7 6 5 4 3 2 1

★

To Walter LaFeber and Bill Moyers

✶

CONTENTS

★

ACKNOWLEDGMENTS

All books are collective enterprises, this one perhaps more so than most. First I would like to thank my editors at *The Nation* and MSNBC for the opportunity to test-drive some of the ideas that appear here. In addition, I am deeply grateful for the wide-ranging help I received from the following individuals: John Moyers, Carol Bernstein Ferry, Eyal Press, Greg Silbert, Haleh Nazeri, Margaret Goud Collins, Patti Cohen, Kai Bird, Michael Kazin, Todd Gitlin, and Anders Stephanson. Diana Silver, the love of my life, was helpful in more ways than I care to explain here. The timely appearance on the planet of Eve Rose Alterman in April 1998 provided important incentive to finish up the book so as to attend to more important matters. Thanks to her, too.

The idea for the book was initially inspired by an essay on Thomas Jefferson's foreign policy authored by my undergraduate thesis advisor, Walter LaFeber. It was funded through the good offices of the World Policy Institute by the Florence and John Shumann foundation at the behest of its president, Bill Moyers. Both men have offered me invaluable assistance and inspiration as I struggled toward its completion. More importantly, both have also served as invaluable teachers to me, not only of American history but also of the nature of scholarship, commitment, and integrity. I dedicate this book to the example set by these two Christian rabbis—Walter LaFeber and Bill Moyers.

✭

As I recall, I was rung for late one night—it was past midnight—to the drawing room, where his lordship had been entertaining three gentlemen since dinner. I had, naturally, been called to the drawing room several times already that night to replenish refreshments, and had observed on these occasions the gentlemen deep in conversation over weighty issues. When I entered the drawing room on this last occasion, however, all the gentlemen stopped talking and looked at me. Then his lordship said:

"Step this way a moment, will you, Stevens? Mr. Spencer here wishes a word with you."

The gentleman in question went on gazing at me for a moment without changing the somewhat languid posture he had adopted in his armchair. Then he said:

"My good man, I have a question for you. We need your help on a certain matter we've been debating. Tell me, do you suppose the debt situation regarding America is a significant factor in the present low levels of trade? Or do you suppose this is a red herring and that the abandonment of the gold standard is at the root of the matter?"

I was naturally a little surprised by this, but then quickly saw the situation for what it was; that is to say, it was clearly expected that I be baffled by the question. Indeed, in the moment or so that it took for me to perceive this and compose a suitable response, I may even have given the outward impression of struggling with the question, for I saw all the gentlemen in the room exchange mirthful smiles.

"I'm very sorry, sir," I said, "but I am unable to be of assistance on this matter."

I was by this point well on top of the situation, but the gentlemen went on laughing covertly. Then Mr. Spencer said:

"Then perhaps you will help us on another matter. Would you say that the currency problem in Europe would be made better or worse if there were to be an arms agreement between the French and the Bolsheviks?"

"I'm very sorry, sir, but I am unable to be of assistance on this matter."

"Oh dear," said Mr. Spencer. "So you can't help us here either."

There was more suppressed laughter before his lordship said: "Very well, Stevens. That will be all."

"Please, Darlington, I have one more question to put to our good man here," Mr. Spencer said. "I very much wanted his help on the question presently vexing many of us, and which we all realize is crucial to how we should shape our foreign policy. My good fellow, please come to our assistance. What was M. Laval really intending, by his recent speech on the situation in North Africa? Are you also of the view that it was simply a ruse to scupper the nationalist fringe of his own domestic party?"

"I'm sorry, sir, but I am unable to assist in this matter."

"You see, gentlemen," Mr. Spencer said, turning to the others, "our good man is unable to assist us in these matters."

This brought fresh laughter, now barely suppressed.

"And yet," Mr. Spencer went on, "we still persist with the notion that this nation's decisions be left in the hands of our good man here and to the few million others like him. Is it any wonder, saddled as we are with our present parliamentary system, that we are unable to find any solution to our many difficulties? Why, you may as well ask a committee of the mothers' union to organize a war campaign."

There was open, hearty laughter at this remark, during which his lordship muttered: "Thank you, Stevens," thus enabling me to take my leave.

—Kazuo Ishiguro, *The Remains of the Day* (1989)

Foreign Policy for the Few

Here each individual is interested not only in his affairs but in the affairs of the state as well. . . . We do not say that a man who takes no interest in politics is a man who minds his own business; we say that he has no business at all.
—Pericles, as recorded by Thucydides in *The Peloponnesian War*

In the winter of 1998, the Clinton administration was preparing to launch an attack on Iraq in retaliation for Saddam Hussein's unwillingness to comply with the United Nations inspection regime. Support for the plan, however, appeared lukewarm in the extreme. Among our erstwhile allies, only England and Canada believed the military route to be the correct one. At home, the plan seemed to raise more questions than answers among the American people. Even Tom Clancy, the right-wing technothriller novelist—and about as reliable a supporter of all forms of military action as one is likely to find anywhere—complained in the *New York Times* that the president had failed to address the nation's most fundamental concerns: "Who has explained to the American people why it is necessary to send our sons and daughters into harm's way?" Clancy asked. "Who has prepared us and the world for the unpalatable consequences of even a successful attack? How likely is failure, and what would be the consequences?"[1]

In an attempt to quell such anxieties, as it simultaneously garnered support at home and demonstrated its resolve abroad, the administration contacted top executives at CNN and arranged for a worldwide broadcast of a national "town meeting" at Ohio State University. The administration sent Secretary of State Madeleine Albright, Secretary of Defense William Cohen, and National Security Advisor Samuel "Sandy"

Berger. As soon as the meeting began, the administration wished it hadn't. First came the loud protests of members of the Spartacist League, the Trotskyite splinter group. When they finally quieted down, an unending barrage of extremely tough and thoughtful questions demonstrated just how ill conceived was the plan for which the Clinton administration was seeking approval.

The problem was not, as administration officials later tried to claim, that the event was hampered by insufficient advance work or too large and unwieldy an audience. Rather, the top national security officials of the United States government were wholly unprepared to answer the kinds of questions with which Ohio citizens had armed themselves. Here are some of the questions asked by members of the audience on that cold February afternoon:

- The American administration has the might and the means to attack the Iraqi state, but does it have the moral right to attack the Iraqi nation? [Cheers, applause.]
- This administration has raised concerns about Iraq's threats to its neighbors, yet none of these neighbors seem too threatened. . . . Furthermore, the international community has been opposed to the bombings. If nobody's asking us for their help, how can you justify further U.S. aggression in the region? [Applause, shouts.]
- If push comes to shove and Saddam will not back down . . . or keep his word, are we ready and willing to send the troops in? [Cheers, applause.]
- President Carter . . . was quoted yesterday as saying that up to 100,000 innocent Iraqi civilians could be killed. Is that something, Secretary Albright, [Shouts, applause] that you think is a realistic possibility? Since we are unsure where Iraq's weapons are, how can we direct a bombing strike against them?
- Why bomb Iraq when other countries have committed similar violations? . . . For example, Turkey has bombed Kurdish citizens. Saudi Arabia has tortured political and religious dissidents. Why does the United States. apply different standards of justice to these countries? [Cheers, applause.][2]

Good questions, every one of them. And the audience at Ohio State asked many more that were equally piercing and intelligent. Yet the gathered administration officials thought such concerns had no merit and were irrelevant to the task at hand. To the viewer at home, it appeared as if the questioners and the government officials were speaking two different languages. In response to the questioner who raised the issue of the inconsistency of the application of U.S. human rights policies, for instance, the secretary of state lectured, "I suggest, sir, that you study carefully what American foreign policy is, what we have said exactly about the cases that you have mentioned. Every one of them have been pointed out. Every one of them we have clearly stated our policy on. And if you would like, as a former professor, I would be delighted to spend fifty minutes with you describing exactly what we are doing on those subjects." But she did not offer a single sentence in response to the question that might fairly be considered an answer.

One anonymous administration official tried to blame the CNN anchors for the public relations debacle, insisting that moderators "Judy [Woodruff] and Bernie [Shaw] looked like they were deer caught in the headlights, they had no control over the management of this."[3] But the true problem was an insurmountable clash of cultures. In the official meeting rooms and academic conferences, to say nothing of high-minded forums such as *Nightline* and *Newshour with Jim Lehrer*, foreign policy discussion is considered a matter for professionals only. When "the public" enters into the discussion, it is usually only in the context of a problem that needs to be managed or an inconvenience that must be finessed. Here was a public empowered by television cameras and a worldwide audience that would not defer and would not go away. The result was not only a genuine roadblock on the administration's road to war, but also a national demonstration of the distance between the governing and the governed when it comes to matters of foreign and military policy.

Speaking on *CBS Evening News*, Dan Rather called the meeting "unruly, disorganized and badly staged."[4] A conservative *Time* magazine essayist complained that the event had been "worthless as a means of preparing the country for war."[5] President Clinton tried to be more generous. He later referred to the Ohio State meeting as "a good old-fashioned American debate," but added, "I believe strongly that most Americans support our policy. They support our resolve."[6] Clinton rushed, however, to undo the damage by throwing his support behind a last-ditch diplomatic effort to avert war by United Nations secretary-general Kofi Annan. Annan succeeded, and this time, war was avoided. The larger lessons of Ohio State, however, remained unlearned. The administration promised better advance work next time but no institutionalized methods of consultation or even mutual education between itself and the public on foreign policy issues. The media, as is its wont, soon forgot about Ohio State and moved on to the next scandal du jour. The problem itself, went away—or so the foreign policy establishment and the media that covers it would like to believe.

The democratization of American foreign policy is a problem that worries precious few people. In the United States, frequently termed "the world's leading democracy" by pundits and politicians, foreign policy has been deliberately shielded from the effects of democratic debate, with virtually no institutionalized democratic participation.* True, we have elections. But elections occur too infrequently to have much of an impact on all but the highest-profile foreign policy decision, and in any case they rarely turn on foreign policy questions. Even in 1968, with an issue as central and divisive as Vietnam, the presidential candidates failed to offer the public a clear choice. During the Cold War, it may have been possible to argue that the survival of the nation itself depended upon the ability of our leaders to make immediate decisions regarding nuclear war. These effectively precluded the untidy mechanisms of the democratic process. Excluding a tiny percentage of decisions that deal with potential terrorist threats, that argument has passed into history along with the Soviet Union. Similarly, it may once have been possible to contend that many Americans were unaffected by most foreign policy decisions. But in an era where a decision to enter into a given trade accord with one nation can literally wipe out an entire industry or geographic community, where the failure to contain environmental destruction on one part of the globe can make life all but unbearable on another, where a new strain of *E. coli* bacteria found in Peruvian carrots can infect conventioneers in Minneapolis, and where tens of millions of Americans have their pension plans invested in global mutual funds, it is anachronistic to the point of willful blindness to argue that "foreign" policy exists apart and distinct from "domestic" policy. How,

---

*The word "democracy" is extremely imprecise. In the course of this book, I will use it as a synonym for the process that the political scientist Robert A. Dahl defines as "polyarchy." Dahl defines a polyarchal system as follows (I paraphrase): 1. The power to make policy decisions is vested in elected officials. 2. Officials are chosen in frequent, free, and fair elections. 3. Suffrage is extended to nearly all adults. 4. The right to run for office is extended to nearly all adults. 5. There is freedom of expression without danger of severe penalties. 6. Citizens can seek alternative sources of information, and such sources are protected by the government. 7. Citizens have the right to form independent associations such as political parties, interest groups, and so forth. See Robert A. Dahl, *Democracy and Its Critics* (New Haven: Yale University Press, 1989), p. 221.

then, can the United States claim to be a functioning democracy when one of the most crucial aspects of public policy allows for almost no democratic participation?

Yet the issue fails to engage. According to a 1997 poll, majorities ranging from 55 to 66 percent say that events in Mexico, Western Europe, Asia, and Canada had little or no impact on them.[7] They prefer to pay attention to those issues that do. Of the thousands of forcign policy monographs published in the past decade by various academics, mandarins, and aspiring secretaries of state, an extremely small percentage focus on the role that the public plays in determining—or even reacting to—those policies.[8] A far greater percentage of the foreign policy community in Washington and in academia is concerned with the problem of improving other nations' democratic practices than with examining the character of our own. The same is true of the specialist's publication *Journal of Democracy*, which has published just a handful of articles even remotely concerned with the United States internal policies. Within the larger populace, and even in the informed debate of the Washington punditocracy, the issue simply does not arise.

At this point the reader might ask if I am not begging an obvious question: Can foreign policy be democratic at all, particularly in a country where most people prefer to remain ignorant of the details of their own politics and culture, much less anyone else's? Indeed, the problem is hardly unique to our time and place. No democracy, it must be admitted at the outset, deals well with this problem; not France, not Germany, not England, not Japan. The conflict may be endemic to democracy itself. Alexis de Tocqueville observed long ago that in the conduct of foreign affairs, "democratic governments do appear decidedly inferior to others." Foreign policy, he lamented, requires none of the good qualities peculiar to democracy but demands the cultivation of those sorely lacking. Democracies found it "difficult to coordinate the details of a great undertaking and to fix on some plan and carry it through with determination" and had "little capacity for combining measures in secret and waiting patiently for the result."[9] The diplomatic historian Walter LaFeber calls this phenomenon "the Tocqueville problem in American history." How, LaFeber wonders, can a "democratic republic, whose vitality rests on the pursuit of individual interests with a minimum of central governmental direction, create the necessary national consensus for the conduct of an effective, and necessarily long-term, foreign policy?"[10]

The problem is real, but hardly insoluble. Much of the American public is indeed ignorant, but it is not stupid. Over time, Americans have demonstrated an impressive consistency of values in foreign policy, one that is easily obscured by the polling data that focuses on immediate reactions to various crises. The public's values, as I argue in the appendix, are a good deal closer to the liberal republican values of the country's original founders than are those of the establishment that professes to represent them. The problem is not that the public does not care. Rather, it has no idea how to force the government to respond to its preferences.

Even if the American people were as incompetent as the members of the foreign policy establishment believe they are, that would be an unacceptable argument for their exclusion from the policy-formation process. In a democracy, a majority of the people have a right to be wrong. "Democracy," insisted Sidney Verba, former president of the American Political Science Association, in a 1995 address to his membership, "implies responsiveness by governing elites to the needs and preferences of the citizenry. More than that, it implies equal responsiveness." The rule of political equality forms the foundational basis of the American political system. It is expressed by our belief in the principle of "one person, one vote."[11]

When Americans complain about the quality of our democracy, their focus is almost always close to home. Crime, drugs, taxes, and schools dominate the agenda while issues of electoral reform and "money politics" floated until recently in the background, most often raised by gadflies such as Ross Perot and Ralph Nader. Yet no nationally significant politician speaks of consulting the American people directly about the conduct of a foreign policy issue, and to my knowledge, no politically significant grassroots leader has put forth a plan to do so either. Despite all the populist anger at "elitist" Washington politicians and bureaucrats that has characterized American debate in recent decades, Americans remain meekly deferential when it comes to foreign policy. In a 1989 survey for the Carnegie Council on Ethics and International Affairs, the Wirthlin Group found that nearly 50 percent of those questioned disagreed with the statement that the "general public is qualified to participate in deciding on U.S. foreign policy."[12]

The U.S. foreign policy establishment, made up of government officials, congressional staffers, insider academics, think-tank partisans, and the lawyers and bankers who shuttle back and forth into these jobs with each change of administration, concur wholeheartedly with this portion of the public. When I first began this study, I approached the head of a prestigious liberal foreign policy think tank in Washington about housing it. "I don't really believe there should be any democracy in foreign policy," he told me. "The people don't know what the [expletive deleted] they want." When I returned to the same think tank to give a talk on the subject of this book to its interns, an extremely self-satisfied young man announced that he did not "see why people who don't know anything about foreign policy should have the same say in what happens as those of us who do."

To argue against the impingement of the democratic process on foreign policy, even in a democracy, is to invoke a long and distinguished political tradition. Both the argument reifying the wisdom of public opinion and the exclusion of matters foreign are products of the Enlightenment mainstream. Jeremy Bentham was the first thinker to propose what he called the value of the "Public Opinion Tribunal." His student James Mill elaborated this notion, insisting that "when various conclusions are, with their evidence, presented with equal care and with equal skill, there is a moral certainty, though some few may be misguided, that the greatest number will judge right, and that the greatest force of evidence, whatever it is, will produce the greatest impression."[13] Both John Locke and Jean-Jacques Rousseau, however, explicitly excluded foreign affairs from their respective litanies of a citizen's rights. "What matters principally to every citizen is the observance of the laws internally, the maintenance of private property, and the security of the individual," explained Rousseau. "As long as all goes well with regard to these three points, let the government negotiate and make treaties with foreign powers."[14] Even James Madison worried about democratic participation in foreign policy because so much could be easily "concealed or disclosed, or disclosed in such parts and at such times as will best suit particular views."[15]

The modern-day foreign policy establishment is less concerned with its own ability to conceal or disclose selectively than with the public's ability to muck up its work with inconvenient interference and ignorant objection. Walter Lippmann stated this concern most boldly in 1955. The "unhappy truth," he wrote, "is that the prevailing public has been destructively wrong at critical junctures. The people have imposed a veto upon the judgments of informed and responsible officials. They have compelled the governments, which usually knew what would have been wiser, or was necessary, or was more expedient, to be too late with too little, or too long with too much, too pacifist in peace and too bellicose in war, too neutralist or appeasing in negotiation or too intransigent."[16]

George F. Kennan, a Lippmann contemporary and among his only equals in terms of the grudging respect received from intellectual adversaries, came to a remarkably similar, even more baldly stated conclusion. Writing two decades after Lippmann, Kennan likened democracy to "one of those prehistoric monsters with a body as long as this room and a brain the size of a pin; he lies there in his primeval mud and pays little attention to his environment: he is slow to wrath—in fact, you practically have to whack his tail to make him aware that his interests are being disturbed; but once he grasps this, he lays about him with such blind determination that he not only destroys his adversary but largely wrecks his native habitat."[17] Kennan believes the American political system is "unsuited, really, to the conduct of foreign affairs of a great power."[18]

Such sentiments are hardly confined to establishment figures of the Lippmann/Kennan generation. Writing in 1972, Kennan's biographer, the estimable John Lewis Gaddis, ended his pathbreaking history of the origins of the Cold War by assigning the primary responsibility to the Communist side, because "the Russian dictator was immune from pressures of Congress, public opinion or the press." Stalin's "absolute powers" gave him "more chances to surmount the international restraints on his policy than were available to his democratic counterparts in the West."[19] In other words, democracy itself was to blame. This view is consistent with that expressed by Adam Ulam, former director of Harvard's Russian Research Center, who likens the interference of democracy in foreign policy to "powerful gusts of popular emotion rather than factual data about the international situation [that should] determine the main lines of American foreign policy."[20] Even former UN ambassador Donald McHenry, addressing the National Issues Convention in Austin, Texas, in January 1996 *on this very issue*, bemoaned the fact that "we have forced our presidents to make policy on what the American people will tolerate, not necessarily what should be done," as if what "should be done" is somehow objectively determinable, while the American people's desires are some sort of illegitimate interference in a process best left to professionals.[21]

To the degree that the makers of U.S. foreign policy recognize a role for the public in policy formation at all, it is usually that of the quietly attentive student. The responsibility of the president, for instance, according to former national security adviser Zbigniew Brzezinski, is not to act in accordance with the wishes of his voters but to "enlighten the public about global complexities and generate support for his policies."[22] That Americans may not wish for their government to invade a particular country should not affect a policymaker's decision-making process, according to former Bush administration official Richard N. Haass. "Interventions tend to rise and fall on their merits. Success will create support that may not have existed beforehand—Grenada and the protection of Gulf shipping are cases in point—while failure will drain any support that might have existed." Grenada, explains Haass, referring to the tiny nutmeg-producing island invaded by U.S. forces under President Reagan, "shows that a president who has the courage to lead will win public support if he acts wisely and effectively."[23] Some officials and former officials have gone so far as to argue that the president's powers to conduct foreign policy are akin to those of a general in the army. When Congress challenged George Bush's friendliness to the Chinese regime in the aftermath of the Tiananmen Square massacre, Secretary of State James Baker was sharply critical. "Leadership on this issue," he insisted, "should come from the president as commander-in-chief."[24] General Maxwell Taylor gave this view added (and ominous) power when he explained to a television journalist in 1971 that "a citizen should know those things he needs to be a good citizen and to discharge his functions."[25] Given what Taylor and his cohorts believed the American people "needed" to know about U.S. policy in Vietnam, his view would appear to contain within it the seeds of tragedy as well as deadly irony.

The elite foreign policy media views itself as very much a part of the policy-making establishment—witness the recent shuttling back and forth of such reporter/policymakers as Leslie H. Gelb, Richard K. Burt, and Strobe Talbott. Its members contribute to the shielding of foreign policy from democratic scrutiny by treating foreign policy as if it occurred without significant domestic ramifications. This is true, incredibly enough, even in stories that profess to be about those ramifications. In a story entitled "Expand NATO? Yes, Say Most Experts, But What Does the Public Think?" New York Times London bureau chief Craig R. Whitney manages to write, in twenty-two paragraphs, only one sentence that deals in any way with what the American public might think. That sentence, written in Europe, asserts that "many Americans apparently believe European security is a problem they no longer need to worry about." It offers no empirical data and appears to have been gleaned telepathically by its author from the London fog.[26]

The most unequivocal, and perhaps most elaborate, explication of this usually unspoken establishment consensus can be found in a book published in 1975 by the Trilateral Commission. Authored by the highly respected Harvard academic Samuel Huntington, The Crisis of Democracy argues that "the problems of governance in the United States stem from an excess of democracy." Huntington reasoned that "effective operation of a democratic political system usually requires some measure of apathy and noninvolvement on the part of some individuals and groups." Such apathy and marginality, he allowed, may be "inherently undemocratic," but it is necessary to "enable democracy to function effectively." In the United States, however, formerly "marginal social groups, as in the case of the blacks, are now . . . overloading the political system authority with demands." The "suicide" of our democracy, Huntington predicted, is more likely to be the product of overindulgence than of any other cause.[27]

All of these arguments rest on the belief that the public is not competent to judge foreign policy choices intelligently and cannot be trusted to act in its own interest. These arguments were initially put forth on a more general basis by Lippmann in his remarkably influential 1922 work, *Public Opinion*. (Lippmann's arguments and John Dewey's response are discussed at some length in chapter 2.) With regard to foreign policy, the arguments implied above were formalized in 1950 by Yale political scientist Gabriel Almond in a work that became the touchstone in this decidedly uncrowded academic field. Almond argued that "the public cannot make an effective foreign policy. It can only support one." Unfortunately, "the orientation of most Americans toward foreign policy is one of mood, and mood is essentially an unstable phenomenon." Americans, Almond discerned, react with indifference to any "foreign policy crisis short of the immediate threat of war."[28] Dexter Perkins, a dean of American diplomatic historians at the time, concurred. He opened his 1952 study of foreign policy and the American system with this observation: "The mass of men have neither the knowledge nor the inclination to understand a complex diplomatic problem in all its ramifications. They can judge only in the large, fixing the mood and general objectives; and policy, to be made intelligible to them, must be stated in broad terms. It is a sound instinct that has made the greatest of American statesmen do this very thing."[29] Hans Morgenthau, perhaps the most influential teacher of "realist" foreign policy principles and guru to establishment figures ranging from Henry Kissinger to Arthur Schlesinger Jr., cautioned his students against paying too much attention to the opinions of everyday people. He urged the country's leaders instead to use their power to mold the public's feelings in accordance with what they knew to be the country's "true national interests." Public opinion, Morgenthau observed, "is not a static thing to be discovered and classified by public opinion polls as plants are by botanists, but . . . a dynamic, ever changing entity to be continuously created and recreated by informed and responsible leadership."[30] (Morgenthau's curiously unexamined implication here is that the nation's "true national interests" *are* static and discoverable.)

To the degree that the issue of democratic participation concerns policymakers at all, they console themselves with the knowledge that in addition to the American people's "moodishess," "indifference," and lack of an "inclination to understand" complex diplomatic problems, the public is also woefully ignorant regarding the essential facts of foreign policy. Examples of this ignorance are not exactly difficult to unearth. A 1993 survey of eight democracies found American citizens dead last in their knowledge of current international events.[31] Eugene Wittkopf points out that the ignorance of so many Americans about such basic facts leaves them open to manipulation by foreign policy elites in the sense that "public support for particular policies may be created where none existed previously."[32]

Knowledge-based surveys fortify the members of the establishment of their superior wisdom. A 1998 survey of presidential appointees and senior civil servants found that fewer than 14 percent believed that common Americans knew enough about issues to make wise decisions about public policy.[33] That number would no doubt shrink even further were the question focused on foreign affairs. When the experts do engage the question of the wishes of the larger public, they generally do so in one of two ways. Most often, they bemoan the loss of the pre-Vietnam "consensus," and they suggest the means for its potential reconstruction. Speaking for the most high-minded traditions of the establishment, former secretary of state Cyrus Vance notes in his memoirs that "our foreign policy should be understood and supported by the American people." Without such support, he worries, our policies are "vulnerable to misunderstanding, public disillusionment and repudiation."[34] But Vance uses Congress as a surrogate for the American people and does not offer much in the way of suggestions for addressing the problem. Like most foreign policy specialists, he holds that success creates its own support.

Vance represents the most venerable traditions of the establishment. He and his peers succeeded Kennan and company, who cared nothing for public support—except when it threatened to interfere with their plans—but they have not yet figured out how to engage the larger public. The Vance generation has spawned yet another group of foreign policy thinkers who, having come of age during the Vietnam war and the

Reagan era, better understand the complexity of their task. This generation has adopted a multicultural model of foreign policy consensus making. Its agenda includes reaching beyond the Ivy League to draw a wider sociological sampling of the population into the establishment's key institutions. In recent years, organizations such as the Council on Foreign Relations and the State Department have gone to considerable lengths to recruit outside the traditional ethnic and geographic bastions of their influence.

In a 1994 *Foreign Affairs* article, tellingly entitled "Say Good-Bye to the Wise Men," Michael Clough, a staff member of the Council on Foreign Relations, takes this line of thought to its logical conclusion by arguing for an entirely new system of foreign policy making. Because power has become decentralized and American society globalized, he maintains, a largely white male Protestant elite can no longer plausibly claim to represent the entire nation. Clough calls on the foreign policy establishment to open itself to a "decentralized and collaborative system, which encourages the initiatives of regional actors, ethnic actors, ethnic groups, and global issue groups to involve themselves in the foreign-policy making process." Such an opening, Clough argues, "would restore public confidence that America's involvement in world affairs is still consistent with their own values."[35]

Clough's solution, while considerably more inclusive than the old days, is only marginally more democratic. It enlarges the circle of foreign policy discussion and debate without addressing its fundamentally antidemocratic character. Clough would extend the current debate beyond the splendid isolation of the Metroliner corridor to the universities and policy centers of the Southwest, Southeast, and Northwest. He would invite representatives of the Asian-American community, the Latino community, the African-American community, women's groups, and nongovernmental organizations (NGOs) to sit at the table with the men from Princeton and Yale. But this invitation would still not begin to expand debate and discussion beyond the mere 5 or 10 percent of the American public who are attentive to foreign policy.[36] Enlarging its recruiting fields may be salutary for the establishment, but it hardly accomplishes the job of democratizing American foreign policy.

The establishment's fear of the public's capacity for judgment in foreign policy that runs from Lippmann and Kennan through Vance and Clough is, however, misplaced. Once we address the issue of insufficient knowledge and information, the alleged deficiency in the quality of the discernment of American people evaporates. Recent research suggests a public that is neither irrational nor "moody," but one whose views on foreign policy are surprisingly consistent. Benjamin Page and Robert Y. Shapiro reviewed thousands of survey items from 1935 through 1990 and concluded that "the American public, as a collective, holds a number of real, stable and sensible opinions about public policy and . . . these opinions develop and change in a reasonable fashion, responding to changing circumstances and to new information." Numerous recent studies have confirmed their conclusions.[37] A series of initiatives undertaken by groups like the Kettering Foundation and the National Issues Forum during the past decade further demonstrate, moreover, that the American people would like to be far more engaged than they are in the crucial foreign policy questions of the day. The Americans who participate in these studies express considerable frustration, even anger, at the unwillingness of policymakers and the media to listen to their concerns seriously and respectfully.[38] But they are intimidated by their own ignorance and by a system of politics that interprets their inability to participate as acquiescence.

The problems are myriad and their costs profound. When the public is unaware of a policy debate, what scholars call the "scope of conflict" is narrowed. Americans may never even hear of a particular policy that seriously affects their interests or offends their values. Even when the public makes a clear choice, it has little means to intervene in the process whereby the policy is determined. Groups that organize themselves for the purposes of guiding these decisions, such as corporate lobbyists, have a much better chance of getting their way than a disorganized public majority. Elites can also mute the democratic voice of the public by controlling the agenda for public discussion. If the punditocracy chooses to discuss only those issues of interest to Beltway insiders in the very terms set by those insiders, then Americans may have great difficulty recognizing their interests in situations where they are clearly at risk.

The problem becomes even more daunting when one considers the complex competing claims to which citizens are subjected in the media. When the debate over NAFTA saturated the media in 1992, just how was the average American consumer to determine whose NAFTA model to believe? How was this American to assess the assumptions that underlay the various contradictory claims of each of the six or seven econometric models that were offered? How many Americans were able to judge President Clinton's insistence that the "the peso would become stronger if NAFTA passes" or his prediction that "NAFTA will create 200,000 American jobs"? (In fact, the peso collapsed two years after passage.) The same questions could be asked about Americans' understanding of the costs of the expansion of NATO, the likely deployment period for U.S. troops in Bosnia or Haiti, and any number of complex topics.[39]

A democratic foreign policy that aspires to express what is most enduring in the values of the American people will need to balance Americans' hopes against their fears and their desire for peace, prosperity, and security against the confusing array of dangers that have cropped up in the post–Cold War world. It will need to do so, moreover, against the background of our government's profoundly truncated abilities to control the nation's destiny in a world where economic and ecological interdependence have rendered much government intervention counterproductive. With the Cold War over, Americans are no longer able to define themselves in terms of what they are not. Hector St. John de Crèvecoeur's 1782 query therefore echoes today with much of its original force: "What is the American, this new man?"[40] More to the point of our inquiry, what are the values that should underlie the foreign policy conducted in his name?

What becomes clear to anyone who studies the problem carefully is that the American people do not accept the foreign policy establishment's definition of the nation's priorities in the world but do not know how to force a reassessment. Most Americans, unlike the members of the foreign policy establishment, do not live to conduct foreign policy; rather, they conduct foreign policy to live.[41] They believe, by vast majorities, that "U.S. foreign policy should service the U.S. domestic agenda rather than remain focused on traditional internationalist problems."[42] In a 1989 poll, designed explicitly to discover the "values" that underlay Americans' foreign policy attitudes, nearly 90 percent of those questioned insisted that "America has a moral responsibility to concentrate on domestic policy before concentrating on foreign policy." Seven years later, a series of focus groups undertaken by the National Issues Forum, a polling and educational organization, determined that almost all participants believed that "domestic needs have been neglected at the expense of foreign affairs."[43] This belief is not the result of ignorance, insufficient education, stupidity, or an inability of the foreign policy establishment to reach the larger public. This is a core American value. At the National Issues Convention in Austin in January 1996, the percentage of participants who believed that the United States would be "better off if we just stayed at home and did not concern ourselves with problems in other parts of the world" increased by 25 percent to nearly one out of two people after each participant had the opportunity to consult with experts, facilitators, and one another. Seventy percent agreed that the "U.S. should shift resources back into helping its own economy now that the Cold War is over."[44] When polled, Americans consistently choose "protecting American jobs" as their most important foreign policy priority, but the goal barely registers among business and opinion elites.[45] Clearly, if it knew how to do so, the public would demand a foreign policy that served those interests, one that focused more on protecting jobs than promoting unfettered trade, one that eschewed far-flung adventures to concentrate on strengthening the American economy and society. Finally, and most importantly, the American people would like to see a foreign policy that ceases to operate as if foreign policy and domestic policy were somehow separate realms. And in this regard, it is the American people who share the viewpoint of the nation's founders and comprehend the world of today with greater realism and sophistication than their alleged intellectual superiors.

Foreign policy experts regard their competence as sufficient reason that they alone should determine the overall direction of U.S. foreign policy. (The day-to-day operation of that policy is unarguably beyond the capacities of any large-scale democratic system.) But the makers of U.S. foreign policy are unwilling to own up to increasing amounts of evidence that the values they believe should underlie the nation's foreign policy are at odds with those of the people in whose name they profess to act and speak.

The values of the foreign policy establishment are less reflective of the political interests of most Americans than of the transnational class of bankers, lobbyists, lawyers, and investors from which they are drawn. These "experts" are so shielded from the struggles of everyday American life that they have become, as John Dewey predicted, "a class with private interests and private knowledge." This development should hardly surprise anyone, nor is it cause for scandal. But it is a reality, and if we are to call ourselves a democracy, we must address it.

The disjunction between elite and mass values in foreign policy has been growing ever since the United States began to take on the accoutrements of empire. Beginning with the Cold War, however, these differences became contradictions, frequently antidemocratic in character. The elites demanded public sacrifice for their policies but employed deceitful means to build support for them. The exposure of these tawdry tactics has done much to destroy public confidence in virtually all American institutions. For instance, according to extensive public research done over a period of decades, the American public views the Vietnam War to have been "more than a mistake" and to have been "fundamentally wrong and immoral." Most members of the elite, committed to the idea of empire and, hence, to the means of defending it, find this view not merely simplistic and wrongheaded but personally offensive. The gulf, moreover, has increased rather than receded with time.[46] When questioned by the National Issues Forum in 1996, members of the public could not credit U.S. foreign policy with a single significant accomplishment that improved their lives, or anyone else's for that matter. Rather, "participants felt that when it comes to foreign affairs, the public has been regularly misled by leaders from both parties for many years."[47]

One must be careful when relying on opinion polls because answers are easily manipulated and most people do not have well-defined views on many foreign policy issues. But polls can be valuable if they are viewed over a significant time continuum, and if the questions are able to elicit a respondent's hierarchy of values rather than simply ill-informed opinions and snap judgments. Since 1978, the Chicago Council on Foreign Relations (CCFR) has tracked the foreign policy views of those it deems to be America's opinion leaders alongside those of the public. In each of these quadrennial polls, a consistently discernible dichotomy crops up between the two categories of respondents. This elite/public discord manifests itself in any number of policy areas. Three times as many working Americans view Japan as a "critical threat" to their well-being than do opinion leaders. The same is true regarding the threat of increased immigration. Eighty-four percent of the public believes that protecting the jobs of American workers is "a very important goal," while barely half of the elite professes to believe this. Perhaps as a result, in the most recent poll, released in early 1995, elite opinion almost uniformly "sympathized with eliminating tariffs" and believed that "NAFTA is mostly good for the U.S." Only 40 percent of working Americans wished to see tariffs eliminated, and only about half of those surveyed were then optimistic about the results of the NAFTA accord.

Regarding military intervention, 84 percent of elite respondents would go to war to defend South Korea from a North Korean invasion, while only 45 percent of the public would; 86 percent of the elite would defend Saudi Arabia if it were attacked by Iraq, while only 58 percent of the public would; the elite is divided 50–50 between using force to support a hypothetical anti-Castro rebellion inside Cuba, while fewer than one in five Americans would be willing to do so.[48] These findings were reinforced by two extensive polls of "Influentials" and the public, undertaken in 1993 and 1997 by Times Mirror and the Pew Foundation, respectively.[49] While the public remains surprisingly supportive of multilateral action taken in conjunction with allies, it consistently rejects the elite view that the U.S. military budget need be orders of magnitude larger than that of our allies. The establishment argument that we must, as the "sole remaining superpower," assume such burdens and responsibilities fails to move them.[50] The differences, moreover, reflect long-term trends and appear to be growing, along with the increasing disparity of wealth between the richest Americans and everyone else.[51]

Historically, the elite's method of dealing with popular disapproval of foreign policy has been simply to ignore it and to cover up evidence of unpopular policies whenever necessary. This was the case for President Franklin Roosevelt, who did so for brave and farsighted reasons between 1939 and 1941, and it remains true today. Unfortunately, Roosevelt's example has led many of his successors to equate their own political interests with the Nazi threat to civilization. Presidents now routinely defy the clearly stated values of the American people and then lie about it. In doing so, they undermine the democratic foundation of our political system. Richard Nixon and Henry Kissinger were guilty of this transgression when they secretly expanded the Vietnam War into Cambodia and then covered up the evidence. Ronald Reagan and Oliver North were equally culpable when they sold missiles to the Ayatollah and used the profits to funnel guns to the Nicaraguan contras. Both of these actions resulted in celebrated scandals, but they did not dissuade future presidents from engaging in the same practices.

Today, presidential actions that defy the unmistakable foreign policy preferences of the American people and are then covered up by their perpetrators are not even considered cause for scandal. For instance, while the public was unarguably unenthusiastic about NAFTA, it did cite "stopping the inflow of illegal drugs" as a top priority in the most recent CCFR poll.[52] During the NAFTA battle, however, according to a *New York Times* report, the Bush administration "often exaggerated the Mexican government's progress in the fight against drugs, playing down corruption and glossing over failures." John P. Waters, a senior official for international drug policy in the Bush White House, explained, "People desperately wanted drugs not to become a complicating factor for NAFTA. There was a degree of illicit activity that was just accepted." Motivated by what one former official called "the bigger picture," the Bush administration went so far as to overlook the killing by corrupt Mexican Army officers of seven U.S. DEA officers who were in hot pursuit of a smuggler's aircraft in Veracruz.[53]

The administration's actions in this incident were not reported until almost five years after it took place. Had Americans wished to vote in 1992 on the basis of the foreign policy issue about which they professed to care most deeply, they would not have had the requisite information. Unless someone happened to be a particularly careful reader of the *New York Times*, a category that excludes more than 99 percent of all U.S. voters, he would probably never have seen or heard any mention of this policy at all. In such cases, democracy is subverted and the peoples' wishes denied.

To protect NAFTA, the U.S. government's whitewash of the involvement of high-level Mexican officials in drug smuggling has continued and even expanded on a bipartisan basis under President Clinton. As an example of conflicts between elite and public goals, it is U.S. foreign policy writ large. Presidents and their advisers understand that the public's natural deference and disinclination to question the details of official policy regarding foreign adversaries gives them enormous latitude to pursue policies in conflict with Americans' professed values and beliefs. In matters of war and peace in particular, Americans' patriotic desire to support their president usually overwhelms their natural bias against involvement in foreign wars. Politicians and members of the punditocracy exploit this phenomenon by deliberately exaggerating potential physical threats to the United States and by manipulating Americans' deep-seated racial fears and insecurities.[54] With regard to trade policy and the protection of American jobs, the elite has managed to exploit the incantatory power of the term "free trade" in order to overcome mass objections to policies that sacrifice workers' wages and job security on the altar of economic efficiency.

To begin to map the potential contours of a new, democratically based foreign policy, we need to be cognizant of a dizzying number of historical trends, issues, and characterological developments within both America and the world at large. The idea, once again, is to identify the enduring collective values of the American people and then to translate these into workable and consistent political policies. Simply reading poll numbers is insufficient, for precious little polling has been done on values as opposed to mere attitudes and opinions. Furthermore, Americans frequently hold conflicting values with varying degrees of intensity, both within themselves as individuals and among themselves as groups. Listen to Ruben Alcala, a retired steelworker in Merrillville, Indiana, explain his feelings about the efficacy of the Clinton administration's Bosnia policy in mid-1995: "I'm not really following it that closely. I can't understand why it's going on so long, or why. It's a shame so many people are suffering. Sometimes I think maybe we should [intervene]. Then I think, no, let them take care of their own. Let someone else solve it. The U.S. is the greatest country in the world. Should we be the world's policeman? No, that's what we got the U.N. for."[55]

Mr. Alcala seems to believe that a UN military force is an alternative to an American intervention. At the moment of his comment, however, the president and his advisers were facing the question of whether to deploy American troops as part of a UN peacekeeping force. Mr. Alcala insists that the United States is the world's "greatest country" but does not begin to define the meaning of those words. Were it to imply U.S. responsibility to help enforce a peace accord in Bosnia, Mr. Alcala immediately terms this the U.S. acting as the "world's policeman" and hence inappropriate. Though he is clearly troubled by "so many people suffering," he is divided between wishing to find some way to alleviate that suffering and simply defining the problem as one outside the realm of his nation's concerns. How, then, to craft a foreign policy that accurately reflects the values that underlie Mr. Alcala's confusing concerns, that honors the genuine pride and patriotism he feels about his country without pandering to his ignorance and fear?

What follows is a rather long-winded and historically minded answer to Mr. Alcala's dilemma. Long-winded because the problem has many layers of complex causes and connective tissue; historical because I believe it is self-defeating to attempt to address a problem without a healthy respect for the historical conditions that shaped it. In the book's first section, I trace the development of the values that underlie U.S. foreign policy to determine the degree to which they were consistent with those of the democratic populace. As the two diverge, I examine the costs of the political elite's failure to hold to the terms of the bargain struck by the Republic's founders. In the second section, I attempt to deconstruct the legacy of this history in the form of the many complex operational constraints on the conduct of a democratic foreign policy in America today. In the third section, I propose a rather immodest institutional reform that could remake the foreign policy process to reflect the democratic values of its people. In case my suggested reforms are not immediately adopted, I outline in an appendix the terms of a democratic foreign policy, given what I understand to be the values and priorities of the American people as we begin the country's third century as the oldest continuously self-governing nation on earth.

★

The Rise and Fall of a Liberal Republic: A Short History

CHAPTER ONE

Virtue, Commerce, and Perpetual Motion

"I am not among those who fear the people."
—Thomas Jefferson, 1816

The historical record of the relationship between America's foreign policy and the democratic desires of its people is decidedly sketchy. Perhaps because historians have shared the elitist biases of foreign policymakers, or perhaps owing to the paucity of reliable data, the historical profession has often failed to do better than offer patriotic clichés or some rough equations that fail to stand up to scrutiny. For instance, Dexter Perkins, perhaps the most respected American diplomatic historian of his day, argued in the 1950s that "In a sense that is true in no such degree in other nations, American diplomatic action has been determined by the people."[1] However, he neglected to present any evidence for this assertion. For generations, Melvin Small observes, "historians interested in public opinion have concentrated on elite opinion and confused the two."[2] The most obvious examples occur when historians equate the views of publishing conglomerates and newspaper editors with those of the masses. Small notes that even Thomas A. Bailey, like Perkins a leading postwar historian, used the words "the people" when he meant "the *Washington Post*."[3] Rare indeed, says Small, is the scholar sufficiently scrupulous to qualify his assertion with a caveat like "the people, who may have agreed with the *New York Times* when it stated editorially. . . ."[4]

Were historians to cite their sources more carefully, however, the problem would still remain. Newspaper editorials are a poor substitute for public opinion. Historically, many publishers have acted as self-conscious cogs in a given politician's machine, or vice versa. (John Quincy Adams once complained of how expensive it was to buy newspaper editors.[5]) Historians and political scientists, moreover, have had a great deal of trouble demonstrating what, if any, effect newspaper editorials have on public views—to say nothing of the difficulty of gauging the public's impact on policymakers. Certainly senior officials regularly credit "public opinion" for inspiring their decisions, but to accept such assertions at face value is naive in the extreme. As Bernard Cohen points out, when a policymaker attributes a decision to the dictates of public opinion, "he is explaining away a variety of complicated delicate political constraints on his and his colleagues' behavior by passing them onto the one legitimate political actor that cannot answer back, defend itself, or take offense at the charge."[6]

Polling data can be helpful when viewed over a sufficient time continuum, but the process did not begin in earnest until the 1930s. Regarding the first 140 years of the nation's history, we are frequently forced to reconstruct the public's views by inference. This task, however, is a thankless one. With the exception of the Founders' generation, Americans have not traditionally cared passionately about foreign affairs beyond issues of war and peace, and neither have their local newspapers. The traditional tools of the historical trade—letters; diaries; and birth, marriage, and death certificates—are of precious little value in reconstructing foreign policy attitudes.

Ironically, the problem of evidence is least apparent in the nation's earliest days. The Revolutionary generation of Americans demonstrated a remarkable commitment to the politics of foreign policy. True, the franchise was limited in many states to propertied white men.[7] But not since ancient Athens, in Gordon Wood's estimable opinion, had even so limited a group appeared to practice the art of self-governance with such passion and dedication. The colonists who made the Revolution were a people obsessed by politics. The Revolution made common people not merely voters, but, for the first time in history, rulers. "The celebration of common people in government," observes Wood, "became the essence of American democracy."[8] And foreign policy, notes Richard Barnet, whose *Rockets' Red Glare* is perhaps the most penetrating examination of the impact of regular people on America's debate on war and peace, became "a burning issue in the infant Republic because it was a metaphor for the political struggle to define what the United States was to be."[9]

Revolutionary Americans argued over the finer points of foreign and military policy in churches, in taverns, at local guild meetings, and at assemblies called specifically for those purposes. Political pamphlets and posters appeared everywhere. In 1776, Tom Paine's *Common Sense* required nineteen editions and perhaps as many as 150,000 copies printed, a degree of saturation that would be equivalent to roughly 20 million copies in today's market.[10] This commitment to public life spilled over into the Republic's early life, filling the wide-open spaces that would determine political precedents for centuries to come.

Battle lines were drawn between Federalists and anti-Federalists. The former, led by Alexander Hamilton, generally supported measures designed to enlarge and strengthen the federal government, while the latter, led by Thomas Jefferson, concerned themselves primarily with restricting the government's capacity for arbitrary and tyrannical rule. Although the divisions between the two sides were serious and significant in their own contexts, for our purposes they obscure more than they reveal. Each side shared an overarching ideological commitment to a vision of political life that was itself conflicted and often self-contradictory: the quest for a simultaneously republican and liberal political order. The conflicts and contradictions between these two ideals defined the ideological parameters of the first century of debate on American democracy and foreign policy. The painful irony of this history is that the perceived practical underpinnings of this ideology—ceaseless commercial and material advancement coupled with increasingly expanded executive power—ultimately undermined the survival of the very values they were intended to uphold.

"Republicanism" is among the most elusive of political concepts.[11] John Adams complained that "there is not a more unintelligible word in the English language."[12] Still, it meant a great deal to the Founders. Self-consciously modeled on what they interpreted to be the values of classical Athens and Rome, updated by Niccolo Machiavelli, the Founders' republicanism sought to regenerate the human spirit by reordering the society that nurtured it. Good government and good people would reinforce each other in a dynamic that called forth the virtuous qualities that lay dormant in the human soul. The very act of self-government would ennoble those who participated in it.[13]

Democracy comprised a rather insignificant portion of these virtues. It was not, moreover, intended to be expanded beyond the class of leisured, well-educated gentlemen whose clearheaded and unsentimental leadership had made the Revolution possible. John Adams, for instance, believed "the people" to be "ignorant, strongly prejudiced, vindictive in their resentments, incapable of being influenced except by their fears of punishment."[14] James Madison simultaneously reinforced and moderated Adams's viewpoint with the Burkean notion that the common people could be trusted to choose their leaders and no more. Madison believed that what political "virtue" rested in common people could be found exclusively in their "intelligence to select men of virtue and wisdom" to lead them. He insisted on the need to "refine and enlarge the public views by passing them through the medium of a chosen body of citizens, whose wisdom may best discern the true interest of their country and whose patriotism and love of justice will be least likely to sacrifice it to temporary or partial considerations."[15] Democratic republicans did not dare argue that the people in eighteenth-century America were competent to rule themselves. Rather, they rested their hopes in the creation of an educated polity. As radical democrat Samuel Adams explained to James Warren during the Continental Congress, "No People will tamely surrender their Liberties, nor can they easily be subdued, when Knowledge is duffused [sic] and Virtue preserved."[16] Sam Adams's abiding faith in the essential educability of the common citizen for democratic governance remained an essential component of American liberal thought through John Dewey's arguments in the mid-twentieth century, while his cousin John's skepticism could still be heard in George Kennan's and Walter Lippmann's respective responses.

As with so many revolutionary leaders, the Wise Men of Philadelphia lost control of the minds they inspired, albeit to a far milder degree than most. All this talk of freedom, liberty, and equality filtered into taverns, churches, and political pamphlets from whence it emerged carrying considerably different connotations. In republican discourse, the working man found a powerful engine for a transformation of his self-understanding. Hating taxes and distrusting most forms of centralized power, white male Americans embraced democratic politics with verve and passion. Authority became so dispersed it almost ceased to exist. Social and political distinctions between the rulers and the ruled following the Revolution all but dissipated. The soil of republican liberty fertilized the roots of democratic self-rule, however inadvertently.[17]

No less important than republicanism to the Founders' conception of politics was John Locke's conception of liberty. Locke, the foremost English philosopher of the seventeenth century, wrote his two treatises on government during the period in which his patron, the Earl of Shaftesbury, sought to exclude James, then Duke of York, from succession to the throne. He therefore argued for a consensual basis of self-government to replace that of divine rights. Lockean liberty was born of the belief that personal freedom was "bounded only by such limits as are necessary if others are to enjoy the same extensive personal freedom."[18] Locke's vision meshed quite easily with the Reformist Protestant character of most Americans' religious self-definition. Locke's *Second Treatise* outlined a social contract whereby individuals, "for the mutual preservation of their lives, liberties, and estates," were willing to forego some of the rights found in "the state of nature" so that they might pursue those rights they deemed to be most important to what the Founders would call "the pursuit of happiness."[19]

Needless to say, Locke's notion of liberty evinced a decidedly problematic relationship to the word's republican connotation. The republican tradition asked its citizens to control their private passions and subordinate their individual interests to the public good, with the latter resting on deference and hierarchy.[20] Liberty, in republican political theory, depends on a sharing of self-government; on deliberating, in Michael Sandel's words, "with fellow citizens about the common good and helping to shape the destiny of the political community."[21] To be "virtuous" in republican terms implied a willingness to sacrifice private interests for the sake of the public good. This required of its citizens a degree of freedom and independence from the petty interests of the marketplace that would prove impossible in a democratic capitalist society that took this same marketplace as its template. How to resolve this dichotomy? One group of historians poses a division that identifies the Federalists as the party of Locke and the anti-Federalists as that of Machiavelli. Another insists that the crucial distinction lies between the ruling and the ruled.[22] But the lines between the two overlap so frequently that they functionally disappear. The conflict between liberalism and republicanism took place not merely between the leaders and the led, but inside the hearts and minds of the men of Philadelphia themselves. The two competing tendencies clashed and meshed in the breast of the American body politic, creating a powerful but unstable hybrid of liberal republicanism. The attempt of American politicians to appeal to these self-contradictory impulses simultaneously—to pursue both "virtue" and "commerce," as it were—defines much of the ideological instability that has characterized American behavior in the world. In foreign policy, the most popular solution would be to apply the rhetoric of the defense of virtue to support a policy driven by the need for expanded commerce, coupled with some decidedly nondemocratic means to help obscure the inherent contradiction.[23]

One significant result of the American Revolution was the repudiation of a key ideological foundation of British parliamentary democracy, that of "virtual representation." In the period leading up to the colonial revolt, the British replied to the colonial slogan "no taxation without representation" with the argument that while the colonies might not send their own representatives to Parliament, they were nevertheless "virtually" represented there. The moral responsibility of each member of the Lords and Commons was not merely the parochial self-interest of his district but the welfare of the entire empire. The leaders of the revolt did not buy this argument when the British made it in 1775 and neither did the merchants, farmers, and mechanics when propertied colonial classes made it following the Revolution. Representation, argued Madison, became "the pivot" on which the whole American system of government turned.[24]

Virtual representation would ultimately achieve a comeback in foreign policy, however, as international affairs reasserted itself as an arena of politics that would become divorced from the rough-and-tumble of local political concerns. This gradual reassertion of privilege was an indirect result of three concurrent trends: the accumulation of the accoutrements of empire by the once tiny colonies, the accretion of de facto executive power by the presidency, and the eclipse of participatory notions of citizenship that accompanied the physical expansion of the nation and its simultaneous population explosion. Between the Revolution and the War of 1812, however, the battles the young nation fought over the character of its external relations were its fiercest. The very survival of the Revolution appeared to rest on the republic's self-definition as an ally of either Britain or France. On the admittedly unscientific means we have for discovering to what degree the battles between Hamiltonian and Jeffersonian factions represented the larger masses, history offers us little evidence to doubt that the two sides represented deep divisions in the larger populace.

The elements of liberal republican foreign policy derived in part from the exigencies of the Americans' strategic dilemma and in part from the precepts of their contradictory political philosophy. A crucial component of the Founders' republicanism was the fear of the corruptive power of luxury. "Commerce produces money, money Luxury, and all three are incompatible with Republicans," wrote John Adams. The foundation of a virtuous government was men who were "sober, industrious and frugal."[25] This view was endorsed across the ideological spectrum by Thomas Paine, who wrote in *Common Sense* that "commerce diminishes the spirit both of patriotism and military defense and would eventually destroy America's soul." In a pattern destined to repeat itself for the next two centuries, the Founders' liberal desires overwhelmed their republican beliefs. Alexander Hamilton, rather than Paine or Adams, became the truest prophet of capitalist America. He believed commerce to be "the most useful as well as the most productive source of national wealth."[26] A commitment to free trade, a philosophical bedrock of classical liberalism, overpowered the Founders' republican fear of moral corruption. The very same John Adams who thought commerce incompatible with republicanism pronounced himself "against all shackles on human trade," insisting "that all the world would gain by setting commerce at perfect liberty."[27] Demonstrating what would become a time-honored practice of knitting a (liberal) economic necessity into a philosophic virtue, Paine too came to believe that commerce could "temper the human mind," help peoples to "know and understand each other," and have a "civilizing effect on all who participated in it."[28] Despondent in 1787, Madison complained to Jefferson of "symptoms, truly alarming, which have tainted the faith of the most orthodox republicans." Americans lacked "industry, economy, temperance and other republican virtues." They had become "a Luxurious, Voluptuous, indolent, expensive people without Economy or Industry."[29] Nothing could have been more warming to Hamilton's Lockean heart, nor have provided more fertile soil for what has become today a two-century-long commitment to the ideology (if not the practice) of free trade.

Americans believed their Revolution was a new "chapter in the history of man," in Jefferson's words.[30] The two great oceans that divided them from the rest of the world's great powers, along with the magnificent physical bounty provided by their lands, constituted, in their eyes, a sign of divine providence. As a consequence, Americans considered themselves to be outside of, and unbounded by, the system of great-power politics that had historically guided relations between nations. "We have it in our power," cried Paine, in a phrase frequently borrowed by Ronald Reagan, "to begin the world all over again." Even the profoundly unsentimental Hamilton can be seen to be imbued with this intoxicating vision. "It seems to have been reserved," he wrote in "Federalist 1," "to the people of this country, by their conduct and example, to decide the important question, whether societies of men are really capable or not, of establishing good government from reflection and choice, or whether they are forever destined to depend, for their political constitutions, on accident and force . . . a wrong election of the part we shall act, may, in this view, deserve to be considered as the general misfortune of mankind." In his choice of words, Hamilton was echoing the no less intoxicated Benjamin Franklin, who wrote from Paris to a friend in 1777, "It is a common observation here that our cause is the cause of all mankind, and that we are fighting for their liberty in defending our own. It is a glorious task assigned to us by Providence, which has, I trust, given us spirit and virtue equal to it."[31]

The Founders blamed the European system of politics between nation states for the breeding of war and poverty. Their natural inclination was to attempt to withdraw themselves entirely from the world of diplomats and armies.[32] Albert Gallatin, then a Republican leader in Congress, attempted to limit the number of American ministers accredited to European capitals. He argued that as the primary purpose of American foreign policy was commercial, mere consuls could handle all the necessary diplomacy. Americans even refused to appoint diplomats with the rank of ambassador until 1893, arguing that the rank smacked of royalism. Gallatin and his Jeffersonian allies also sharply opposed Federalist plans to expand the navy, which they insisted would threaten the survival of republican institutions at home.[33] Americans sought to enjoy the material benefits of liberal trade while simultaneously protecting their fragile republican institutions from the degenerative moral viruses running rampant in the Old World. No matter how just the cause of a foreign power might be, the Founders counseled abstention.

In what would become the Magna Carta of early American foreign policy, President Washington in his farewell address counseled his countrymen to keep their society pure by remaining above the petty animosities of European politics and to value peace above almost any other goal. While he recommended "harmony" and "liberal intercourse" with all nations, Americans were never to "seek nor grant exclusive favors or preferences." "There can be no greater error," Washington insisted, "than to expect or calculate upon real favors from nation to nation."[34] Washington's almost visceral loathing of war was born of his experience of command. His hope that the United States "never unsheathe the sword except in self-defense" and his "devout" prayer "that we remain at peace to the end of time" provided the central themes of the farewell address.[35]

The Founders enshrined in the Constitution their abhorrence of war by explicitly vesting in Congress, rather than the president, war-making powers. As Madison wrote to Jefferson, "The Constitution supposes what the History of all Governments demonstrates, that the Executive is the branch of power most interested in war, and most prone to it. It has accordingly with studied care, vested the question of war in the Legislature."[36] Jefferson called this decision an "effectual check to the dog of war."[37] The Federalists did not dispute this argument. Even Hamilton, who consistently argued for a strong executive with a large standing army and war-making capability at his disposal, nevertheless agreed that "it is the peculiar and exclusive province of Congress, when the nation is at peace, to change that state into a state of war."[38] Indeed, only one delegate to either the Philadelphia convention or any of the state ratifying conventions, Pierce Butler, even suggested that presidents be constitutionally vested with the power to begin a war. When Elbridge Gerry responded that he "never expected to hear in a republic a motion to empower the Executive alone to declare war," Butler disowned the idea. "The point," John Hart Ely contends, was "to 'clog the road to combat' by requiring the concurrence of a number of people of various points of view."[39]

The final peace treaty of 1783 left Canada in English hands. Any number of American politicians predicted renewed war, owing perhaps to Hamilton's analysis in "Federalist Six" that "it has . . . become a sort of axiom in politics, that vicinity, or nearness of situation, constitutes a nation's natural enemies."[40] Nevertheless, these same Americans favored a policy of tilting toward England, in part for balance-of-power reasons and in part because they saw themselves in some important fashion as "modified Englishmen" and viewed French revolutionary fervor with fear and apprehension.[41] To the Jeffersonians, however, whose most profound emotional attachments remained with France for its (perceived) crusade on behalf of liberty, England represented the embodiment of monarchist tyranny. Economic self-interest reinforced the ideological proclivities of both sides. To Hamilton, who hoped to midwife a powerful commercial economy in America, the center of the world lay clearly within the British empire. But France was the prime market for the agricultural goods of the South.

The two sides fought each other viciously through Washington's two presidential terms, for neither group recognized a division between foreign and domestic affairs. Virtually every local issue, notes Richard Barnet, "was mixed up in some way with foreign affairs: matters of trade; navigation on the Mississippi, the St. Lawrence, or rivers further to the West held either by Britain, France, or Spain; dealings with Indian tribes and frontier security. . . ."[42] The degree of popular involvement in the questions of war and peace is astonishing by contemporary standards. When the French emissary "Citizen Genet" arrived in 1793 to seek

American support for the French Revolutionary War with England, gro-
cers, bakers, sail makers, and lawyers organized themselves into voluntary brigades should war with England ensue.[43] When John Jay concluded a treaty to resolve Anglo-American tensions by largely placating
the British two years later, opponents burned him in effigy and pelted
his representatives with rotten vegetables at every opportunity. When
Congressman Frederick Muhlenberg changed his mind on the treaty and
voted in favor of its implementation, he lost his next election and
received a stab wound from his brother-in-law for his troubles.[44] Anti-
Federalist political clubs, called "democratic societies" and "republican
societies," also sprouted up during this period in Philadelphia, Norfolk,
Lexington, and other major cities to support the pro-French Jeffersonians
against the pro-British Hamiltonians. The Federalists regularly attacked
the societies as "nurseries of sedition" and insisted that the people who
created them were lacking in political and constitutional legitimacy. But
they also set up some societies of their own. Together, these helped lay
the groundwork for the creation of the American two-party political
system.[45]

How to assuage the demands of an extremely unwieldy democratic
process while at the same time conducting a patient, effective foreign
policy that would secure the blessings of trade without entangling the
New World in corrupt Old World political arrangements? Here lies the
crux of America's still unresolved "Tocqueville problem." In the opening
moments of the new nation's history, this tension submerged itself in the
personal prestige of General Washington. On the basis of his understanding of the Constitution's "advise and consent" clause, Washington
initially attempted to consult with the Senate in advance of negotiating
treaties. During his first visit there, on August 22, 1789, to discuss a
potential treaty with southern Indians, Washington found his dignity so
profoundly affronted that he immediately retreated and allegedly said
he "would be damned if he ever went there again."[46] After this, Washington did not much concern himself with the democratic basis of his
foreign policy. He sought to portray himself as somehow above the Jay
treaty controversy (while politicking furiously for it), and pretended to
ignore the creation of competing political parties as well. Despite the
incident just described, the persuasive power of the Revolutionary general's special standing decreased the political necessities of democratic
consultation conversely.

Unfortunately, Washington's suprapolitical pose would set a precedent
for future occupants of his office who wished to compromise the demo-

cratic accountability of their diplomatic endeavors. Washington observed in his farewell address that "in proportion as the structure of a government gives force to public opinion, it is essential that public opinion should be enlightened."[47] At the same time, however, he inaugurated a tradition of presidential secrecy in foreign affairs that would ultimately make such enlightenment impossible. For instance, in 1790 Washington presented the Senate with a secret article for a treaty with the Creek Indians, and later, in 1795, he refused to supply the House with details of the treaty that Jay had negotiated with Great Britain. In the latter case, he demanded that the legislature appropriate funds to carry out its terms, but these he refused to identify despite repeated requests, insisting that his "duty to [his] office forbade it.[48] The great enlightenment philosopher John Stuart Mill has asked how, without publicity, democratic citizens might be expected to "check or encourage what they were not permitted to see?"[49] Virtually every one of Washington's successors has sought to evade this question—an evasion that lies at the epicenter of the failure of the U.S. political system to apply the principle of democratic accountability to the conduct of its foreign policy.

John Adams enjoyed none of Washington's majestic political advantages. The nascent uprisings that continuously simmered throughout Washington's two terms threatened to explode into organized violence and perhaps even civil war as Washington retired to Mount Vernon. Planning for war with France, Adams helped push through the Alien and Sedition Acts of 1798 as an unsuccessful means of silencing his most intemperate critics. The curtailment of free speech the acts entailed energized the opposition and threatened the entire basis of the Federalist project when Republicans responded with the Virginia and Kentucky statutes designed to nullify them. With his own party leading the country toward an ill-considered war, Adams unselfishly sacrificed his hopes for reelection for a peaceful compromise. The second president believed his final political act was the "most disinterested and meritorious action of [his] life." He would later write, "I desire no other inscription over my gravestone than: 'Here lies John Adams, who took upon himself the responsibility of the peace with France in the year 1800.'"[50] By willfully forfeiting the election of 1800 to keep the country at peace, Adams set a standard for statesmanship that few presidents have sought to equal.

Historians tend to treat President Thomas Jefferson's foreign policy—in particular, the Louisiana Purchase—as a paradox, if not a betrayal.[51] Here was the ur-Jeffersonian adopting decidedly heavy-handed Hamiltonian methods to achieve what appeared to be expansionist, aggrandizing Hamiltonian goals. Indeed, while Jefferson had once championed the rights of the House of Representatives in the treaty-making process, as president he expected the same body to authorize enormous sums of money to be used at his discretion while refusing to offer any details to the elected representatives of the people.

There is an important point here, to be certain. But to focus exclusively on the betrayal is to miss the significance of the philosophy that underlay it. This would be a costly mistake, since Jefferson's willingness to face up to a philosophical contradiction of liberal republicanism, as he understood it, helped determine the contours of the next century of American foreign policy.

Jefferson shared with Tom Paine a view of human relations that divided society into two groups: the "productive classes," including laborers, farmers, artisans, small merchants, and manufacturers; and "the state," which consisted of the "plundering classes" of government officials, standing armies, blue-water navies, and holders of government monopolies. War, wrote Paine, was a tool of the plundering classes designed to expropriate the value of the labor of the productive classes, and to distract the common man from "looking into the defects and abuses of government." Its practice was encouraged by governments because without it, the plundering classes would "have no excuse for its enormous revenue and taxation, except it can prove that, somewhere or another, it has enemies."[52] Jefferson the politician was forever haunted by the degraded lives and specter of mass poverty he observed among the landless peasants of France. He became convinced that this potential tragedy was the worst that could befall a republican nation. If the American people ever sank to a similar level, he reasoned, American liberties would sink irretrievably with them.

Jefferson's fear led him on an urgent search for the origins of the Old World's unhappy state. He concluded that the European peasant's wretched condition derived first and foremost from his landlessness.[53] To Jefferson, yeoman farmers were "the chosen people of God, if ever He had a chosen people, in whose breasts He has made His peculiar deposit for substantial and genuine virtue."[54] Jefferson so profoundly believed that republican citizenship depended on property that he once proposed that his home state of Virginia grant a minimum of fifty acres to any man who owned less. With Madison, he believed that political liberty could survive only under conditions of economic and social equality. The central task of Jeffersonian statecraft was thus to create and maintain an open and roughly equal society where all had access to enough land to support republican virtue. This task was complicated, however, by Jefferson's belief, enunciated by Paine, that as societies grew in wealth and power, liberty and equality simultaneously eroded. Though human nature remained constant, economic and social environments might be constructed to minimize concentrations of wealth, dampen personal ambitions, and thus water the tree of republican liberty. But because even yeoman farmers operated in a capitalist marketplace with highly developed commercial networks—Locke dogged Machiavelli at every step—they needed to continue to grow in order to maintain their prosperity, and hence their virtue.[55]

Jefferson's solution lay in the great open spaces of the American West. These spaces would draw Americans out of the morally corrupt cities of the East and encourage the social equality that republican liberty required. "By enlarging the empire of liberty," Jefferson believed, "we multiply its auxiliaries, and provide new sources of renovation, should its principles, at any time, degenerate, in those portions of our country which gave them birth."[56] The Republic's growth across the North American continent would prevent, or at least indefinitely delay, the cyclical process of growth, maturity, and decay through which all past societies had traveled. Jefferson's project, however, was fraught with two great ironies. The more obvious one was the necessity that he adopt Hamiltonian methods—and thereby establish Hamiltonian precedents—to free his nation from what he perceived to be its nightmarish Hamiltonian future. By purchasing Louisiana without explicit congressional sanction, Jefferson transgressed what had previously been a sacred political boundary—his own understanding of the Constitution. The second great irony of Jefferson's decision, of no less gravity and importance for the future of both American democracy and its foreign policy, was his equation of the preservation of republican virtue and liberal prosperity with ceaseless physical expansion. Jefferson could conceive of no other path to assure the survival of republican virtue and democratic governance. Though he hated war, and all of the expropriation of local power and prerogatives it involved, Jefferson was willing to threaten war alongside his enemy, Britain, against his beloved France in order to secure the cherished agricultural lebensraum represented by the Louisiana territory. Such calculations by future American presidents in pursuit of further expansion would eventually strangle the very goals and principles in whose pursuit Jefferson made his original Faustian bargain.

The sale came about when Spain ceded the trans-Mississippi region known as Louisiana (except for New Orleans) to France. In October 1802, the Spanish commander in New Orleans closed the Mississippi River to American commerce, depriving westerners of the major outlet for their agricultural produce. Upon hearing rumors that Spain planned to transfer New Orleans to France, Jefferson was ready to use force, but first, in early 1803, he sent James Monroe to Paris with instructions to try to buy New Orleans and West Florida. Monroe found France's foreign minister, Talleyrand, ready to sell all of Louisiana. A slave rebellion in Haiti made its food production irrelevant, and with war with England on the horizon, Napoleon preferred to have his troops back in Europe. The result was Jefferson's congressionally unsanctioned decision to purchase a land mass as large as all thirteen colonies added together. Claiming the survival of the nation was at stake, President Jefferson asserted a "higher obligation" than "scrupulous adherence to [the] written law" of the United States Constitution.[57]

Jefferson and his countrymen saw no contradiction between their antipathy toward Old World power politics and their own continual territorial acquisition. Their displacement of the French and the British from the western territories seemed a matter of divine destiny rather than foreign policy. Upon leaving office in 1809, Jefferson told Madison that after Florida, Cuba, and Canada were annexed, the United States would constitute "such an empire for liberty as [the world] has never surveyed since the creation. And I am persuaded no constitution was ever before so well calculated as ours for extensive empire and self-government."[58] Indeed, it was Madison's own theory of the "extended republic" that had lain the groundwork for Jefferson's sublime confidence. ("This form of government," Madison wrote in 1787, "in order to effect its purposes, must operate not within a small but an extensive sphere."[59]) Like his predecessor, he rested his belief in America's destiny on the premise that the United States would continue to expand almost indefinitely, but without resort to military conquest. Madison, too, condemned war as the root of all evil—the precursor of taxes and armies and all other "instruments for hiring the many under the domination of the few."[60] Indeed, the idea of purchasing Louisiana, argues one Jefferson biographer, "could only have arisen in a nation and with an administration determined to settle international disputes without resort to force."[61] But in the republican political imagination, the wars fought with Native Americans to secure the western territories explicitly did not qualify as such.

The Native American simply did not figure in the Founders' calcula-tions. In 1780, Virginia's governor, Thomas Jefferson, wrote Revolution-ary frontier leader George Rogers Clark in words that would become painfully close to prophecy, "If we are to wage a campaign against these Indians, the end proposed should be their extermination, or their removal beyond the lakes of the Illinois River. The same world will scarcely do for them and us."[62] After purchasing the Louisiana territory from France, Jefferson secured legislation to allow him to rule over its population of Shawnee, Pottawatomie, Cherokee, Creek, Chickasaw, Choctaw, and Seminole Indians as a virtual dictator until the place could be populated by proper Anglo-Saxons capable of self-government.[63]

In the early decades of the Republic, U.S. foreign policy reflected the conflicts that shaped the character of American life itself: the desire to "do good" in terms of republican virtue while "doing well" in terms of liberal commerce; the desire to stand with the conservative, established power of the British versus the almost hysterical vision of liberty repre-sented by the French Revolution; the desire to stand outside and above the conflicts that characterized the European state system while employ-ing brutal military tactics to create sufficient space to avoid the cycle of war and poverty that the state system allegedly created. With almost every action cloaked in the language of religious predestination, the for-eign policy of the Founding Fathers presented a faithful replica of the tensions that tore at the infant American (white male) character. Under-lying all of it was a hierarchical system of racial exclusion that viewed Negroes as chattel and Latins and Indians as savages. Republican free-dom existed only for those in the imagined community of Revolutionar-ies.[64] It rested, moreover, on consistent presidential subversion of the fundamental constitutional constraints of the office's democratically enjoined powers.

The War of 1812 was primarily a tribute to President James Madison's political incompetence. The British proved willing to concede on the cru-cial issues, but the message did not reach the president until after he asked Congress for a declaration of war. Westerners demanded war once they discovered that Native American warriors were being armed by England through Canada, and Madison could not convince them other-wise. The western representatives elected the militant "War Hawk," Henry Clay, Speaker of the House and forced Madison to toe their bel-ligerent line. Because Madison's opponent, New York governor DeWitt Clinton, was unambiguously antiwar, the election provided a clear choice, with the West demanding war, the middle states divided, and New England clearly for peace. (The region's merchants were so infuriated by the war's disastrous impact on their trade with Britain that some threatened to secede.) Madison's desultory war message failed to sway the war's opponents, and a nasty seventeen-day congressional debate resulted. It would be the last time that a President would ask Congress for the formal power to go to war while uncertain of ultimately having his way.[65]

Following the war's inconclusive conclusion, however, Britain retreated from its former colonies, and the United States found itself freed from the political implications of European conflict. For military purposes, at least, the nation was invulnerable. It marched west. While thirteen colonies had made the Revolution, by 1824 there were twenty-four states. The population doubled every twenty-second year and showed no signs of abatement. That America would continue to expand into the West seemed no less natural than the fact that the sun would continue to set there.

Nowhere was the political character of the newly confident young nation better revealed than in President Monroe's 1823 enunciation of the Monroe Doctrine, viewed by many historians as the cornerstone of American diplomacy. The doctrine was inspired by reports that Czar Alexander intended to extend Russian territorial claims southward along the Pacific coast, coupled with indications that the French, backed by Russia, Prussia, and Austria, were planning to use military force to reassert control over the newly independent Spanish colonies in Latin America.[66] The president declared any attempt on the part of the European powers to "extend their system to any portion of this hemisphere as dangerous to our peace and safety." Henceforth, the Americas would be ruled exclusively by Americans.[67]

For all of its subsequent rhetorical power, the Monroe Doctrine was irrelevant to its stated purposes. Its enforcement power rested solely on the power of the British navy, hardly an instrument under the control of Congress or the president. It was (and is) also meaningless as a matter of international law. The alleged success of the Monroe Doctrine was therefore a kind of useful fiction made possible by the world's lack of interest. Masked beneath its rhetoric, however, was a formula that would come to embody U.S. foreign policy for the ensuing 150 years. It combined soaring idealism with a sense of separation from the Old World while at the same time proclaiming the American right to unbridled expansion as if completely ignorant of the civilizations that already occupied those spaces.

Like Jefferson and Madison, John Quincy Adams, Monroe's secretary of state and the genius behind the doctrine, fully expected the United States to dominate the entire continent one day. He declared, in 1811, that North America was "destined . . . to be peopled by one nation, speaking one language, professing one general system of religious and political principles, and accustomed to one general tenor of social usages and customs."[68] But Adams was simultaneously enthralled by the commercial possibilities of South America. His masterful negotiation with Spain's Don Luis de Onis in 1819 not only secured Florida and created a boundary that extended all the way to the Pacific, but also laid a foundation for the Monroe Doctrine and a claim to the Oregon territory. It therefore helped determine the direction of American expansionism for half a century.[69] Adams's commitment to an American global commercial empire explains the fervor with which the Monroe Doctrine proclaimed American primacy over the entire hemisphere, when previously the mind's eye of U.S. foreign policy had gazed exclusively north and west. William Appleman Williams points to this as the moment when Adams became aware that the infant nation had acquired the financial might and sophistication to pursue its objectives economically rather than militarily, something Washington had foretold in his farewell address. Explaining to the Congress what Washington had meant, Adams pointedly drew the obvious conclusion. "Must we not say," he asked rhetorically, "that the period which he predicted as then not far off has arrived?" Economic predominance, notes Williams, "would mean effective control without limiting America's freedom of action."[70]

Adams may well be the most successful diplomat in American history. His deeply held beliefs were wholly consistent with the liberal republican philosophy of the Founders and the exceptional principles outlined in Washington's farewell address. Adams achieved even greater heights of eloquence in 1821, when he issued a blistering warning for the ages:

> Wherever the standard of freedom and independence has been or shall be unfurled, there will her [America's] heart, her benedictions and her prayers be. But she goes not abroad, in search of monsters to destroy. She is the well-wisher to the freedom and independence of all. She is the champion and vindicator only of her own. . . . She well knows that by once enlisting under other banners than her own, were they even the banners of foreign independence, she would involve herself, beyond the power of extrication, in all the wars of interest and intrigue, of individual avarice, envy, and ambition, which assume the colors and usurp the stan-

dard of freedom. . . . She might become the dictatress of the world; she would no longer be the ruler of her own spirit.[71]

But like both Washington and Jefferson, Adams found he could not achieve his ambitious foreign policy without sacrificing his equally ambitious standards of republican virtue and democratic governance. When Adams defended Andrew Jackson's 1818 invasion of Florida, he employed the same lies and evasions to which his predecessors had resorted. To justify his president's policies in Central America, Secretary of State Adams sent Congress purposely incomplete sets of documents to create the illusion of democratic participation in the foreign policy process while actually subverting it. When challenged by opponents to these policies in the West, he published a series of letters under the pseudonym "Phocion" to mislead unsuspecting readers.[72]

Adams replaced Monroe as president in the three-way contest of 1824, only to be soundly trounced by Andrew Jackson, the war hero, four years later. With the expansion of the franchise to even unpropertied white males (save in Mississippi and Rhode Island), the direct election of senators in most states, and the massive increase in physical distances traveled by voters' representatives, Americans' definition of citizenship underwent a gradual transformation. Past practices had kept election winners close to home and losers ready to take advantage of any perceived distance between elector and electee. After each session, Robert Wiebe notes, "legislators were expected to come home and talk about it: what had they done? Why? What would they do next?"[73] But the rituals of self-governance as practiced in the New England colonies were no longer appropriate in a nation growing so large and so populous.

The cost of politics rose continuously as ambitious men amassed political empires of local machines and newspaper chains to back their candidacies. Politics became a career rather than an avocation, and its prohibitive entry fee disqualified all but the well-to-do. These new developments also had the effect of divorcing the representatives and the represented, as presidents and senators grew ever more physically remote from the people under whose direction they theoretically acted. Harriet Martineau, a British traveler who spent two years in America during the mid-1830s, arrived expecting to see Americans talking incessantly of politics. Instead, she discovered a pervasive political ennui. A fervent democrat, Martineau lamented the "almost insane dread of responsibility that had taken over the Republic."[74] Alexis de Tocqueville, who also traveled during this period, coined the word "individualism" to describe a "calm and considered feeling which disposes each citizen to isolate himself from the mass of his fellows and withdraw into the circle of family and friends. With this little society formed to his taste, he gladly leaves the greater society to look after itself."[75]

The distancing of the people from their representatives might also be seen as the inevitable result of the enormous economic and technological transformations stirring in America in the early part of the nineteenth century. While the great capitalist enterprises of the robber barons were still decades away, the nature of labor was changing. A work force that had been made up of small, largely self-employed and self-reliant tradesmen and farmers was now giving way to an increasing number of factory wage workers. John Dewey notes, paradoxically, that the theory of the freely choosing individual self that undergirded the Jacksonian political revolution "was framed at just the time when the individual was counting for less in the direction of social affairs, at a time when mechanical forces and vast impersonal organizations were determining the frame of things." Modern economic forces liberated the individual from traditional communal ties as they simultaneously disempowered individuals and local communities. The "crisis of self-government and the erosion of [republican] community," Michael Sandel argues, were therefore closely connected.[76]

The final nail in the coffin of republican political culture in America proved to be the degree to which the inexorable dynamic of expansion and empire came to strangle the sinews of democratic practice. Excluding the tariff battles that regularly divided Congress and occasionally brought the representatives to blows, U.S. foreign policy operated on the principle of virtual representation. Most often, the policy reflected what was either an underlying consensus of the politically active or else a negative consensus that such matters were not worth active politicking. Following the Treaty of Ghent, however, and with it the end of American involvement in the affairs of Great Power politics, citizens had little inspiration to occupy themselves with matters of foreign affairs. Westward expansion was considered a matter of destiny rather than policy.

Though many Americans understood that the annexation of Texas, and later, half of Mexico, could well bring simmering regional tensions to their boiling point, many nevertheless felt helpless to resist what appeared to be a kind of perpetual motion machine. U.S. Treasury Secretary Robert J. Walker said nothing controversial in 1847 when he explained, in an official government report, that "a higher than any earthly power" had guided America's expansion and "still guards and directs our destiny, impels us onward and has selected our great and happy country as a model and ultimate center of attraction for all the nations of the world."[77] "Expand or die" became what Walter LaFeber calls the "shadowy underside of American thinking" as populations continued to double each generation. Millions of immigrants from Germany and Ireland flooded the northeastern cities, and soil-depleting farming techniques (and increasing numbers of slaves) impelled southeastern landholders to demand more and more western territory.[78] These tensions, coupled with President James K. Polk's decidedly underhanded political tactics, eventually exploded in the Mexican War. Polk threatened war with both Britain and Mexico during his aggressive 1844 campaign.[79] When the British proved conciliatory, he made war on the Mexicans. As with the organized slaughter and displacement of Native Americans, the injustices suffered by the Mexicans in a war described by Ulysses S. Grant as "one of the most unjust waged by a stronger against a weaker nation" concerned precious few Americans.[80] Combining both the philosophy of Manifest Destiny with the racial hierarchy that underlay the nation's Indian policies, the *New York Evening Post* (founded by Alexander Hamilton) observed, "Providence has so ordained it. . . . The Mexicans are aboriginal Indians, and they must share the destiny of their race."[81]

Polk's conquest of Mexico did more than simply add a million square miles to the union and set the stage for America's bloodiest conflict. His actions in Mexico also set the stage for what would become the "imperial" American presidency of the twentieth century. In the decade of Polk's election, Tocqueville pointed out that it was "chiefly in foreign relations that the executive power of the nation finds occasion to exert its skill and its strength." In foreign policy, he noted, the president "possesses almost royal prerogatives."[82]

What Polk demonstrated, as John Quincy Adams noted at the time, was that "the President of the United States has but to declare that War exists with any nation and the War is essentially declared." Congress never declared war against Mexico. It simply "recognized" the existence of war, as the president demanded, based on Polk's false claim that the Mexicans had attacked an American army detachment on American soil.[83] (He had, in fact, instructed his generals to take actions designed to provoke the conflict.) Indeed, in January 1848, the House nearly passed a resolution proclaiming that the conflict had been "unnecessarily and unconstitutionally begun by the President of the United States."[84] Polk presented no evidence that war was necessary. No organized political force was pushing for it, and much of the fighting was over before the public knew it had begun.

To be fair, the war announcement did inspire considerable enthusiasm. Large pro-war demonstrations took place in Baltimore, New York, Indianapolis, and elsewhere. "A military ardor pervades all ranks," Herman Melville wrote his brother. "Nothing is talked of but the 'Halls of Montezumas.' Mexico must be thoroughly chastised," Walt Whitman chimed in.[85] Given the degree of public euphoria, it took a brave, one-term-only Illinois congressman to focus on the dangers inherent in Polk's constitutional end run. As young Abe Lincoln stated in 1848:

Allow the President to invade a neighboring nation, whenever *he* shall deem it necessary to repel an invasion, and you allow him to do so, *whenever he may choose to say* he deems it necessary for such purpose—and you allow him to make war at pleasure. Study to see if you can fix *any limit* to his power in this respect, after you have given him so much as you propose. . . . You may say to him, "I see no probability of the British invading us," but he will say to you, "be silent; I see it, if you don't."

The provision of the Constitution giving the war-making power to Congress was dictated, as I understand it, by the following reasons: Kings had always been involving and impoverishing their people in wars, pretending generally, if not always, that the good of the people was the object. This our [Constitutional] convention understood to be the most oppressive of all Kingly oppressions; and they resolved to so frame the Constitution that *no one* man should hold the power of bringing this oppression upon us.[86]

Lincoln here invokes the same fears that haunted Washington, Jefferson, and Madison sixty years earlier, as well as those of Monroe and John Quincy Adams. Together these men defined an American foreign policy tradition that sought to avoid war at *almost* all costs, lest it lead naturally to impoverishment, tyranny, and the destruction of the necessary physical foundations of republican virtue. This fear constituted perhaps the single defining ideal of republican foreign policy, and it was this belief upon which Polk trampled in pursuit of Manifest Destiny.

Polk, however, was not without his own precedent in the Founders' own compromises between their republican hopes and the liberal expansionist demands that underwrote them. Jefferson's "empire of liberty" was hardly rhetorical. President Jefferson had threatened war and willingly subverted his own understanding of the Constitution in pursuit of Louisiana. Madison, with Monroe as his secretary of state, had gone to war in 1812 for reasons that, while complex, were also not unrelated to the success of his beloved "extended republic." Monroe and Adams had uncritically endorsed the view of their predecessors that the success of the republican experiment was almost wholly dependent on the continued availability of fertile land for America's free men. Representative John Quincy Adams, who denounced Polk's chicanery as "duplicitous diplomacy" and demanded "all of the documents" relating to what he termed Polk's "usurpation" of Congress's power to declare war, was hardly in a position to complain.[87] "Virtue" depended on expansion, however unvirtuously undertaken. The commerce that the cultivation of such land produced tended to undermine virtue over time, but this tension was preferable to its certain destruction by war, inequality, and oppression within the self-defined category of worthy citizenship. That each of these exquisitely morally sensitive and subtle thinkers thought little of subverting the intention of the Constitution even while pursuing a war of unapologetic terrorism against the Native Americans adds further emphasis to our understanding that, for all their fear of Jefferson's war/impoverishment/oppression iron triangle, the material bottom line of republican foreign policy was unbridled expansionism.

Before the Civil War, the executive branch of the U.S. federal government did not really qualify as a "state" in the familiar European sense of the term. The German philosopher G. W. F. Hegel could find none of its necessary underpinnings in the American government.[88] The ratio of U.S. federal expenditure to gross domestic product usually equaled 15 to 20 percent of that routinely achieved in European nations.[89] In the case of most citizens, the federal government existed primarily in the abstract. The citizenry paid no federal taxes and drove on no federal roads. The federal government's mandates extended only to six areas of the economy: internal improvements, subsidies (mainly to shipping), tariffs, public lands disposal, patents, and currency. Most of these mandates involved the promotion of commerce. Almost none of them involved what we now call "regulation."[90] In fact, until the war, most Americans probably never had reason to encounter a single federal government agent in their entire lives. The Civil War changed all this, threatening constitutionally guaranteed civil liberties, accelerating the accumulation of power in the executive, and further complicating the relationship between U.S. democracy and foreign policy. The United States, as Garry Wills has pointed out, became a singular rather than collective pronoun.

The centralization of federal power had significant implications for the conduct of a democratic foreign policy, none of them auspicious. With the institution of the draft, the income tax, and the massive logistical and propaganda efforts necessary to defeat the secessionist states, the American government began to acquire the accoutrements of power that would later preclude even the possibility of a democratic foreign policy debate. Barely two weeks after the fall of Fort Sumter, Lincoln suspended the writ of habeus corpus. In August 1862 the War Department authorized U.S. officials to arrest and detain persons engaged in any "disloyal practice." The same orders permitted civilians to be tried before military commissions.[91] The extraordinary changes that resulted from, or took place during, the Civil War—to say nothing of Reconstruction and its ensuing military occupation of the South—are beyond the purview of this discussion. But in many important ways, America in the 1870s was no longer the same country it had been in the 1850s.

As in antebellum America, foreign policy beyond the western plains remained a minor consideration. The business of Reconstruction and reconciliation took up most of the nation's political energy, and its commercial development continued unimpeded. The explosive energy of the burgeoning capitalist machine that defeated the South expanded into Central and South America, remaking governments and reordering those societies in its wake. The nation ran its first trade surplus in 1874 and would continue to do so for the following ninety-seven years. The 1880s, moreover, saw the creation of America's first genuinely multinational corporations as Singer Sewing Machine, Standard Oil, and Kodak Camera began investing overseas in order to facilitate their foreign sales. Tariff battles, with the Democrats representing free traders and Republicans representing protectionists, helped to define the two parties in an era of little discernible ideological conflict, but plenty of commercial and economic competition.

For the purposes of constructing the ideology of modern American foreign policy, the 1890s proved to be the pivotal decade. The year 1890 marked the construction of the U.S. Navy's first battleship and the publication of Alfred Thayer Mahan's opus, *The Influence of Sea Power on History*. Mahan was a great admirer of the British naval empire and had turned a lifetime of study into a strategic argument for the United States to mimic England's path of naval superiority and unilateral intervention as a means of maintaining a global empire. He hated Thomas Jefferson and consciously sought to undermine his hold on the American political imagination. Mahan's America required a powerful national government willing to use war and intimidation for what Henry Kissinger would later term, *raison d'état.*[92] Like many an American grand strategist, Mahan spoke of using amoral means to achieve an inspirational end, in this case, America's "great mission" to remake non-Western civilization in our image. This mission dovetailed nicely with American economic interests—another repetitive pattern in American history, though Mahan insisted that "mere utilitarian arguments . . . have never convinced nor converted mankind." Citizens refused to "be commanded by peace, presented as the tutelary deity of the stock-market."[93] Not coincidentally, however, stock markets did just fine under Mahanian strategic tutelage. As U.S. manufacturers grew in power and scope, their interests began to lie less in protection, which raised the cost of their raw materials, than in free trade, which offered them unfettered access to world markets. These interests, together with Mahan's arguments, would provide the foundation for the birth of a global navy—another of the founders' nightmares. American business leaders, acting as the best organized and most persuasive of democratic actors, were claiming vast new markets in the Far East and appreciated the military means to enforce an "open door" policy there should the nation's erstwhile trading partners behave uncooperatively.[94]

As Mahan was revolutionizing the American military's understanding of its strategic function, the U.S. census bureau was finalizing work on a propitious report announcing the "end" of America's western frontier. Three years later, on July 12, 1893, amid the hoopla of the celebrated "White City" of the Chicago World's Fair, a young Wisconsin historian named Frederick Jackson Turner constructed from this raw material a new manifesto. The western frontier, he argued, "with its new opportunities, its continuous touch with the simplicity of primitive society, furnish[ed] the forces dominating American life." Expansion promoted individualism, which "from the beginning, promoted democracy." The frontier had been "a magic fountain of youth in which America continuously bathed and rejuvenated." It mitigated class fissures, encouraged democratic habits, and fertilized republican virtues, providing Americans with a degree of independence and equality unknown elsewhere on the planet.[95] While Turner himself was no less interested in the expansion of the American spirit than of its landmass, his interpreters understood his thesis to imply the Jeffersonian equation that free land equals democratic governance and republican virtue. Its disappearance therefore endangered the American experiment itself. The Turnerist response to this crisis was to jettison the fundamental aims that animated the foreign policies of Washington, Jefferson, and Adams in order to embrace the expansion that supported them. This turnabout demanded exactly the kinds of foreign military conquests that in the republican imagination would guarantee the destruction of political virtue. Poised on the cusp of empire, America had outgrown its Revolutionary republican ideals. Armed and educated by Turner and Mahan, the nation went in search of foreign monsters to destroy.

The democratic appeal of Turnerism was undeniable. The Turner thesis, notes William Appleman Williams, "rolled through the universities and into popular literature as a tidal wave." Turner's compact historical survey gave Americans a worldview that settled their uneasiness, calmed their confusion, eased their doubts, and provided a philosophical foundation for their imperial dreams. Combining America's new understanding of virtue with its historic attachment to commerce, the new secular gospel tapped into deep wells of American self-interest and self-perception. Despite its inherent self-contradictions, or more likely because of them, its appeal spread across political, economic, and religious lines, uniting Democrats and Republicans, financiers and workers, atheists and missionaries.[96] Sacrificing principles of limited and constitutional government, Turnerism nevertheless paid heed to the ideal that had provided their necessary foundation: rugged republican individualism based on ceaseless expansion. Undergirded by Mahan, it cast aside those aspects of Jeffersonianism that had become inconsistent with an ideology of unlimited expansion and laid the groundwork for neoimperialist foreign policy based on economic manipulation and backed up by the occasional Marine landing.

Turner entered the back door of Theodore Roosevelt's White House through the influence of Brooks Adams, who closely advised the president and his secretary of state, John Hay, during Roosevelt's two terms. Confronting the same data as Turner, Adams counseled a policy of expansion, both commercial and political, into Asia, which required a navy of the sort Mahan envisioned. Turner's influence arrived more directly in Woodrow Wilson's administration. Williams calls the historian an "unseen intellectual roomer in the [Wilson] White House." Wilson and Turner had been extremely close at Johns Hopkins University in the 1880s. Wilson relied extensively on Turner's frontier thesis in presenting his own interpretation of American history, going so far as to write, "All I ever wrote on the subject came from him." This may have been an exaggeration, but it would be hard to miss Turner's influence on Wilson's thinking. In an essay on American expansion after 1896, Wilson explained, "The spaces of their own continent were occupied and reduced to the uses of civilization; they had no frontiers. . . . These new frontiers in the Indies and in the Far Pacific came to them as if out of the very necessity of the new career before them." The impact of Turner's thesis can be seen as far into the future as Franklin Roosevelt's speech before the San Francisco Commonwealth Club during the 1932 presidential campaign, just one year shy of the essay's fortieth anniversary. "Our last frontier has long since been reached," FDR announced. "There is no safety valve in the form of a Western prairie. . . . Our task now is not discovery or exploitation of natural resources, or necessarily producing more goods. It is the . . . less dramatic business of administering resources and plants already in hand, of seeking to reestablish foreign markets for our surplus production."[97]

While secular issues dominated both men's philosophies, the glue that joined Mahan and Turner together in many Americans' understanding was the power of the nation's growing missionary sensibility. Many Americans believed Protestant Christianity to be a spiritual precondition for modernization. Participants and spectators at the World Congress Auxiliary to the 1893 Columbian Exposition, where Turner first revealed his thesis, frequently called the World's Fair, the "Divine Exposition," or the "New Jerusalem." The organizer of the Exposition's Religious Congress proclaimed the American purpose "of building up the Kingdom of Christ in America is to engage with fresh ardor in efforts to Christianize India and Africa, Turkey and China."[98] Five years later, American religious leaders argued strenuously for annexation of the Philippines following their conquest in the Spanish-American War, so that they might be "uplifted and civilized by God's grace" in the carefully chosen words of President William McKinley.[99] This decision, hardly coincidentally, marks the beginning of America's acquisition of formal sovereignty over nonwhite, non-English-speaking peoples abroad—exactly the primary danger to the foundations of republican virtue most feared by the Founders.

What virtues such arrangements may have offered the black, brown, and red inhabitants of the hemisphere were subsumed in America's now dominant ideology of Lockean liberalism, Protestant Christianity, and ceaseless expansion. A nation that is sufficiently powerful to impose its will in so many fashions simultaneously need never face up to potential contradictions regarding just where that will may lead.

Tocqueville believed that "the sovereignty of the people and the freedom of the press are . . . two correlative things."[100] Quite a bit had transpired with regard to the media's relationship to democracy in the ensuing half-century. Technological innovation and the growth of advertising brought the cost of newspaper production down to less than a penny per paper by 1841. Before the onset of the penny press, one paper in America was sold for every fourteen or fifteen inhabitants. By 1880, this ratio fell to nearly one paper per person.[101] But the precise role played by the new mass-circulation newspapers is enormously difficult to pin down. Certainly, the explosion in circulation contributed powerfully to President McKin-ley's decision to go to war with Spain in 1898. Joseph Pulitzer's *New York World* increased its daily circulation from 150,000 in 1896 to more than 800,000 in 1898 as a result of its coverage of Cuba. The paper greatly agi-tated the atmosphere in which foreign policy decision making took place. The trumpeting of various insults to America's honor, outrages to com-mon decency, and the alleged terrorist explosion aboard the U.S. battle-ship *Maine* in the winter of 1898 created an irresistible political momen-tum for war.[102] "The Whole Country Thrills with the War Fever," shouted William Randolph Hearst's *New York Journal* on its front page three days after the explosion. On its best day, the *Journal* printed 1,068,000 copies, and its managing editor, Arthur Brisbane, complained that this number was 200,000 too few.[103] Pulitzer's *World*, which sent its correspondents to interview more than a hundred American women in the aftermath of the *Maine* tragedy, discovered "American Women Ready to Give Up Hus-bands, Sons, and Sweethearts to Defend Nation's Honor."[104]

Evidence is inconclusive as to whether McKinley himself wanted war. Powerful interests, including the Rockefeller, Morgan, and Pullman empires, all doubted its value.[105] The president frequently appealed to the public for patience. But if it was patience he wanted, he was presi-dent of the wrong country. When it came, the war proved every bit as divisive as all the rest of America's wars, save the one forced upon us in 1941. That it appeared to be inspired by a popular outcry, clearly manip-ulated by less than savory elements of the popular media, gave further impetus to those who believed that such decisions must be kept out of the fray of democratic debate.

Yellow journalism, the *Maine*, Cuban propagandists working through the American media with imagined atrocity stories, and the internal threat felt by Republicans coming from free-silver Democrats all combined to create a popular drumbeat for war that no president could ignore.[106] "American Friends of Cuba" gathered 300,000 signatures in three weeks demanding it; both houses of Congress treated the public to daily atrocity reports while attempting to recognize the belligerency on their own.[107] The National Association of Manufacturers, founded in 1895, was already clamoring for the creation of new markets. Pacific bases were required to protect the merchant marine. Massachusetts mill owners were pressuring their representatives to "take the strongest possible action" to find a place to sell their cotton goods.[108] Spain was willing to capitulate on virtually every term the Americans demanded, but this seemed somehow beside the point. Congress and the yellow press demanded a "splendid little war" to fight.[109] When the president hesitated in asking Congress for a declaration of war after the *Maine* explosion, the *Chicago Tribune* editors wondered what the president "hoped to accomplish by this desperate defiance of the popular will." The *World* demanded that Spain make amends within forty-eight hours "under a threat of bombardment." Teddy Roosevelt, then assistant navy secretary, publicly called for the United States to expel Spain from the New World and privately termed the president a "white-livered cur" with "no more back-bone than a chocolate éclair."[110] The *Journal*'s huge banner headline called for "Armed Intervention at Once!"[111] When war finally came, on April 25, Hearst's paper boasted, "HOW DO YOU LIKE THE JOURNAL'S WAR?"[112] Just how exaggerated this claim was is difficult to say.

Once the fighting began, it seemed almost churlish for Americans to refuse to pick off the Philippines from the rotting Spanish empire as well, and President McKinley claimed to act under divine advisement in doing so. But William James noted that despite all the talk of "raising and educating inferior races," imperialism had become a "peculiarly exciting kind of sport" for Americans.[113] Anti-imperialists drew strength from the fearfully nonwhite skins of the Philippines' inhabitants, coupled with what remained of Americans' republican reflexes, which recoiled from the acquisition of corruptive empires. The debate over the issue grew clouded, however, when William Jennings Bryan instructed anti-imperialist Senate Democrats to vote in favor of McKinley's expansionist treaty with Spain in the hopes that its passage would provide a clear target for his anti-imperialist presidential campaign in 1900. This was foolishness on a grand scale. Americans are nothing if not pragmatic. They are therefore loath to reopen settled controversies on mere matters of principle. Regarding nonterritorial expansion, moreover, Americans' racism and residual republicanism conflicted with their now dominant belief in Manifest Destiny, as Anders Stephanson convincingly demonstrates.[114] But Bryan's folly ensured that the United States would take responsibility for the brutal subjugation of the Philippines while simultaneously short-circuiting what might have been a seminal debate on the question of expansion and imperialism before the question became moot.

By the end of the nineteenth century, America's leaders had repudiated the central republican principles enunciated by Washington, Jefferson, Madison, Monroe, and the two Adamses. The problem, quite appropriately, was expansion. The Founders had sidestepped their own warning to future generations to uphold peace at almost any cost by creating a racial hierarchy that somehow defined military campaigns that resulted in the large-scale killing of Indians and Mexicans as "peaceful." (Witness President Roosevelt's 1901 remark that when the U.S. government fought "wars with barbarous or semi-barbarous peoples," this was not war, but merely the exercise of "a most regrettable but necessary international police duty which must be performed for the sake of the welfare of mankind."[115]) Jefferson's Louisiana Purchase, moreover, delayed the choice between virtue and empire by allowing this expansion to take place with only aboriginal victims in its path. But the Jeffersonian republican vision turned out to be a kind of devil's bargain, even judged on his own racist terms. Believing he was providing an alternative vision to Alexander Hamilton's hopes for an unequal, urbanized commercialized economy, Jefferson gambled that by ignoring what he understood to be the constitutional limits on his power as president, he could provide his country with sufficient arable land to house a nation of republican yeoman farmers in perpetuity. Instead, his successors seized Jefferson's example of ignoring constitutional strictures on the president's powers in foreign policy and placed this power at the foot of a commercial economy that grew and expanded into a great power beyond Alexander Hamilton's imagination. When the land ran out, the expansion and abuses of presidential power continued to escalate, leading to foreign wars of conquest, entangling alliances, the creation of a large standing army, and the trampling of the very republican values this expansion had been intended to protect. Lockean liberalism, adjusted for empire building and missionary reform, became the American creed. America's unsolved Tocqueville problem, festering quietly in the nineteenth century, would grow like a cancerous tumor on its constitution in the twentieth.

CHAPTER TWO

Slouching toward Rome

Public opinion is the voice of the devil.
—Theodore Roosevelt

During the first half of the twentieth century, the forces that had combined to weaken the bonds between the leaders and the led in the
nation's first century spawned new and more challenging barriers to a
foreign policy process based on democratic rule and republican principle. War, industrialization, immigration, class conflict, and the acquisition of empire frequently overwhelmed the American political system to
the point where democracy often appeared an afterthought when it
appeared at all.

Theodore Roosevelt and Woodrow Wilson may not have agreed on
much, but both men held a profoundly expansive view of presidential
power. Each man continued to enlarge the foreign policy prerogatives of
his office. Neither president believed his responsibilities to voters
included an honest accounting of the nation's foreign and military alternatives. Wilson's decision to enter into World War I, moreover, resulted
in a number of temporary curtailments of Americans' rights of free
speech. Franklin Roosevelt built on this legacy, making permanent many
of the limits on public discussion and knowledge his predecessors had
instituted on a temporary basis. The failure of the public to master the
intricacies of public policy—and its apparent disinclination even to try—
led America's most influential intellectuals to question the efficacy of
democracy itself. Progressivism, the twentieth century's response to the
liberal republican dilemma in the context of a capitalist economy and a
growing American empire, became, in some instances, antidemocratic.
The net result of these trends would prepare the groundwork for a con-

certed U.S. government effort by the end of World War II to limit the public's right to even the most fundamental information relating to matters of "national security." Such secrecy caused a cycle of self-fulfilling prophecies. When citizens are denied the information they need to make informed political choices, intelligent democratic decision making becomes impossible.

President Theodore Roosevelt had little use for public opinion. When he dispatched American troops in Latin America, admittedly less frequently than did either Taft or Wilson, he rarely consulted Congress or anyone else.[1] When the Senate refused to approve a treaty allowing the United States to operate the custom houses of Santo Domingo, he simply concluded the deal by executive agreement. He employed the same tactic to acquiesce, in secret, to Japan's decision to establish a military protectorate over Korea. Roosevelt, the former police chief, believed that "the increasing interdependence and complexity of international political and economic relations render it incumbent on all civilized and orderly powers to insist on the proper policing of the world."[2] His police plans included vigorous diplomatic, and, when necessary, military, intervention in those areas he deemed to be America's responsibilities, and he was not about to allow Congress or the American people to interfere in these plans in any fashion.[3] When Congress refused to pay for his plans to dispatch the country's shiny new Great White Fleet of sixteen battleships around the world, he simply sent them halfway and then dared the legislative branch to refuse to pay to bring them back.

Even more than Roosevelt, perhaps, Wilson believed that at critical times, "the pleasure of the people" had to give way to presidential power. "He *exercises* power and we *obey*," he wrote in an early study of the workings of constitutional government.[4] No American president has ever used force more frequently than Thomas Woodrow Wilson. From April 1914 to July 1918 alone, Wilson committed U.S. troops in Haiti, in the Dominican Republic, in World War I, in northern Russia, in Siberia, and twice in Mexico. Excluding the World War, none of these military operations was congressionally authorized. Wilson also used his personal advisor, Colonel Edward M. House, as a kind of private secretary of state, empowered to speak for him but unanswerable to Congress.[5] Public debate in all these cases was minimal at best.

Both men operated from an understanding of American interests that stood diametrically opposed to the principled noninterference and self-disciplined pursuit of peace outlined by the Founders. Roosevelt's "corollary" to the Monroe Doctrine asserted a U.S. right to meddle inter-nally in the affairs of a Latin American nation whenever Roosevelt deemed another country to have been unable or unwilling "to do justice at home or abroad," or to have taken an action that "violated the rights of the United States or invited foreign aggression." Though he was a generally cautious statesman and superb foreign policy tactician, Roo-sevelt nevertheless operated from a world-historical view imbued with a sense of glorious mission. On the global stage, as on the North American continent, "civilization" was contesting "barbarism" for control of man's destiny. America's responsibility lay in expanding the power of the force of light without risking its own limited civilizing resources in the process.[6] While Roosevelt was a confident but prudent policeman, Woodrow Wilson was an intoxicated one. To Wilson, absolutely nothing that concerned humanity could be "foreign or indifferent to" the inter-ests of the United States.[7] As the planet's "only idealistic nation," charged with "redeem[ing] the world by giving it peace and justice, " America had not merely a right, but a duty to slay foreign monsters.[8] No goal was too ambitious for Wilson's missionary aims. When asked to explain his Mexican policy to a British emissary in 1914, Wilson confi-dently explained, "I am going to teach the South American republics to elect good men."[9] Wilson even attempted to interpret Washington's farewell address in a manner that would be consistent with such pro-nouncements, but a more sweeping reversal of the Founders' foreign policy principles is difficult to imagine.[10]

While Roosevelt and Wilson were similarly untroubled by the consti-tutional implications of frequent foreign and military intervention, they practiced these policies in pursuit of opposing goals. Roosevelt directed America's burgeoning power to foster a stable, lawful world trading order. He had no interest in allowing unruly natives to gum up the works of the marketplace with rebellions and revolutions unless ab-solutely necessary to secure American interests. Wilson, on the other hand, represented the full flowering of America's missionary sensibility. Wilson announced in 1915 that America could "not confine our enthusi-asm for individual liberty and free national development to the incidents and movements of affairs which affect only ourselves. We feel it wher-ever there is a people that tries to walk in these difficult paths of inde-pendence and right."[11]

The tradition to which Wilson hearkened predated America itself. In his landmark 1952 essay, "Errand Into the Wilderness," Perry Miller sug-gested that the Puritan crossing of the Atlantic had been "an essential maneuver in the drama of Christendom." The Puritans left England not as indigent refugees, but as "an organized task force of Christians" bent on creating a model of a reformed society that their fellow Englishman at home could emulate." The Puritans came to create, in the words of their leader John Winthrop, "a City upon a Hill, [for] the eyes of all people are upon us." Sacvan Bercovitch believes Miller's claims were overly modest. The Puritan rescue of the Reformation, insists Bercovitch, provides the essential American myth that even today continues to shape the lens through which Americans view the rest of the world. "The New England Puritans fired their gaze on the future" and forged a faith in progress that "gave America the status of visible sainthood," according to Bercovitch. They "used the Biblical myth of Exodus and conquest to justify imperialism before the fact." Herman Melville spoke of the United States as "the Israel of our time," a "political messiah, bearing the ark of the liberties of the world." Ronald Reagan quoted Winthrop in a nationally televised debate more than a century later.[12]

The missionary impulse in American foreign policy has always been present; indeed, its presence in the rhetoric of the Revolution and in the character of the men and women who made it, led Washington and John Quincy Adams to warn against it. In addition to its religious roots, the impulse also has Lockean underpinnings, clearest perhaps in the language of the Declaration of Independence. If Americans find it "self-evident that all men are created equal, that they are endowed by their Creator with certain unalienable rights," then it can hardly be said that foreigners are not endowed with these same rights as well.[13] While the doctrine found its most eloquent expression in the passionate prose of Tom Paine—also a favorite of President Reagan's—the ideology of millennial internationalism is present even in the writings of such conservative figures as Alexander Hamilton and John Adams. The latter proclaimed the founding of the colonies to be "the opening of a grand scene and design in Providence for the illumination of the ignorant, and the emancipation of the slavish part of mankind all over the earth."[14]

Politicians in the United States frequently invoke the language of altruism and uplift to justify actions that happen to increase the power, prestige, or commercial wealth of the nation—witness William McKinley on the "Christianizing" slaughter of the Filipinos.[15] Such benefits to Americans are usually said to be incidental to the main purpose of raising up indigent peoples, but just how seriously one takes these denials is usually a function of one's own ideological preconceptions. Europeans generally consider such talk by Americans to be unmitigated hypocrisy. Woodrow Wilson claimed to fight to "make the world safe for democracy." But he also noted, "If America is not to have free enterprise, then she can have freedom of no sort whatever. . . . We need foreign markets."[16]

Throughout the period under discussion, U.S. politics were dominated by a spirit of what is termed progressive reform, though the meaning of the term has become, if anything, even more confusing than that of republicanism. Following the Civil War and Reconstruction, as America experienced the simultaneous shocks of the loss of the frontier, the triumph of market capitalism, a massive influx of European and Asian immigrants, and the perceived unmooring of the rigorous religious beliefs that had sustained earlier generations, progressives attempted to reconstruct society though the use of modern techniques of social scientific inquiry and organization.[17] Progressivism had too many conflicting tendencies to be usefully considered a movement, but may be understood as a series of attempts to find new meaning in the American experience given the multiplicity of threats to the familiar myths that had hitherto sustained public life. Robert Wiebe, progressivism's most influential interpreter, terms the period one of a "search for order" in which politicians, the clergy, muckraking journalists, businesspeople, and various civic crusaders grappled with the inherent anarchy of capitalist economic life by attempting to introduce elements of stability and rational organization. They shared, according to Wiebe, an urge for a more efficient system of production, a growing reliance on executive decision making, an acceptance of bureaucracy, and a desire for the kinds of reforms that might be likely to reduce or eliminate the possibility of social chaos. Progressivism might be seen as an attempt to discover a republican political response to the destruction of the communal foundation that supported the Founders' republican hopes.

A republican community is possible, in a racist imagination, only among a homogeneous people. While Native Americans no longer existed in sufficient numbers to pose a threat to such hopes and Blacks remained politically quiescent, shackled by laws and economic conditions that prevented them from exercising their constitutional rights, the progressive imagination was nevertheless dogged by the perceived dangers implied by the massive immigration the United States experienced between 1880 and 1924. According to the 1910 census, more than a quarter of the U.S. population was either born abroad or had two foreign-born parents.[18]

Americans began to feel these new immigrants threatened their well-being and political stability, potentially paralyzing the nation's ability to continue to cohere. Early reactions on both the right and the left manifested a heavily racist anti-Asian component, but many Caucasian ethnic groups did not fare much better. A nativist writer named Madison Grant wrote a best-selling book in 1916 warning Americans of the dangers of "race suicide." These anxieties were stoked in nearly every strata of society. For instance in 1891 approximately 30,000 Italian immigrants resided in New Orleans. On March 4 of that year, a mob of white nativists lynched eleven Italians following the acquittal of one of their countrymen on a murder charge. Theodore Roosevelt called the action "a rather good thing" and boasted about it before "various dago diplomats."[19]

Viewed from the pastoral perspective of the would-be Jeffersonian yeoman farmer, the new immigrants brought to the United States previously unimaginable chaos. On the day von Moltke's troops crossed into Belgium in August 1914, German-Americans marched at a Bavarian volksfest in Harlem River Park and sent a congratulatory telegram to King Ludwig of Bavaria. In Chicago, Slavs and Germans fought in the streets. In Cincinnati, Russian Jews formed a volunteer regiment to fight alongside the Germans against the czar. Woodrow Wilson believed at the time that public opinion precluded any course other than neutrality, "since otherwise our mixed populations would wage war against each other."[20] What Wilson could not see, however, was that while the ethnic character of America may have been changing, the character of the foreign policy–making elite remained exclusively Anglo-American. U.S. foreign policy still operated in the realm of virtual representation. Irish, Italian, German, and Russian Jewish Americans may have fought one another over control of various industrial plants, and even for a few mayoralties. They could cause street demonstrations and the occasional labor strike. But in the early part of the century, none had yet developed the resources to challenge the entrenched Anglo-American hegemony over U.S. foreign policy.

The Populist movement of the late nineteenth century also frightened many Americans with its confrontational brand of class-based politics. Events like Chicago's Haymarket Square Riot of 1886 and the 1901 assassination of President McKinley by an immigrant anarchist led to worry among many Anglo-Americans that immigrants were injecting into American society a European style of political and class confrontation. As early as 1889, Professor Woodrow Wilson warned, "One hundred years ago we gained, and Europe lost, self-command, self-possession.

But since then we have been steadily receiving into our midst and to full participation in our national life the very people whom their home politics have familiarized with revolution: our own equable blood we have suffered to receive into it the most feverish blood of the restless old world."[21] This fear echoed that of Henry Watterson, the powerful owner/editor of the *Louisville Courier-Journal*. To Watterson, however, foreign policy, in the form of a new empire, appeared to promise a solution to these dangers. "We escape the menace and peril of socialism and agrarianism," he explained, "as England has escaped them, by a policy of colonization and conquest. From a provincial puddle of petty sovereignties held together by a rope of sand we rise to the dignity and prowess of an imperial republic incomparably greater than Rome. . . . We risk Caesarism, certainly; but even Caesarism is preferable to anarchism." Senator E. O. Wolcott of Colorado concurred. "It may well be that this people have found," he mused, "the one course which shall lead to the perpetuity of our institutions and the safety and stability of the Republic."[22]

Although it galvanized many politically contradictory campaigns, progressivism did inspire a reasonably coherent political manifesto: Herbert Croly's *Promise of American Life*. Soon to be the founding editor of the *New Republic*, Croly was enormously well connected in New York politics. His 1909 tome sought to marry Roosevelt's vigorous nationalism with the classical republican values of the Founders, tempered by the deeply Calvinistic sense of sin and redemption he detected in his supreme hero, Abraham Lincoln. His vision, notes John Patrick Diggins, is in some respects reminiscent of Samuel Adams's deeply republican hope for a new "Christian Sparta."[23] America's "promise," Croly argued, had been undermined by the "inevitable outcome of the chaotic individualism of our political and economic organization." What was necessary to regain that promise was not merely "the maximum amount of economic freedom," but "a certain measure of discipline" and "a large measure of individual subordination and self-denial."[24] Like Mahan, Croly fought to exorcise the ghost of Thomas Jefferson, arguing on behalf of a strong central government to help create and strengthen the institutions necessary to better discipline the new order of economic life. No less important to Croly's vision, however, was the necessity of America's transformation into a society based on "an instinctive familiarity of association, upon a quick communication of sympathy, upon the easy and effortless sense of companionship."[25] Traumatized by the violent class warfare of the period, Croly invokes the hope for a classless Christian community pursued by nearly every American religious reformer since the Mathers sailed the Atlantic.

America's immigration explosion helps explain the paradox of the Progressive era's expansive notions of democracy combined with fears of the attitudes and influence of the masses. Eager to separate themselves from the hordes of unkempt foreigners, many political reformers wrapped themselves in the trappings of proper Protestant reserve. The unifying concept of the American "People," Robert Wiebe points out, was a casualty of these forces. "Conceptually," he writes, "the People lost coherence and deteriorated into a mass of people, myopic, and gullible." Progressive politics began to focus far less on democracy and more on efficiency. Reformers frequently spoke of "the human herd," in Randolph Bourne's scathing phrase.[26] Meanwhile, as Progressive reform removed more and more contentious issues from the hurly-burly of democratic exchange, voter turnout dropped from 80 percent in 1896 to 50 percent in 1924.[27]

Both Roosevelt's and Wilson's foreign policies can be viewed as the projection of domestic Progressive anxieties upon the world stage. Herbert Croly believed that the Spanish-American War initiated the Progressive era because it offered a "tremendous impulse to the work of reform."[28] Progressives were enthusiastic in their support of Roosevelt's "big stick diplomacy" because it gave them a sense of control in domestic life. Roosevelt's success in winning public support for his foreign initiatives, whether in America, East Asia, or Europe, rested, in Robert Dallek's reading, on an "instinctive ability to relate overseas actions to progressive concerns." Whether he was taking the Canal Zone, policing the Caribbean, supporting the "open door" policy in Asia, mediating the Russo-Japanese War, sailing the battleship fleet around the globe, or promoting the Algeciras settlement, Roosevelt was advancing the Progressive struggle for moral democracy, law, and social order. These adventures also, Dallek notes, "gave progressives an exhilarating feeling of power, of a newfound ability to control seemingly unmanageable forces like the ones besetting them at home. Frustrated by their inability to find effective solutions to the country's deeply troubling problems, progressive crusaders took comfort from Roosevelt's seeming mastery of foreign affairs."[29]

Woodrow Wilson's foreign policies can be explained similarly. By insisting on democratic rule in Mexico, Wilson sought to achieve abroad what he had been elected to do at home. When the Mexicans resisted,

Wilson , insisted in a nationally publicized speech that the problems in Mexico lay "at the heart of all our national problems. . . . We should prove ourselves untrue to our own traditions if we proved ourselves untrue friends to them."[30] By equating the achievement of Mexican democracy (and the protection of private property) with that in the United States, Wilson allowed himself to be driven to extremes that bedeviled his presidency and further eroded the congressional role in foreign policy. When Wilson failed in the spring of 1914 in his attempts to "teach the South American republics to elect good men"—men who would not expropriate the property of U.S. corporations—the president seized on an insignificant incident to ask Congress for permission to retaliate. Then, instead of waiting for proper authorization, he ordered the navy to occupy Veracruz.

Progressives placed hardly less import on the need for expanding foreign markets than republicans had on the need for endless supplies of arable land. Sometimes this required the imposition of order on a revolutionary nation, as in Spain or Mexico, while in others, such as Cuba, Nicaragua, Panama, and to some degree China, it required the fostering of revolution, only to reimpose order once a more sympathetic regime had been installed. In all cases, it required a rhetorical bob and weave in public, with a claim to support "democracy" abroad as it undermined its practice at home.

Not surprisingly, many Progressives viewed America's entry into World War I as yet another opportunity to jump-start domestic reform at home. The *New Republic* viewed the opening of the war as the means for the United States to achieve "a clearer understanding of the relation between our democratic national ideal and our international obligations, and such an understanding should bring with it a political and economic organization better able to redeem its obligations."[31] Before Wilson decided to intervene, the magazine argued that just because "a whole people clamors for a war, and gets it, there is no cause for calling the war democratic." Now it was calling the Allies' cause "unmistakably the cause of liberalism and the hope of an enduring peace."[32] Progressives had so imbibed the wine of Wilsonianism that they championed imperialism as the prelude to world government. The necessary "surrender of sovereignty," Walter Lippmann wrote, "will be much easier if it occurs first in outlying portions of the earth," conveniently for those lucky enough to be living at its center.[33]

John Dewey, America's foremost progressive philosopher, shared this enthusiasm. An avowed socialist and pacifist, Dewey defended American intervention in the war on the grounds that it would provide a unique opportunity to reorganize the world into a democratic social order. "Industrial Democracy is on the way," Dewey naively declared in July 1917. "The Rule of the Workmen and the Soldiers will not be confined to Russia."[34] But Dewey never defined what he meant by democracy during these years. Like Lippmann, he seemed ready to toss a career's worth of searching overboard in order to jump on Wilson's warship. Dewey, too, proved quite susceptible to the idealization of the moral qualities of his own country.[35] He abandoned "the task of making our own country detailedly fit for peace" during this period, Randolph Bourne ruefully commented, in exchange for the "gradual working up of the conviction that we were ordained as a nation to lead all erring brothers towards the light of liberty and democracy."[36]

With the help of these progressive intellectuals, Wilson successfully fused support for the war with the newly defined ideals of democracy at home. He argued that the war would be an unequaled opportunity for international reform that in turn was the essential precondition for the success of future domestic reform.[37] Wilson had come to power as an avatar of popular democracy. He therefore became a kind of ideological bridge over which some progressives moved from neutrality to intervention. This line was echoed in Croly's *New Republic* by its founders, Lippmann and Dewey, and by progressive intellectuals including Charles Beard and Frank Cobb in the *New Republic*, the *Nation*, and the *New York World*.

Tocqueville had warned that "all those who seek to destroy the liberties of a democratic nation ought to know that war is the surest and shortest means to accomplish it."[38] Wilson understood that "Once lead this people into war, and they'll forget there ever was such a thing as tolerance. To fight you must be brutal and ruthless, and the spirit of ruthless brutality will enter into the very fiber of our national life."[39] These views were rooted in experience. With the onset of the war, democratic debate ceased entirely, and progressive reform stopped dead in its proverbial tracks.

Herbert Gutman teaches us that "the central value of historical understanding is that it transforms historical givens into historical contingencies . . . [enabling] us to see the structures in which we live . . . as only one among many other possible experiences."[40] In this case, history records the victory of the "War Progressives," such as Roosevelt, Wilson, Croly, and Lippmann, over those of the "Peace Progressives," such as Robert LaFollette and William Borah, but rarely notes the significant results this victory had for the democratic future of U.S. foreign policy. In addition to being antimilitarist and anti-interventionist, the Peace Progressives forged a vigorous campaign for the democratization of U.S. foreign policy. During the 1915–1916 debate on Wilson's preparedness plans, they demanded a nationwide referendum on whether America should enter the war. Had these efforts struck a more responsive chord in the body politic, the structure of U.S. foreign policy making, as well as the content of U.S. foreign policy, would have been dramatically altered.[41]

Instead, the war constricted democratic debate. Though as early as 1912 the War Department directed that certain war-related records be considered "confidential," it was not until the United States had entered World War I that it adopted a formal classification system patterned after British and French systems. Considerably more worrisome from a democratic standpoint were the hundreds of prosecutions brought under the Espionage Act of 1917 and the Sedition Act of May 1918. The former provided laws preventing the dissemination of information relating to vital military or naval installations or equipment, or "classified information" relating to cryptographic and communication systems and facilities. The latter made it a crime to say anything "scornful or disrespectful" of the government, the Constitution, the flag, or the uniform. Socialist presidential candidate Eugene V. Debs received a ten-year prison sentence for opposing the war. Motion-picture producer Robert Goldstein received a ten-year prison sentence (later reduced to three) and was fined $5,000 for including a scene in his Revolutionary War epic that showed British soldiers bayoneting women and children. A Wisconsin official received a thirty-month sentence for criticizing a Red Cross fund-raising drive. As many as 8,000 to 10,000 Americans faced imprisonment, official suppression, deportation, or mob violence during the war.[42] Even the Post Office became a tool of repression. The Espionage Act instructed the Postmaster General to withhold mailing privileges to publications deemed injurious to the war effort. At least seventy-five publications were banned under this authority. The Masses, International Socialist Review, and other journals that opposed the war were barred from the mail, but so also was the Freeman's Journal and the Catholic Register—the latter for quoting Thomas Jefferson's opinion that Ireland should be an independent republic.

The Wilson administration also created two new agencies, the Censorship Board and the Committee on Public Information, which exercised broad discretion over what could be published by the press. In addition to conducting censorship, the committee also undertook a massive propaganda alert aimed at promoting popular support for the war. Committee head George Creel placed advertisements in the *Saturday Evening Post* and other magazines calling on readers to report to the Justice Department "the man who spreads pessimistic stories . . . cries for peace, or belittles our effort to win the war."[43] All of this went beyond censorship, Bruce Porter notes, "into that quintessentially modern form of state power: the manipulation of public opinion."[44] Such manipulation constitutes one of the most difficult—and constant—challenges for anyone seeking to bring democracy to bear on the making of foreign policy.

Popular disenchantment engendered by the Versailles settlement, Wilson's inability to sell his vision of a League of Nations, and the widespread belief that the war had been foisted on the American public by a conspiracy of unsavory weapons producers killed off not only what republican idealism underlay progressive reform but also many Americans' faith in democracy itself. Wilson had professed a desire to extend the principle of democratic government to include popular control over foreign policy. Hence his insistence on "open covenants, openly arrived at."[45] But his inept politicking and political megalomania insured that these covenants would have just the opposite effect. Wilson undermined his announced intentions by insisting on the ratification of a peace agreement that perpetuated the most unjust and exploitative aspects of the colonial system and put American forces in the position of upholding and enforcing them. Wilson's commitment to the moral force of public opinion, moreover, was absolute in the abstract but frequently lacking in matters concrete. When the Japanese raised the issue of race equality at the League of Nations Commission, the president replied, "How can you treat on its merits in this quiet room a question which will not be treated on its merits when it gets out of this room?" As E. H. Carr observes, "it became a commonplace for statesmen at Geneva and elsewhere to explain that they themselves had every desire to be reasonable, but that public opinion in their countries was inexorable."[46] Democracy, in other words, was the obstacle, both real and imagined, to a democratic peace. In the United States, pro-peace Progressives, working together with the likes of Henry Cabot Lodge, overrode the president and the president's exclusive control of foreign policy information. Given their opposing motivations, however—with sympathy for the Bolsheviks on the one side and fear and horror on the other—the left/right alliance that defeated Wilson on the League of Nations was decidedly unstable. While it briefly asserted the primacy of constitutional and democratic procedures in the conduct of U.S. foreign relations, it could not create alternative mechanisms to ensure that such consultations would be institutionalized. Their victory, moreover, resulted as much from Wilson's weakness, both physical and political, as from the reassertion of democratic principle or practice in foreign policy.

America also closeted its republican ambitions at home and abroad. Immigration was restricted and foreign adventurism curtailed. Moneymaking coupled with a Jazz Age commitment to frivolousness replaced political reform as the governing cultural idea of the period. As the political system opened itself up to nearly unmediated manipulation by business elites, Niccolo Machiavelli disappeared from democratic discourse and John Locke reigned triumphant.

It was against this unpromising background that Walter Lippmann and John Dewey conducted the most important debate on America's democratic character since the publication of the *Federalist Papers*. A founding editor of the *New Republic*, Lippmann had written two important books in which he addressed central problems of classical republicanism, including the corruption of government by commerce, and the potential for the creation of a virtuous society by means of its political system.[47] Coming off the experience of the dashed hopes of the Progressive movement coupled with the failure of the League and Versailles—he had been one of the authors of the Fourteen Points—the young public philosopher began to think about what had gone wrong. The result was a series of three books, the most important of which, *Public Opinion*, John Dewey would term "perhaps the most effective indictment of democracy ever penned."[48]

Public Opinion may be seen as an eloquent epitaph for Americans' hopes for progressive, democratic reform based on classical republican principles. In it, Lippmann examined what he believed were the necessary preconditions for the operation of a successful democratic republic—a competent, civic-minded citizenry with access to relevant details of public policy—and decided that the entire notion was dangerously utopian and ought to be shelved. In Lippmann's view, at the heart of republican theory stood the "omnicompetent" citizen: "It was believed that if only he could be taught more facts, if only he would take more interest, if only he would listen to more lectures and read more reports, he would gradually be trained to direct public affairs." Unfortunately, Lippmann concluded, "The whole assumption is false."[49]

In republicanism the legislative branch is considered sovereign because it best represents the hearts and minds of the people. In Lippmann's analysis, however, sovereignty now rested with the media, the modern institution that shaped citizens' opinions and hence "manufactured" consent for the governing class. But the press, he argued, "is very much more frail than the democratic theory has yet admitted. It is too frail to carry the whole burden of popular sovereignty."[50]

According to Lippmann, the social and political events that determine our collective destiny are well beyond the public's range of experience and expertise to understand. Only through incomplete, poorly comprehended media reports are these events made accessible. "Public opinion," therefore, is shaped in response to people's "maps" or "images" of the world and not to the world itself. "For the most part," Lippmann wrote, "we do not first see, and then define, we define first and then see."[51] Mass political consciousness does not pertain to the factual "environment," but to an intermediary "pseudoenvironment." To complicate matters, this pseudoenvironment is further corrupted by the manner in which it is received. Citizens have only limited time and attention to devote to issues of public concern. News is designed for mass consumption, and hence the media must employ a relatively simple vocabulary and linear story line to discuss highly complex and decidedly nonlinear situations. The competition for readership (and advertising dollars) drives the press to present news reports in ways that sensationalize and oversimplify, while more-significant information goes unreported and unremarked upon.

Given both the economic and professional limitations of the practice of journalism, Lippmann argued, news "comes [to us] helter-skelter." This is fine for baseball box scores, a transatlantic flight, or the death of a monarch. But where the picture is more complex, "as for example, in the matter of a success of a policy or the social conditions among a foreign people—where the real answer is neither yes or no, but subtle and a matter of balanced evidence," then journalism "causes no end of derangement, misunderstanding and even misinterpretation."[52]

Lippmann's pseudoenvironment is not composed merely of the information we receive; it consists, in equal measure, of what Lippmann termed "the pictures in our heads." Voters react to the news in light of a personal history that contains certain stereotypes, predispositions, and emotional associations that determine their interpretations of the news. We emphasize that which confirms our original beliefs and disregard or denigrate what might contradict them. What emerges is a kind of polydimensional censorship. Lippmann compared the average citizen to a deaf spectator sitting in the back row of a sporting event. "He does not know what is happening, why it is happening, what ought to happen; he lives in a world which he cannot see, does not understand and is unable to direct."[53]

Democracy in modern society is surprisingly undemocratic. It operates with only "a very small percentage of those who are theoretically supposed to govern."[54] In truth, only a "specialized class of men" whose minds can pierce the pseudoenvironment can perceive the common interest, which is invisible to the general populace. Since the specialized class "acts upon information that is not common property, in situations that the public at large does not conceive," it is highly questionable to what extent the government could be exercising the will of the people.[55] "There is no prospect, in any time which we can conceive, that the whole invisible environment will be so clear to all men that they will spontaneously arrive at sound public opinions on the whole business of government. If there were a prospect, it is extremely doubtful whether many of us would wish to be bothered."[56]

Lippmann also explained (as did Tocqueville) why Madison's hope that representatives would "refine and enlarge" the views of their districts proved in vain. Thomas Jefferson may have dreamed of a well-informed citizenry of civic-minded, virtuous yeoman farmers, but in the modern era such optimism was no longer sustainable. The problem was not merely that representatives found it easier to pander but that they preferred the security of a false picture of the world to the difficult task of attempting to create a more complex and daunting whole. "Even if the theory were applied, and the districts always send the wisest men, the sum of a combination of local impressions is not a wide enough base for national policy and no base at all in the control of foreign policy. Since the real effects of most laws are subtle and hidden, they cannot be understood by filtering local experiences through local states of mind." The representative "needs to know the local pictures, but unless he possesses instruments for calibrating them, one picture is as good as the next." Significantly, notes John Diggins, the only leader in American history to profess awareness of this dilemma, Alexander Hamilton, was never elected to public office.[57]

Lippmann understood reality to be "picturable." Truth can be discovered by matching an independent, objective reality against a language that corresponds to it. That picture, however, is available only to insiders who are proscribed from telling their democratic constituents the "whole truth" by "penalty of political death."[58] No one expects a steelworker, musician, or banker to understand physics, Lippmann believed; why should they be expected to understand politics? In keeping with his Platonic inclinations, Lippmann proposed if not a "philosopher king" then a philosophically grounded aristocracy. Men do not desire "self-government for its own sake," he argued; "they desire it for the sake of results." One should judge a democracy not by its degree of self-governance, but by "whether it is producing a certain minimum of health, of decent housing, of material necessities, of education, of freedom, of pleasures of beauty."[59] What is needed, Lippmann noted, is a network of organized intelligence gatherers shielded from the dangers of democratic interference. It is, after all, "because they are compelled to act without a reliable picture of the world that governments, schools, newspapers and churches make such small headway against the more obvious failings of democracy."[60]

Lippmann wisely dropped his "specialized class of men" proposal, but his attack on the operational deficiencies of democracy left a powerful legacy. He strengthened progressive beliefs that the problems of society could be profitably solved in an environment of social scientific inquiry rather than through intellectual exchange in the marketplace of ideas.

John Dewey replied to Lippmann in the May 3, 1922, issue of *New Republic* , and later in an important though extremely tendentious book, *The Public and Its Problems*, published in 1927.[61] Dewey conceded that voters were not "omnicompetent"—that is, they were not "competent to frame policies, to judge their results, competent to know . . . what is for his own good"—and passionately shared Lippmann's republican hope that government could be formed to inspire generosity and civic-mindedness in the citizenry.[62] But he violently disagreed with Lippmann's sanguine trust in the beneficence of elites. "A class of experts," he insisted, "is inevitably so removed from common interests as to become a class with private interests and private knowledge, which in social matters is not knowledge at all."[63] Only in genuine community with the public can the government identify and respond to the public's interests. An expert shoemaker may know best how to fix a shoe, but only its wearer knows where it pinches and when it needs fixing. "Democracy must begin at home . . . and its home is in the neighborly community."[64]

Dewey placed enormous emphasis on capitalism and the growth of technology, which he believed was a double-edged sword for democracy. "Invent the printing press and democracy is inevitable," wrote Thomas Carlyle. Add to this, elaborated Dewey, "the railway, the telegraph, mass manufacture and concentration of population in urban centers, and some form of democratic government is, humanly speaking, inevitable."[65] The advent of mass communication creates strong public interest and almost necessitates some kind of popular input in government. "The Great Society, created by steam and electricity, may be a society, but it is no community." The inexorable advance of technology, coupled with capitalist relations of production (markets plus mass production), created new and impersonal modes of behavior. This mechanical understanding of an individual's role in society, according to Dewey, became "the outstanding fact of modern life."[66] "Indifference," noted Dewey, "is the evidence of current apathy, and apathy is testimony to the fact the public is so bewildered that it cannot find itself."[67]

While Lippmann argued for what James W. Carey calls a "spectator theory of knowledge," Dewey viewed knowledge as a function of "communication and association."[68] Systematic inquiry, reified by Lippmann, was to Dewey only the beginning of knowledge. "Vision is a spectator," he wrote. "Hearing is a participator."[69] The basis of democracy is not information, but conversation—and the cultivation of what might be called a "culture of communication." Democracy required what Dewey termed "certain vital habits: the ability to follow an argument, grasp the point of view of another, expand the boundaries of understanding, debate the alternative purposes that might be pursued." Habit, he argued, "is the mainspring of human action, and habits are formed for the most part under the influence of the customs of a group."[70] The media's job, in Dewey's conception, "is to interest the public in the public interest."[71]

The Lippmann/Dewey debate is simultaneously one of the most edifying and most depressing moments in the history of American political discourse. It is edifying because it is one of the only instances when the substantive operational questions of effective democratic participation have ever been placed at the center of political debate. Both the originality and the disciplined lines of inquiry of their respective theses command respect and a degree of awe for each writer's amazing prophetic insight. Lippmann's critique of commercially driven sensationalism, and Dewey's of the fracturing impact on the "public" of technological advance, demonstrate remarkable foresight and understanding of developments they could not possibly have anticipated. Although both writers provided trenchant diagnoses of the maladies afflicting American democracy, neither came up with a remotely pragmatic prescription. Lippmann abandoned his network of organized intelligence gatherers as unworkable in a democratic context but never came up with a suitable replacement. Instead he spent the balance of his career seeking to elevate the character of public discourse by example—creating a new form of journalist, the insider pundit, who went beyond the box score coverage of the news in hopes of providing consumers with sufficient context and information to allow them to better match the "pictures in their heads" with the world outside. This effort, while noble in many ways, was fundamentally flawed for the very reasons Dewey predicted. As a member of the governing class, Lippmann ceased to identify with the "group" he professed to represent and became instead a sophisticated propagandist for the interests of the political elite. Moreover, his example, though widely emulated in professional journalism, was woefully insufficient to inspire the kinds of habits and mores that Dewey correctly identified as necessary for the healthy functioning of a democratic culture.[72]

But Dewey was hardly more successful. His penetrating critique of Lippmann's unapologetically elitist and overly schematic understanding of the role of information in a democratic discourse was never fortified by a workable notion of how, exactly, to inspire the culture of communication necessary to sustain its alternative. Dewey understood its necessity. "By what means," he asked, "shall [the public's] inchoate and amorphous estate be organized into effective political action relevant to present social needs and opportunities?"[73] How, asks Hilary Puttnam, was American society to "develop the capacities of all its men and women to think for themselves, to participate in the design and testing of social policies, and to judge results?"[74] Dewey's inability to formulate a response, however, pointed to a consistent weakness in his prescriptions. He rarely bothered to work out the mechanisms through which his reforms might be achieved.[75] The question therefore remains: Exactly how, in an increasingly urban capitalist society and given all of the strains and weaknesses of public discourse that both philosophers identified, does one craft a culture conducive to the creation and sustenance of a body politic made up of the modern-day equivalents of Jefferson's civic-minded yeoman farmers? And how, to complicate matters further, would one apply these criteria to America's Tocqueville problem—the need to conduct foreign policy on a sound, democratic basis?

The intellectual achievement of the Lippmann/Dewey debates comes into stark relief when viewed in the context of the era in which it took place. Interwar American political culture was characterized by rampant nativism, jingoism, and isolationism. The period's politicians can boast some significant diplomatic achievements, including perhaps the most significant conventional arms–limitation agreement ever signed between potential adversaries, but the purposeful insularity of American political culture in this period made it difficult to pursue any kind of concerted strategy in world affairs.

By the time of Franklin Roosevelt's presidency, which followed the collapse of the international financial system and the growth of fascism in Europe and bolshevism in Russia, Americans were more eager than ever to try to isolate themselves from the nefarious influence of the Old World. Indeed, the rhetoric of the period often recalled that of the republican Revolutionaries such as Paine and Jefferson who feared the corruptive influences of Europe on the infant nation more than a century and a half earlier. According to one 1934 poll, 95 percent of the American people believed the United States should not get into a European war in the future for any reason.[76] American isolationism enjoyed a particularly broad and diverse basis of support. Its leaders included socialist and religious pacifists who had supported Wilson and political descendants of Republican imperialists who had followed McKinley and Roosevelt. Spokesmen such as Idaho's William E. Borah and California's Hiram W. Johnson represented both progressive reform and nativist xenophobia. Many were not isolationists but unilateralists, interested in intervention but only on America's terms. Others were simply pacifists. Another group professed to place the bar for intervention higher than the wars taking place in Europe and Asia. Nativism, in an era that saw the growth of the KKK, also played a large role. Nor was American business immune to isolationism's siren song. Some firms, led by du Pont, Standard Oil, General Motors, and Union Carbide, even worked closely— sometimes secretly and illegally—with Nazi German firms as late as 1941, with Ford and GM subsidiaries producing half of Hitler's tanks.[77] The America First Committee, organized in 1940 by two Yale students, R. Douglas Stuart Jr., the son of a high Quaker Oats executive, and Kingman Brewster Jr., later the university's president, attracted such liberals as Chester Bowles, William Benton, Robert Hutchins, and socialist Norman Thomas.[78]

Ironically, perhaps, one of the most effective techniques the isolationists discovered to try to tighten its legislative straitjacket on Roosevelt's foreign policy was to attempt to subject that policy to democratic control. In December 1937, with war raging in the Pacific, Japanese planes attacked the U.S. gunboat *Panay*, killing three American soldiers. Tokyo officials quickly condemned the attack as an error and apologized. The next day, Representative Louis Ludlow of Indiana introduced a constitutional amendment stating that, except in cases of invasion, "the authority of Congress to declare war shall not become effective until confirmed by a majority of all votes cast in a nationwide referendum." A 1937 Gallup poll found three-quarters of Americans supported the amendment.[79] President Roosevelt had to intervene personally and at a cost of considerable political capital to defeat this amendment, 209–188.[80]

Roosevelt, who in the campaign of 1932 had been elected almost without reference to foreign affairs, saw isolationism as pernicious nonsense espoused by people with suspect motives. "A free nation," he declared, had the right "to expect full cooperation from all groups." Those preaching appeasement, encouraging skepticism, or otherwise promoting disunity, he declared, were little more than "Fifth Columnists."[81] He used every means at his disposal to discredit the isolationists and build support for American entry into the European war, but he had few illusions regarding the political obstacles he faced in doing so. "I am the captain of the ship but I never forget it is the seas which control the captain," Roosevelt once explained. "Events and public opinion are the limitations on my power and the implements of it. No matter what legal powers I have, what I can do is conditioned by the seas around me."[82] Nevertheless, George Kennan later commented that FDR "influenced public opinion less through the power of his words than through the quiet shaping, in a manner conducive to his own purposes, of the environmental factors, the external factors, in which the formulation of wartime policy had to proceed."[83] Roosevelt's patience for legal and constitutional restraints, however, was decidedly minimal. Following his secret meeting with FDR aboard a ship in Newfoundland in August 1941, Winston Churchill told his War Cabinet, "The President . . . said he would wage war, but not declare it" because of isolationist opposition in Congress, "and that he would become more and more provocative. If the Germans did not like it, they could attack American forces."[84] Accordingly, FDR did not shrink from allowing U.S. ships to engage German and Italian raiders on the high seas, therefore risking, if not exactly provoking, war decidedly without congressional authorization.[85]

As the threat from Nazi Germany became more apparent each day, Roosevelt did what virtually every president had done before him: he compromised Americans' constitutional freedoms and attempted to bring the control of information under some sort of official discipline, going so far as to deliberately mislead his citizens when he believed it would further the overall cause of preserving his freedom of action. In March 1940, Roosevelt issued Executive Order 8381, marking all official military documents under the authority of the Secretary of War or the Secretary of the Navy as secret, confidential, or restricted.[86]

Severely constrained by the nativist and isolationist sentiments of Congress and much of the nation, Roosevelt did much to escape the foreign policy handcuffs with which Congress tried to bind him.[87] FDR's problems derived from both the left and the right. The 1935 Senate Munitions Committee reported on the efforts of so-called "merchants of death" to entice the country into World War I. Numerous sensationalist journalists, pro-German business interests, peace groups, women's groups, and traditional "America First" isolationists joined to create what was then the largest peace movement in the nation's history. Between 1935 and 1937, the Emergency Peace Campaign, a group that lobbied hard for a strengthening of the already restrictive neutrality acts, enjoyed subsidiaries in more than 1,200 American cities. Against the background of the 1937 Neutrality Act, Roosevelt added a "cash and carry" provision to sell the Allies materiel and made his case to Congress and the nation in deliberately misleading terms by presenting a step toward belligerency as a measure to avoid war. Permitting England and France to buy American weapons, he assured the country, "offers far greater safeguards than we now possess or have ever possessed to protect American lives and property." When FDR agreed in 1940 to lease destroyers to Great Britain in exchange for British naval bases in the Caribbean, he did so without asking for any congressional authorization, based on nothing more than his attorney general's extremely questionable interpretation of the Constitution and a promise by his Republican opponent, Wendell Wilkie, not to object. He also deployed warships in the Atlantic, in the Azores, and off Greenland and landed U.S. troops in Iceland without even informing Congress or the American people. These actions may have been consistent with the Supreme Court's expansive interpretations of the Constitution during this period, but they could hardly have been more contemptuous of a citizen's fundamental democratic right to judge his leaders on the basis of their actions.[88]

As the European war grew in intensity, FDR stepped up his methods of deception. During the 1940 election campaign, just as Lyndon Johnson would do twenty-four years later, Roosevelt repeatedly assured Americans that their sons would not be sent to fight in "foreign wars." On November 2, he stated flatly, "Your President says this country is not going to war."[89] In early September 1941, however, the U.S. destroyer *Greer* had been issued secret orders to escort British convoys and aid in the effort to sink German submarines. It tracked a German U-boat for three hours and signaled its location to British forces before the sub turned and attacked. In an eerie foreshadowing of the 1964 Gulf of Tonkin incident, the *Greer* escaped unharmed, but FDR used the incident to denounce Germany. "I tell you the blunt fact," Roosevelt explained, "that this German submarine fired first . . . without warning and with deliberate desire to sink her." He never told Americans how the ship actually provoked the submarine. "You know I am a juggler," Roosevelt later told a friend. "I never let my right hand know what my left hand does. I am perfectly willing to mislead and tell untruths if it will help win the war."[90] FDR used the alleged incident to step up U.S. participation in the undeclared war against Germany in the North Atlantic. One month later, three U.S. warships were torpedoed, and one sank while on convoy duty in the North Atlantic. One hundred seventy-two men were lost. FDR was then able to persuade Congress to repeal what remained of the Neutrality Act's restraint upon his power to act as he saw fit.[91] Employing this analogy, Senator J. William Fulbright would later remark, "FDR's deviousness in a good cause made it much easier for [LBJ] to practice the same kind of deviousness in a bad cause."[92]

FDR did not limit his attempts to manipulate opinion to official statements and diplomatic maneuvers. He also worked closely with William Allen White's "Committee to Defend America by Aiding the Allies," which had been formed in 1940 with the encouragement of the administration. (White was actually reviving a much smaller committee that had been dedicated to revising the neutrality laws.) The Committee soon had 850,000 members in almost nine hundred cities. In addition to White's own efforts, it regularly broadcast the pro-interventionist speeches and statements of *Time* magazine magnate Henry Luce, Harvard president James B. Conant, and, to Roosevelt's profound joy, Charles Lindbergh's mother-in-law. "Why don't you call me pusillanimous?" the president once asked, when shown a mock-up of a full-page newspaper advertisement attacking his administration for its refusal to come to the aid of the allies.[93]

The mammoth effort to reeducate Americans about the need for an engaged foreign policy in time of peril required further expansion in the number of government workers involved in producing pro-war propaganda as well as a concerted effort to enlist the entertainment and broadcast industries to shape opinion. Each new agency created a public relations staff. These were supplemented by those of the Office of Government Reports, created in 1939, and the Division of Information of the Office of Emergency Management. In July, the Hays office established the Motion Picture Committee Cooperating for National Defense to evaluate requests from government public relations offices to make the appropriate facilities or technical advice available to them. The government controlled the foreign film market and, through the military, the contractual availability of some of Hollywood's biggest stars. It would have been bad business for any studio to resist its machinations. Hollywood studios such as Warner Brothers and MGM offered to make any movie Roosevelt desired. Such fare was frequently shown with a "March of [Henry Luce's] TIME" docudrama, which also reinforced FDR's interventionist assumptions.[94] Office of War Information head Elmer Davis placed a premium on this type of communication as he explained, "The easiest way to inject a propaganda idea into most people's minds is to let it go through the medium of an entertainment picture when they do not realize they are being propagandized."[95]

Roosevelt's informal manipulation of the media, through intimate press conferences and beautifully scripted and acted "fireside chats," went a long way toward shaping press coverage of his administration. Still, Roosevelt was not one to take chances, if he could help it, with a media he could not control. Faced with concerted pressure from the White House, NBC and CBS soon eliminated anti-Roosevelt voices from their regular schedules, the latter firing one of its most popular commentators, Boake Carter, at the explicit request of the White House. By 1938, virtually everything the American people heard on radio supported Roosevelt's view of events. The four most popular radio commentators—H.V. Kaltenborn, Elmer Davis, Raymond Gram Swing, and Edward R. Murrow—were all outspoken and persistent advocates of military intervention.[96]

By 1941, the constitutional provisions outlining how Americans were to go to war in an open, accountable process had broken down. FDR secretly placed U.S. ships in areas where incidents could force Americans into war. He then misled the American people about his actions. He allowed the FBI to wiretap phones and open mail of suspected Axis sympathizers and let the FBI spy on congressmen who merely criticized him. With Pearl Harbor in December, moreover, came a growing preoccupation with secrecy. In September 1942 the Office of War Information issued a regulation controlling the identification, handling, and dissemination of sensitive information. It defined three categories of information: Secret, Confidential, and Restricted. The authority for this OWI regulation has not been identified by historians, but for the first time in our history a classification system went beyond mere intelligence.[97]

Finally, we have the matter of the atom bomb. Few would argue with the need to protect all information related to the wartime Manhattan Project. But in August 1946, President Harry S. Truman signed the McMahon/Atomic Energy Act, America's first legislative act to protect secrecy in peacetime. Its provisions were far more stringent than those related to previous national security classifications. Atomic information was "born secret." Any person demonstrated to have acquired or disseminated "any document, writing, sketch, photograph, plan, model, instrument, appliances, note or information involving or incorporating restricted data" with "the intent to injure the United States" was subject to life imprisonment or death.[98] A recent report estimated that at last count, in the Department of Energy alone thirty-two million pages of documents—the equivalent of thirty-two Washington Monuments if stacked on top of one another—had been classified as secret under this act.[99] These papers contain details of atomic experiments conducted by the government against its own citizens that resulted in the maiming and crippling of innocent and frequently mentally incompetent victims—yet another legacy of the continued destruction of America's democratic rights and republican principles resulting from the constitutional compromises engendered by war. Would the American people have approved such atrocities had they been given the choice? Such questions are unanswerable in a context where democratic decision making has been usurped.

During the isolationist/internationalist debate, Walter Lippmann had worried that the United States remained overly immature to adapt itself to the role history seemed to intend for it. "What Rome was to the ancient world, what Great Britain has been to the modern world, America is to be in the world of tomorrow," Lippmann wrote in 1929. "We cling to the mentality of a little nation on the frontiers of the civilized world, though we have the opportunity, the power, and the responsibilities of a very great nation at the center of the civilized world." Charles Beard, the isolationist historian, read these words ten years later on the eve of the European war and lamented their implications for the fate of what remained of republican rule. "These are ornate, glistening, masculine words," he wrote. "But are they true words and what do they mean in terms of action? Rome conquered, ruled and robbed other peoples from the frontier in Scotland to the sands of Arabia, from the Rhine to the Sahara, and then crumbled to ruins."[100]

Just as the Founders believed that republican virtue would be impossible to maintain without unbridled expansion, their inheritors would find that the dynamics that such expansion created—an imperial president, the restriction of the free flow of information, and a deliberately misled voting public—would strangle not only the hope for republican virtue but the lifeline of democracy itself. It may have been an unavoidable bargain, but it was also, in many ways, a tragic one.

CHAPTER THREE

Present Dangers

No nation could preserve its freedom in the midst of continual warfare.
—James Madison, 1795

Today, no war has been declared, [but] the danger has never been more
clear and its presence has never been more imminent.
—John F. Kennedy, 1962

The Cold War succeeded where America's hot wars had failed; it fundamentally compromised Americans' basic democratic rights on what
appears to be a permanent basis. Containment policy, the doctrine that
guided U.S. attempts to counter the Soviets throughout the Cold War,
proved to be far more than a mere defense strategy; rather it provided an
entirely new paradigm for American citizenship. Individuality and free
expression, while routinely celebrated in political rhetoric, fell victim to
a demand for corporate loyalty to the concept of "national security."
That term's connotative flexibility, moreover, offered its guardians enormous opportunity to censor information and limit debate.[1] In some
ways, this redefinition of American identity can be seen as the logical
culmination of the trends discerned by both Herbert Croly, who called
for a corporatist self-definition for Americans, and Walter Lippmann,
who argued that ordinary Americans lacked the necessary political
sophistication to decide their collective fate. In Cold War America, the
constitutional rights of the individual would be subordinate to the security imperatives of the whole. Owing to the compelling demand for
secrecy as well as the cumbersome nature of democratic practices in a
time of national emergency, all key decisions regarding the best interest
of the nation would be made exclusively by those with access to the (nec-

essarily) secret relevant data. Because nuclear attack could take place at almost any moment, permanent wartime discipline would be required at all times. Reaction time, and with it space for democratic debate, shrank to the number of minutes required to confirm a missile launch. To question the new paradigm was to transgress the parameters of responsible debate and thereby threaten the organic health of the body politic.

The crucial document of the period was an April 1950 internal report to President Truman entitled *NSC-68*. Though classified until 1975, it functioned within the government as the operational blueprint for containment policy, following George Kennan's theological treatise known as the "long telegram," which detailed the author's understanding of the ideological basis for Soviet expansionism and the need for a firm U.S. response. As the end product of extensive bureaucratic negotiation, *NSC-68* lacked Kennan's romantic flair for poetic explication. But its prescriptive elements were clear, present, and dangerous to constitutional democracy. Believing that the Kremlin leaders were possessed of a "new fanatic faith" and were seeking "absolute authority over the rest of the world," the authors argued that "the integrity of our system will not be jeopardized by any measures, covert or overt, violent or non-violent, which serve the purposes of frustrating the Kremlin design."[2] Communism, as Louis Hartz noted in 1955, was allowed to redefine "the issue of our internal freedom in terms of our external life."[3] The former proved no match for the latter.

The discovery of the wartime potential of the atom, the problem of Soviet espionage, the "loss" of China, and the belief of so many Americans that the victory over Germany necessitated an equally grim battle with Stalin's empire contributed to the creation of a political culture in which paranoia prospered and debate fizzled. Franklin Roosevelt had initiated many of the practices that would form the basis for the new secrecy policies, but he did so only in wartime, and without the requisite enthusiasm to turn the policy into a crusade. Fearing the political implications of appearing "soft on Communism," the Truman administration used secrecy and loyalty investigation as a strategic centerpiece of its domestic "toughness" pose. The secrecy disease soon infected virtually every significant aspect of U.S. foreign policy. In many important areas, government secrecy restrictions removed foreign policy as a topic of democratic debate. Few voters had access to the information necessary to make a reasoned decision about their leaders. Wars were conducted in secret, executive agreements signed and commitments made, all without Congress or the American people being informed. Citizens could not judge a president's foreign policy because they had no way of knowing what it was. To pursue such information during this period, moreover, was to court accusations of murky associations and dubious loyalty.

The explosion of the first atomic bomb in the summer of 1945 changed much in American life. Following the already stringent provisions of the McMahon/Atomic Energy Act, President Truman issued an executive order authorizing, for the first time, all federal agencies to classify information as "secret" and "top secret." Initially, the order provoked alarm and outrage in the media and among conservative Republicans. The Associated Press Managing Editors' Association protested that the order applied military classifications to civilian agencies, failed to offer a clear-cut definition of "national security," and provided no appeal or review system for challenging the decisions of officials. Twenty-five (primarily Republican) members of Congress issued a statement that argued: "Uncontrolled public discussion is the American tradition and is the greatest enemy of tyranny. There is evidence that no man can criticize our Government today and escape intemperate reprisals. This is an alarming situation."[4] The 1952 GOP platform promised "not to infringe by censorship or gag order the right of a free people to know what their government is doing."[5]

Such arguments lost their resonance, however, with the Republican victory in 1952. The Eisenhower administration found that it enjoyed the political prerogatives of secrecy no less than its predecessors. Soon, the Migratory Bird Conservation Commission and the Indian Arts and Crafts Board were stamping documents "top secret."[6] By 1993, a Government Accounting Office report reviewing only documents thirty years old or older found more than 304 million pages still classified.[7] Prior to the 1967 Freedom of Information Act, the public enjoyed no statutory right whatever to any portion of this mountain of secrets. But because the act specifically exempts documents "to be kept secret in the interest of national defense or foreign policy," it often proves useless where democracy most needs it.[8]

The secrecy virus not only prevented Americans from gaining the information they required to make informed electoral judgments and from learning about secret wars in Laos, secret U.S. involvement in coups in Africa and Latin America, and secret U.S. attempts to subvert elections in Europe and Japan; it also allowed the government to violate Americans' most basic rights without any sanction whatever. For instance, the U.S.

Public Health Service knowingly allowed uranium miners to be exposed to cancer-causing levels of radon because the Atomic Energy Commission refused to allow the agency to inform Americans of the dangers involved. The deleterious public health effects of atmospheric nuclear testing were also withheld and concealed.[9] In a recently declassified 1947 memo, a military official in the Atomic Energy Agency observed, "It is desirable that no document be released which refers to experiments with humans and might have [an] adverse effect on public opinion or result in legal suits," and recommended the reclassification of these documents to "secret."[10] National security was not even mentioned. Violations of citizens' civil liberties by various law-enforcement bodies—some of whose very existence was kept secret—would soon become routine.

Once contracted, the secrecy virus proved impossible for presidents and their subordinates to shake off. As recently as 1982, for instance, President Reagan issued Executive Order 12356, which allowed bureaucrats to classify documents on the mere expectation of "identifiable damage" to national security without requiring any identifiable standards of proof. It also empowered the government to reclassify previously declassified documents, which it promptly did. A year later, Reagan issued an order requiring all government employees with access to classified information to sign a lifetime publication-review agreement. Reagan's order was eventually rescinded, but not before 200,000 people were forced to choose between signing and resigning.[11]

In addition to atomic secrecy, the new secret foreign policy apparatus vastly expanded the government's ability to control information irrespective of constitutional safeguards. Article 1, Section 9 of the Constitution requires that a "regular statement and account of the receipts and expenditures of all public monies shall be published from time to time." But the National Security Act of 1947, which created the Central Intelligence Agency (CIA), ensured that the secret government would be answerable to no one.[12] Lawmakers were initially sensitive to this problem. During the deliberations on the act, Walter Pforzheimer, legislative liaison for the CIA's predecessor, the Central Intelligence Group, withdrew a clause that would have allowed the new organization to use "covert and unvouchered funds" because he feared it would "open up a can of worms." Two years later, with almost no public debate, Congress empowered the agency to perform covert operations of a type for which "the U.S. Government can plausibly disclaim any responsibility." These included "propaganda; economic warfare; preventive direct action, including sabotage, anti-sabotage, demolition, and evacuation measures: subversion against hostile states, including assistance to underground resistance movements, guerrilla and refugee liberation groups, and support of indigenous anti-Communist elements in threatened countries of the free world."[13] The worms were loose.

Initially, the CIA played entirely by its own rules, without any federal or congressional oversight. When in 1955 and again in 1959 the president did create small bureaucratic bodies for this ostensible purpose, they attempted little and accomplished nothing. Congress, too, displayed bipartisan kid gloves. Senator Leverett Saltonstall, the ranking Republican on the Armed Services Committee, explained, "It is not a question on the part of CIA officials to speak to us. Instead, it is a question of our reluctance, if you will, to seek information and knowledge on subjects which I, personally, not as a Member of Congress and as a citizen, would rather not have, unless I believed it to be my responsibility to have, because it might involve the lives of American citizens." Democratic Majority Leader Mike Mansfield responded, "I see. The Senator is to be commended."[14]

The CIA closed its perfect circle of secrecy by forcing its officers to sign lifetime censorship oaths, which were later enforced by the Supreme Court. Protected by its veil, the CIA became a law unto itself. Edward Pessen catalogues the kinds of operations the agency has routinely undertaken that contradict either U.S. law, international law, or both:

Since 1947, the CIA has hired and protected Nazi war criminals, falsified their records, employed them to promote the subversion of the Soviet bloc, spirited some of them into the United States where citizenship was conferred to them. It spent untold millions of dollars bribing foreign nationals and heads of state. It subsidized publishers and editors in the United States and overseas and created its own ostensibly private corporations. It induced major American corporations to undertake covert CIA projects. It engaged university administrators, scholars, journalists, union leaders and other Americans to serve CIA purposes abroad. It disseminated false information or disinformation purportedly prepared or written by the sources that such "black information" was designed to embarrass or destroy. It financed and organized operations designed to undermine, destabilize and overthrow governments of which it disapproved, not drawing the line at assassination of uncongenial individuals and government leaders. It trained foreign police and military forces in the technique of torture and murder of "subversives." It helped organize and in some cases participated in clandestine invasions of and actual wars against nations with which the United States was at peace. And in blatant violation of the law creating it, the CIA kept files and spied on American citizens, tampered with and opened the mail of hundreds and thousands, and conducted drug experiments on unwitting American victims.[15]

Various congressional efforts to investigate these actions have been sporadic and halfhearted, directed as much toward protecting the agency as toward revealing its actions.[16] Even the agency's budget remained an official, though poorly guarded, secret through 1997. When, following journalistic revelations, the congressional investigation reports hinted at the sums involved during the 1970s, Congress censored the reports and appropriated money to plug the leak. The official attitude toward democratic control of the CIA was neatly demonstrated in an exchange between Vice President Nelson Rockefeller, head of President Ford's commission of inquiry, and CIA Director William Colby. "Bill," asked the vice president, "Do you really have to present all this material to us? We realize there are secrets that you fellows need to keep and so nobody here is going to take it amiss if you feel there are some questions you can't answer quite as fully as you seem to feel you have to." Colby later wrote that he "got the message, quite unmistakably."[17]

Because the CIA was essentially unaccountable in the conduct of foreign policy, its actions—presidentially or otherwise directed—undermined the right of American citizens to make informed judgments about their leaders. In 1953, when the agency overthrew Mohammed Mossedeq, the legitimately elected leader of Iran, his removal was reported in the American press as a popular rebellion, and the U.S. government did nothing to correct this false impression.[18] The CIA then destroyed all records relating to its role.[19] When the Eisenhower administration ordered the CIA to sponsor a coup against the leftist regime of Guatemalan president Jacobo Arbenz a year later, UN ambassador Henry Cabot Lodge called the action "a revolt of Guatemalans against Guatemalans." Secretary of State John Foster Dulles added that "the situation is being cured by the Guatemalans themselves."[20] The courts prohibited the CIA from destroying these documents, but even under pressure from a Freedom of Information Act lawsuit, it has seen fit to release barely 1,400 of 180,000 relevant pages nearly half a century after the ostensible crisis took place. The CIA, notes Theodore Draper, therefore "acted in the name of the American people but could not afford to let the American people ever know what they had done."[21]

According to longtime CIA covert operations veteran Richard Bissell, "the success in Guatemala, combined with the previous success in Iran in 1953, led Washington policymakers to overestimate the agency's abilities in the area of covert action. For many policymakers outside the CIA, cover action became a quick fix, an easy way to deal with hostile foreign leaders and renegade nation-states."[22] Four years after Guatemala, the CIA recruited pilots to ferry B-26 bombers from the Philippines to fly combat missions against Indonesian president Achmed Sukarno's forces during a bloody coup there. Secretary Dulles promised Congress, "We are not intervening in the internal affairs of this country. . . ." President Eisenhower stated at a press conference, "Our policy is one of careful neutrality and proper deportment all the way through, so as not to be taking sides."[23] (The agency also produced and distributed pornographic films allegedly starring Sukarno, including one that showed him coupling with a beautiful blonde Soviet agent.) The CIA covertly backed coups in the Dominican Republic (1965) and Chile (1973), and it attempted to murder the heads of state of Cuba and the Belgian Congo— where Patrice Lamumba was indeed killed—among others. It even fought an entire air war in Laos. The agency was briefly reined in by a spasm of congressional assertiveness in the mid-1970s but was soon unleashed again by the election of Ronald Reagan and the appointment of CIA director William Casey. In 1984, Congress learned that the CIA had, on its own authority, mined Nicaragua's harbors, thereby committing the United States to an act of war.[24] Eleven years later, the agency was forced to admit that it had secretly retained on its payroll in Guatemala the torturer and murderer of the husband of U.S. citizen Jennifer Harbury. The State Department officer who, acting on his conscience, informed a member of Congress about this episode soon lost his security clearance and his job. This occurred despite the clear language of the Lloyd-LaFollette Act of 1913, which insists that the right of federal employees "to furnish information to either House of Congress, or to a committee or member thereof, may not be interfered with or denied." Whatever the laws may say, the fact is that no matter how deeply Americans may care about the actions taken by their government in their name, their secret government will remain impervious to democratic control.

Free speech and free expression also suffered grievous blows during the Cold War as the fear of treason and espionage gave various local officials and powerful private individuals both the right and the ability to limit dissent and punish nonconformist beliefs. The limits on free expression undertaken during the Cold War were hardly unprecedented in American history, but their seriousness and longevity caused severe and lasting damage to the quality of the nation's democratic debate.

No nation can conduct a war without a means to prosecute traitors and spies, and the United States is no exception. The Alien Act of 1798 gave President Adams the authority "to order all such aliens as he shall judge dangerous to the peace and safety of the United States, or shall have reasonable grounds to suspect are concerned in any treasonable secret machinations against the government thereof, to depart out of the territory of the United States within such time as shall be expressed in such order."[25] The Sedition Act prohibited the publication of any "false scandalous and malicious writing" directed against any branch of the U.S. government with intent to "defame" it, bring it "into disrepute," or excite against it "the hatred of the good people of the United States" for the purpose of "opposing or resisting any law" or any lawful presidential act, or to "aid, encourage, or abet any hostile designs or any foreign nation against the United States, their people or government."[26]

These acts are indeed serious blemishes on the reputations of the men who supported them, but they never evolved into a powerful means of limiting debate. The Alien Act was never enforced, and only twenty-five people were ever arrested for violating the Sedition Act. Moreover, the Alien Act had a provision for automatic expiration two years from its date of passage, and the Sedition Act similarly expired automatically in March 1801. Both acts also explicitly allowed truth as a defense, a provision that would be dropped when Congress passed a similar act in 1918. The violent reaction against these acts, particularly evident in the defiant Kentucky and Virginia nullification resolutions of 1799, also provide a decided contrast with the Cold War era.

The harmful fallout from the 1798 acts ensured that no censorship efforts would be undertaken again until the Civil War. Initially, all Union censorship was voluntary. When that failed, newspapers were prosecuted for publishing "false reports," which Union officials deemed anything potentially harmful to their cause. Stories were censored, editors were arrested, and one correspondent was even ordered shot by Secretary of War Edwin Stanton. (Neither the order nor the reporter was ultimately executed.) In February 1862, the military took over the telegraph lines and refused to allow transmission of messages of which it disapproved. The Post Office did the same with the mail.[27] These provisions, however, also expired with Lee's surrender.

World War I proved the most serious threat yet to American freedom of expression. War correspondents were required to post a $1,000 bond to the government to cover the cost of maintenance and equipment and a $10,000 bond to ensure that the correspondent would conduct himself "as a gentleman of the press." ("Ladies of the press" were few and far between.) If the military decided the correspondent hadn't lived up to that description, the funds were forfeited.[28] The Espionage Act of 1917 and the Trading with the Enemy Act used the same flexible standard employed during the Civil War. They also empowered the Postmaster General to censor the foreign language press while allowing the president to censor all internal communications. In May 1918, the Sedition Act dispensed with the need for the government to prove injury for offensive speech. In *Schenck v. United States*, Oliver Wendell Holmes upheld the Espionage Act, noting that conduct that would be legal in normal times could be punishable in a time of "clear and present danger." Unfortunately for the future of freedom of expression in the United States, he did little to define this weighty and highly malleable term.

These laws, and the atmosphere to which they contributed, led to a series of raids against radical political organizations by Attorney General A. Mitchell Palmer in the World War I's immediate aftermath. Palmer instructed the FBI to focus on infiltrating and disrupting communist organizations and lobbied incessantly for passage of a peacetime sedition act, which President Wilson endorsed but Congress successfully resisted.[29]

These were hardly trivial matters. Following World War II, however, such liberties that had been merely threatened were withdrawn entirely. While many at the highest levels of government were no doubt sincere in their belief that the ideological struggle with Moscow necessitated severe restrictions of free speech, unscrupulous officials and ambitious politicians were also eager to protect their policies from democratic scrutiny. Richard Freeland observes that as the Truman administration sought domestic support for its expansive foreign policy agenda, including the Truman Doctrine and the Marshall Plan, it faced an uphill battle. Public opinion appeared to be drifting away from foreign policy and world affairs. Large majorities of Americans polled were supporting a more conciliatory approach to US-Soviet relations than that favored by Truman and his advisers.[30] The administration responded by conscientiously communicating the Soviet problem in terms "clearer than truth."[31] With his political fortunes flagging and his reelection prospects dim, President Truman seized on a strategic memo written by his young legal adviser, Clark Clifford, together with James T. Rowe, advising him to move leftward on domestic issues while simultaneously exploiting the prospect of increased Cold War tensions to stifle dissension and dissatisfaction with his leadership. "The worse matters get, up to a fairly certain point—real danger of imminent war—the more is there a sense of crisis. In times of crisis the American citizen tends to back up his president," the authors wrote. To head off a challenge by fired secretary of agriculture (and former vice president) Henry Wallace, Clifford advised the president to "identify him and isolate him in the public mind with the Communists."[32] This was perfectly congenial to Truman, who considered Wallace a "pacifist 100 percent," allied to "parlor pinks" and acting as "a sabotage front for Uncle Joe Stalin."[33]

The Clifford/Truman strategy succeeded in part because the Wallace campaign was indeed heavily communist and therefore proved an easy target. Its effect on public debate, however, was to further equate dissent from the hard-line Cold War position with sympathy for Communism and the Soviet Union. In the future, no major party candidate would dare diverge from the 1948 consensus without fear of being labeled "soft" and hence unfit for the burdens of office. While the American people may or may not have shared the unquestioned assumptions regarding the best means to pursue peace and prosperity in the world during the next four decades, the parameters of responsible debate were never sufficiently shifted to allow for an alternative. In this manner, Truman and Clifford's effective use of the Cold War to "isolate" Wallace and "identify" his positions with those of the communists, backed up by even nastier Republican charges, had the effect of closing off public debate and democratic discussion for two generations.

Even by 1947, to dissent from or to question in public the wisdom of U.S. Cold War policies at an official level became cause for dismissal. On March 22, 1947, responding to the recommendations of a special commission on loyalty and national security, President Truman established the Federal Employee Program, creating a system of boards in each department of the government—under the ultimate supervision of a central Loyalty Review Board—to conduct investigations and hearings identifying disloyal individuals. Precedents for this program were set during World War II, when first the armed services and then the Civil Service Commission were authorized to dismiss "suspect" employees. The Department of Justice received $100,000 to investigate federal employees suspected of belonging to "subversive organizations." FDR had authorized the FBI to make dismissals based on "credible evidence" rather than simply "suspicion." He also limited the program's duration and did not allow the establishment of a permanent loyalty bureaucracy.[34] Those standards disappeared from President Truman's program by 1950. The Loyalty Board loosened its standard for dismissal to "reasonable doubt exists as to the loyalty of the person involved." Under Eisenhower's security or "suitability" program, hearing and review procedures were abolished entirely.[35]

The McCarran Act, passed on September 23, 1950, authorized preventive detention of suspected subversives and required Communist Party members to register with the attorney general. Senator William Langer, a Midwestern Republican, called the act "the greatest threat to American civil liberties since the Alien and Sedition laws of 1798." He railed against the bill for five hours before collapsing in exhaustion on the Senate floor. Only six senators, concurred, however. FBI chief J. Edgar Hoover opposed the bill because the FBI already had 20,000 people in its security index and did not appreciate the extra work involved in registering every single communist.[36]

Hoover launched his counterintelligence program (COINTELPRO) in 1956 in response to a bus boycott launched by the Black citizens of Montgomery, Alabama. COINTELPRO focused on organizations like the NAACP, Martin Luther King's Southern Christian Leadership Coalition, and a variety of communist and communist front groups before expanding to include the antiwar movement in 1969. Such programs were scaled back by Attorney General Edward Levi in 1976 but were reauthorized by Ronald Reagan in 1981 under Executive Order 12333. Two years later, Reagan's attorney general, William French Smith, abandoned the "probable cause" standard for investigations and allowed the FBI to "anticipate or prevent crime" and thereby investigate any organization it chose. COINTELPRO was just one of the FBI's antisubversive initiatives to compromise debate. Under the guise of fighting Communism, Hoover and the FBI targeted progressives and liberals for campaigns of slander and defamation while operating wiretaps, mail intercepts, and illegal break-ins. Almost always, these operations were justified within the government under the rubric of national security.[37] Outside the government, similar strictures on freedom of expression were put into place as institutions ranging from Harvard University to the Congress of Industrial Organizations (CIO) scrambled to placate the official keepers of an extremely exacting standard of paranoia. While denouncing the excesses of the likes of Senator McCarthy and his aide-de-camp, Roy Cohn, officials at Harvard encouraged tenured faculty to name names to investigators and forced junior faculty to cooperate with all "civic authorities."[38] The CIO expelled its radical members as its president, Philip Murray, termed them "dirty, filthy traitors of American trade-unionism."[39] In 1948, the Department of Justice convicted the top leaders of the U.S. Communist Party under the 1940 Smith Act, prohibiting the "teaching and advocating" of subversive doctrines. Several hundred party members were also sent to jail. Eisenhower's 1954 State of the Union address even proposed depriving Communists of their citizenship.[40]

The power of the Soviet empire provided an irresistible weapon for nefarious politicians to silence democratic debate. Even the recitation of economic statistics became occasion to question a person's patriotism. During the 1956 election, in what would become a staple of political debate, when the average annual growth rate dropped from 4.3 percent in the last six years of Truman's presidency to 2.5 percent under Eisenhower, Democratic presidential nominee Adlai Stevenson observed that the economy had become sluggish. Vice President Richard Nixon replied, "Mr. Stevenson has been guilty, probably without being aware that he was doing so, of spreading pro-Communist propaganda as he has attacked with violent fury the economic system of the United States."[41]

Just how serious a military threat the Soviets did in fact pose to the American people remains an enormously disputatious subject. Clearly Joseph Stalin was no democrat and may prove to be the greatest mass murderer in human history. The Soviet secrecy obsession, coupled with its iron-fisted treatment of those unlucky enough to live within the borders of its empire, offered considerable cause for genuine concern among those who did not. While no one could accurately gauge the intentions of the mercurially murderous Soviet leader, a measure of caution was clearly in order. Free-speech advocates who reject *all* restrictions on secret information are clearly guilty of naive utopianism. Such considerations, however, do not begin to exonerate the official U.S. practice of deception and disinformation when it came to the actions of the Soviet Union. Tempting as a clear lie is when compared to a complex truth, its employment has the effect of poisoning debate and creating its own dynamic. This dynamic occurred time and again during the Cold War as American officials, sometimes deliberately, sometimes acting in the grip of ideological misperception, misled the American people about its own actions as well as those of the USSR. They did so, moreover, with the active support of some intellectuals and some even historians. Early in the Cold War, Thomas A. Bailey, a dean of diplomatic historians, wrote, "Deception of the people may in fact become necessary . . . the yielding of some of our democratic control of foreign affairs is the price we have to pay for greater physical security."[42] The postwar era, in this regard, was "conceived in sin," as Franklin Roosevelt refused to come clean to the American people about the degree of bargaining and give-and-take he had engaged in at the Yalta peace conference. His refusal to acknowledge its ambiguities later allowed his successor, Truman, and Republican conservatives to use the conference as a metaphor for the duplicity of either Soviet diplomats (in Truman's view) or Roosevelt Democrats (according to the Republicans.) Much of Joe McCarthy's (and Congressman Richard Nixon's) political oxygen derived from the presence of Alger Hiss at the conference and the apparent double-dealing that had taken place there but had never been honestly explained to the American people. While some of what took place at Yalta necessitated temporary secrecy during the war, this excuse evaporated with the Japanese surrender in August 1945. This is not an argument for Wilson's naive hope for "open covenants, openly arrived at." It is an argument for giving the American people the basic facts about what they were being asked to approve after the fact. In what would constitute an oft-repeated pattern throughout the Cold War, the government's unwillingness to trust the American people with the ambivalent truths of diplomacy and foreign policy—to state its cases in terms that were "clearer than truth"—resulted in a political dynamic that ultimately raged out of control.

In most cases, as with Yalta, this deception turned out to be both self-defeating and unnecessary. Over and over, America's leaders demanded that the information necessary to understand the true demands made upon them was too sensitive to share with the general public. "If you only knew what I know . . ." became the most common official refrain of the Cold War. Yet most often, this position marked an unwillingness to defend a speciously conceived policy against the rigors of democratic debate. Shortly after leaving office, former secretary of state Dean Rusk admitted, "I really do not know of any secrets which have a significant bearing upon the ability of the public to make their judgments about major issues of foreign policy."[43]

The atmosphere of constant threat, coupled with the danger posed by nuclear weapons, allowed the president to usurp virtually all war-making powers from Congress, thereby creating exactly the situation that the Founders had sought to avoid when they drafted the Constitution. Wars always result in the expansion of executive power, and American history is replete with examples of presidents ignoring constitutional strictures to prosecute wars they deem necessary. But none did so on the scale carried out during the Cold War, which does not—either constitutionally or ontologically—qualify as a war at all.

The trouble began with Korea. When President Truman was about to order the Korean intervention, Republican Senate Minority Leader Robert A. Taft urged him to ask Congress for a joint resolution before doing so. Truman refused, though Congress would have happily complied. Taft maintained that Truman's refusal to come before Congress "violated all the precedents which have been established as to the limitations of the President's power to make war. . . . If the President can intervene in Korea without Congressional approval, he can go to war in Malaya or Indonesia or Iran or South America."[44] Robert Taft would prove a prophet without honor in Cold War America.

The president argued, with some legal justification, that the UN Security Council's resolution in favor of war gave him all the constitutional authority he required. But as conservative legal scholar Robert Bork has pointed out, Truman received this authority from the UN only because the Soviets were boycotting the Security Council and hence were not present to veto it. Technically, the president appeared to have this right, as the 1945 UN participation act stipulates that "the President shall not be deemed to require the authorization of Congress to make available to the Security Council . . . the armed forces, facilities, or assistance provided therein."[45] Still, Truman's high-handed methods raise troubling questions of both efficacy and legality. "The President's Constitutional powers can hardly be said to ebb and flow with the veto of the Soviet Union in the Security Council," Bork notes.[46] In any case, Truman authorized the troops to be sent to Korea well before the Security Council passed its resolution. Secretary of State Dean Acheson later acknowledged that he and Truman used the UN merely to ratify decisions that they had taken earlier in the day: "It wasn't until 3:00 in the afternoon [on June 27] that the UN asked us to do what we said we were going to . . . in the morning." Truman and Acheson went to the UN before going to Congress because they had fewer concerns about political opposition there. Had Acheson consulted Congress first, he later noted, "you might have completely muddied up the situation" just as the Founders intended. When Acheson finally did brief congressional leaders on the decision, he did not even bother to mention the Security Council vote.[47] Truman, however, argued that the commander-in-chief clause gave him the authority "to send troops anywhere in the world" without congressional authorization, particularly to uphold the government's "obligations under the United Nations."[48] He also believed that he enjoyed the authority to seize newspapers, radio stations, or both and "to act for whatever is for the best for the country."[49] More Americans would die in this nonwar than in the wars of 1812, 1846, and 1898 combined.[50]

In Vietnam, executive usurpation was gradual and perhaps less dramatic. But it could hardly have been less consistent with democratic processes. Congress authorized spending for the war under the August 1964 Gulf of Tonkin resolution, which followed a murky incident involving two alleged North Vietnamese attacks on U.S. vessels off its shores. (At least one of these attacks turned out not to have occurred.) Administration officials had actually drawn up the authorization three months earlier but had waited for a political pretext to put it to use.[51] Members of the Johnson administration were less than truthful with both Congress and the American people about the nature of the "attack," even given their own limited knowledge and understanding of what had taken place, and Congress did not conduct its own investigation. Thus were loosed the dogs of war purely on the basis of the word of a president who, like his successor, could not be trusted.[52]

Of the many ironies of the Cold War, few offer such poetic justice as the results of deliberate government deception for the ambitions of the perpetrators. The politicians who subverted constitutional and democratic practices during the Cold War frequently ended up subverting themselves—or at least their parties—in the process. Franklin Roosevelt's refusal to come clean with regard to Yalta left his party open to the charge that they were dupes of the nefarious Russians and could not be trusted to deal with them. Harry Truman's refusal to engage Congress over Korea resulted in a seemingly interminable war that helped Eisenhower win the election in 1952. Lyndon Johnson's various double-dealings over Tonkin and Vietnam led to the destruction of his presidency, and much the same can be said about Richard Nixon. In each case, presidential dishonesty damaged the cause of not only American democracy but also the efficacy of its foreign policy. The Tocqueville problem, it seemed, worked in reverse as well: the failure to conduct a foreign policy openly and honestly and thereby retain the democratic support of American citizens resulted in the subversion of that policy from within.

Congressional efforts to rein in the executive's ability to commit the country to war have proven only sporadically effective. Angry at its inability to control first Johnson's and then Nixon's expansion of the war in Indochina, Congress passed a number of minor laws attempting to force the president to inform the legislative body of the nation's actions overseas. Most significantly, it also passed the War Powers Act in 1972 and the War Powers Resolution in 1973. Together these laws compel the president to inform Congress within forty-eight hours should U.S. troops be committed to a war zone and prohibit the president from deploying troops for more than sixty days without explicit congressional sanction. But a president's ability to put U.S. troops in harm's way of his own accord turns out to be a kind of de facto war-making power as Congress has proven unwilling to repudiate a presidential use of force even when a majority of its members say they disapprove. Not wanting to appear disloyal when American troops are under fire, Congress has feared the political implications of invoking the act, and presidents, disputing its constitutionality, have generally refused to be bound by it. Presidents Gerald Ford and Ronald Reagan violated it in Cambodia (1975) and Grenada (1983), respectively, as did President George Bush when ordering troops into Panama (1989). Bush's Persian Gulf conflict (1990–91) and President Bill Clinton's incursions into Haiti (1993) and Bosnia (1995) were undertaken in a manner consistent with the spirit of the law, in that Congress was given the opportunity to vote on these deployments, but without adhering to its specific provisions. In fact, Congress has invoked the resolution only once, regarding Reagan's intervention in Lebanon, and then only to approve of the president's decision. "Perhaps not since the Volstead Act ushered in the Prohibition era," notes John Hart Ely, "has a federal law been talked about more and respected less than the War Powers Resolution of 1973."[53]

Political censorship has been a problem of erratic significance since the beginning of the Cold War. While the government has not avoided censorship entirely, in most cases calls for voluntary restraint usually received sufficient support from mainstream media organizations to make it unnecessary. This was particularly true during World War II. Nevertheless, Franklin Roosevelt felt compelled to employ censorship on occasion to smooth potentially perilous political waters. For example, during the early, most difficult period of the war, FDR forbade the publication of the names of dead or dying U.S. soldiers. And army censors read every outgoing letter written by every member of the U.S. military and deleted whatever they considered objectionable.

Both Churchill and FDR also agreed to Joseph Stalin's request to bar the press from attending the Yalta peace conference in February 1945.

This veil of secrecy helped contribute to the variety of myths that cropped up about the conference, including those relating to FDR's health and his delegation's alleged treachery that would later poison U.S. political discourse throughout the postwar period.[54] Harry Truman agreed to the same provisions at Potsdam in July 1945, though this time some reporters were at least allowed into the city. Again, a U.S. president sided with Stalin against Churchill, agreeing that brief, nondescript press releases would be the only news given out. Republican conservatives such as Alexander Wiley from Wisconsin called it "censorship and a ghastly example of dictatorial behavior," but such complaints soon disappeared.[55] As Theodore F. Koop has noted, "So firmly had the idea of checking with a government authority been implanted in the minds of radio and newspapermen, that it was difficult for them to reconvert to peacetime freedom."[56]

Following the war, the administration launched Operation Shamrock, through which it gained access to intelligence transmitted by foreign governments through RCA Global, ITT World Communications, and Western Union International. The program was a violation of the 1934 Federal Communications Act, but it continued until the press discovered it in 1975.[57]

The postwar American government had a definite idea about the role of a free press in the Cold War. As James Forrestal, the nation's first secretary of defense, explained, "The American press should be an instrument of our foreign policy."[58] This policy was soon put into practice. In the late 1940s, the U.S. army revoked the credentials of eleven reporters and denied them to fifty others on the grounds of alleged Communist connections. The State Department adopted a policy of denying passports to reporters whose travels were "not in the interest of the U.S." A reporter for the Communist Party newspaper the *Daily Worker* was not even allowed to leave the country. The American Society of Newspaper Editors briefly protested these strictures before its members decided to learn how to live within them.

Most reporters, however, internalized the values that Forrestal and others were seeking to inculcate, thereby obviating the need for actual censorship. Early into the Cold War, the media's definition of "news" became contingent upon the government's official edicts. During the CIA's Iranian coup in the summer of 1953, for instance, *New York Times* reporter Kenneth Love authored an accurate report of events for CIA director Allen Dulles and a deliberately false one for his readers.[59] At Dulles's request, *Times* publisher Arthur Sulzberger kept reporter Sidney Gruson out of

Guatemala during the period leading up to that country's 1954 coup. Dulles made this request because he questioned Gruson's loyalty, though he presented no hard evidence to back up his allegations.[60] Robert Miller, who reported on the Korean War for the Associated Press, explained, "There are certain facts and stories from Korea that editors and publishers have printed that are pure fabrication. Many of us who sent stories knew they were false, but we had to write them because they were official releases from responsible military headquarters and were released for publication, even though the people responsible knew they were untrue."[61]

Reporters, editors, and media owners were enthusiastically enlisted in the struggle, willfully compromising their responsibilities to their audiences in hopes of serving the government's national security interests. NBC founder David Sarnoff tried to create a media-government Cold War partnership. He authored a forty-two-page memo entitled "Program for a Political Offensive against International Communism" for President Eisenhower. It envisioned the use of radio and television to disseminate U.S. government propaganda worldwide and railed against left-leaning media outlets that were not inclined to cooperate.[62] *New York Times* editors killed stories about U.S. spy programs in the Soviet Union and the "imminent" invasion of the Bay of Pigs.[63] *Times* editor Lester Markel captured the journalistic ethos of the Cold War era quite plainly when he explained, "The question of how much news . . . shall be released and when, must be left largely in the hands of the government."[64] It fell, irony of ironies, to Richard Nixon to defend the idea of a free and vigorous press, pursuing the news wherever it might lead. "The whole concept of a return to secrecy in peacetime demonstrates a profound misunderstanding of the role of a free press as opposed to a controlled press," he insisted in response to President Kennedy's demand for voluntary restraint. Such internal policing, Nixon warned, would "inevitably encourage government officials to further withhold information to which the public is entitled." Moreover, "the plea for security could well become a cloak for errors, misjudgments, and other failings of government."[65]

During the Vietnam era, the media developed a reputation for fearlessness and dragon slaying. Today many soldiers and conservatives blame the media's relentlessness for sapping the nation's will. Following the 1968 Tet Offensive, Dean Rusk faced hostile questioning from reporters for perhaps the first time in his career. His response to his questioners: "There gets to be a point where the question is, 'Which side are you on?' "[66] Those who credit the media for bringing the ugly reality of the war into American living rooms are overly generous. From August

1965 to August 1970, the worst years of the war, only 76 of 2,300 television reports actually contained any battle scenes. Most often they featured Vietnamese rather than American casualties.[67]

The Nixon administration's blatant untruths regarding U.S. policy in Vietnam and Cambodia, coupled with its illegal conduct at home, did encourage investigative reporting in the early 1970s into further official deception. But this era proved brief indeed. The ascension of the media to the status of the de facto fourth branch of government gave it a heightened sense of responsibility for the maintenance of political order and public confidence. Bob Woodward, the most admired investigative reporter of his time, revealed the degree of cooperation between the press and the national security establishment in 1994 when he remarked about former top CIA official Bobby Inman, "It was well-known among reporters [that] if you had sensitive information, he would respond and try to guide you and say that this is where national security would be harmed and this is where it won't. This was the Cold War. This was when the Russians might find out where our submarines are because we're going to print one word or code phrase in the newspaper. It was a dangerous era, and it would have been absolute madness for editors not to go to the government."[68] The inability of the U.S. media to discover the enormous political machinations necessary to construct William Casey's and Oliver North's Iran-Contra operation until a tiny Lebanese newspaper revealed it in 1987 demonstrated just how helpless these institutions remained in the face of a concerted government effort to mislead them. Woodward himself was completing a book on Casey while the entire operation was conducted under his nose.

During the 1991 Persian Gulf War, some news reports traveled more slowly to the home front than during the battle of Bull Run. The Pentagon regularly censored U.S. journalists, though this often turned out to be unnecessary.[69] When ABC News discovered, via its own satellites, that the Bush administration had deliberately misled the country regarding one of its primary justifications for the entire emergency—Iraq's alleged massing of troops on the Saudi border—the network *chose* to kill the story.[70] Such tendencies constitute a fundamental repudiation of the responsibilities inherent in the First Amendment and a breakdown in a foundational aspect of democratic theory. "How," asked John Stuart Mill, can citizens either "check or encourage what they are not permitted to see?"[71]

Among the most significant costs to American democracy that resulted from the Cold War strictures on democratic debate lay not in what was said or done by public officials but in what was left unsaid and undone by everyday Americans. Sissela Bok has written of the "casual way in which enemyhood is so often bestowed" by the official lie. A 1954 U.S. Army pamphlet entitled *How to Spot a Communist* explained that "a communist could be 'spotted' by his or her 'predisposition to discuss civil rights, social and religious discrimination, the immigration laws, [and] antisubversive legislation.' " Communists supposedly used "such giveaway terms as 'chauvinism,' 'book burning,' 'colonialism,' 'demagogy,' 'witch hunt,' 'reactionary,' 'progressive,' and 'exploitation.' " A naval intelligence officer told a reporter that "intelligent people are very likely to be attracted to communism." The pervasiveness of these beliefs were revealed in a public opinion poll, taken at the time, that demonstrated that while not many Americans claimed ever to have met a true Communist, they imagined that people who were "always talking about world peace," who "read too much, who had an affinity for causes," and who, if they were white, had black friends, were "Reds."[72]

Ellen W. Schrecker points out that officially inspired Cold War paranoia did much to constrict the political space for debate in Cold War America. It destroyed and delegitimated not only the spy-infested Communist Party but also an entire field of activities and beliefs associated with activism, class consciousness, progressive internationalism, and social change. Non-Communist leaders like Walter White of the NAACP, who in the early 1940s had openly espoused anticolonialism and solidarity with movements in Africa, by the 1950s abandoned such nations and backed the status quo there. "Black Americans abandoned the Pan-African movement," writes Schrecker, "and when they finally reconnected . . . did so in cultural or nationalist terms rather than in the language of economic exploitation that people like [W. E. B.] Du Bois had used." The labor movement lost its militant edge, giving up on issues of international solidarity and social democratic reform. Conservatism lost its libertarian cast. Isolationism withered and noninterventionism died. During the Korean War, dissenting interpretations of world events, especially ones that remotely paralleled those advanced by the Communist Party, came to be treated as signs of disloyalty. Peace became a dangerous issue. No significant opposition arose to challenge Truman's war in Korea. Nor did the United States enjoy any serious public debate about the use of nuclear weapons, though American leaders repeatedly contemplated their use. Communist-linked groups had raised the issue, and that was that. The cost to American life and culture in discoveries never made, movies never filmed, novels never written, unions never organized, movements never inspired, political alliances never formed, civil liberties never demanded, and ideas never imagined is incalculable.[73]

Perhaps the greatest loss to American democracy from the Cold War was the destruction of the people's trust in their leaders. On May 5, 1960, when Soviet premier Nikita Khrushchev disclosed that an American plane had been shot down inside Soviet territory, the White House responded that a NASA "weather research plane" on a flight inside Turkey had been missing and might have drifted into Soviet territory. The government identified the pilot, Francis Gary Powers, as a civilian employed by Lockheed Aircraft. In fact, Powers was a CIA spy, which Khrushchev triumphantly disclosed to the Supreme Soviet a day later. The U.S. government continued to lie until May 9, when President Eisenhower admitted the spy flights, took personal responsibility for them, and implied they would continue. In 1962, when reporter David Kraslow asked Eisenhower about his "greatest regret" as president, Eisenhower replied, "The lie we told. I didn't realize how high a price we had to pay for that lie."[74]

But how to marry the government's right to lie with the public's right to information? Quite simply, by divorce. When President Kennedy's official spokesmen asserted the American government's "inherent" right to lie to its own people during peacetime, they illustrated the degree to which the makers of U.S. foreign policy believed themselves to be wholly unaccountable to democratic control.[75] After 150 years of republicanism, Madison's greatest fear had been realized. As he predicted, the state of "continual warfare" strangled his proudest creation.

★

The Anatomy of Pseudodemocracy

The New World Order: Trading Away Democracy

No nation was ever ruined by trade, even, seemingly, the most disad-
vantageous.
—Benjamin Franklin, 1774

Thank God I am not a free-trader. In this country, the pernicious indul-
gence in the doctrine of free-trade seems inevitably to produce fatty
degeneration of the moral fibre.
—Theodore Roosevelt, 1895

The surprise end to the Cold War in the late 1980s left the United States
woefully unprepared to pursue a democratic foreign policy in the new
global order. The steady compromise of constitutionally guaranteed
liberties and the inexorable expropriation of power by the executive
outlined in previous chapters left the vast majority of Americans with
no voice whatsoever in foreign policy–making circles. The Cold War
closed the circle, cutting off Americans' access to the insider debate
and curing them of the habit of trying to behave as citizens of a democracy.

Meanwhile, the foreign policy establishment, which had assumed
exclusive responsibility for both the conduct and the debate of U.S. foreign policy, remained intellectually imprisoned wholly obsolete notions
of global power based on Cold War calculations. It was therefore unable
to sort out new priorities in an area where both power and threats had
grown diffuse within global markets and environmental degradation.
While many Americans displayed increasing unease with the new rules
of the global marketplace, almost no one within the policy-making elite
questioned the nation's official fealty to the twin values of free trade and
economic efficiency. As the power of global corporations to bargain

down wages and standards increasingly threatened American workers' job security, health, and safety as well as communities' environmental quality of life, workers and their families could find no effective allies in their government to help them fight to retain a measure of democratic control over their lives and communities. The Cold War finally severed the tenuous link between the nation's democratic ethos and its foreign policy practices.

The demarcation line between foreign and domestic policies had never been as neat and clean as was pretended during the Cold War. By the 1990s it had largely erased itself. The global revolution that exploded the sclerotic sinews of the Evil Empire turned out to be less democratic than capitalist. Its irresistible force carried such power that even the hermetic leaders of Albania were forced to capitulate overnight. In the United States, home of the globe's least restrictive economy and most ideologically procapitalist political system, the creative/destructive powers of global capital flowed through citizens' daily lives with the charge of an invisible lightning storm.

By the beginning of the 1980s the restrictive power of the global market was already apparent. In 1981, following forty years in the political wilderness, Socialist French president François Mitterrand attempted to pay off a veritable Mount Sinai of accumulated political debts by jump-starting his economy through an injection of public spending. The international bond market reacted with no less power than a German panzer division (though with far greater swiftness and precision). To stave off a ruinous run on the franc, Mitterrand was immediately forced to retreat. The bond market, rather than the Eysée Palace, was the ultimate sovereign of the French economy.

Twelve years later, Bill Clinton learned a similar lesson—less dramatically, perhaps, but no less brutally. While the U.S. economy is many times larger than the French, it is only marginally less vulnerable to the strictures of the global market. Approximately $150 billion worth of U.S. government bonds change hands daily across an electronic global network that has no on/off switch. By the time of Clinton's election in November 1992, the government's outstanding obligations to private bondholders exceeded $1 trillion. Having held the White House for only four of the previous twenty-four years, numerous Democratic constituencies believed they had accumulated a considerable stack of IOUs in the form of deferred social spending. Indeed, the primary theme of

Clinton's winning election campaign had been the promise of significant public investment in order to, as the campaign phrased it, "put people first."

This phase of the Clinton presidency ended literally before it began. Even before Clinton sat down at his new desk in the Oval Office, Federal Reserve Chair Alan Greenspan explained to the president-elect that while he had won the election fair and square, the bond market would simply not hear of an investment package of the size and scope Clinton had promised in his campaign. Otherwise, U.S. bonds would be unloaded overnight, and the dollar would be forced into a downward spiral. The result would be either runaway inflation or, more likely, a (Greenspan-directed) stiff rise in interest rates, which would cause an immediate recession. A more modest administration "stimulus package" fared no better, despite its having been pared down to meet Greenspan's objections. Reportedly, at one point an exasperated Clinton complained, "You mean to tell me that the success of the program and my re-election hinges on the Federal Reserve and a bunch of fucking bond-traders?"[1] While the media treated the budget battle between Clinton, Greenspan, and Republican leader Bob Dole as political psychodrama, its true lesson was the irrelevance of 1992 election—and of democracy itself—to the fundamental direction of the U.S. economy.[2]

The scope and intensity of global capital's power to order American lives and communities has vastly outrun the system's ability to understand and assimilate it. The result, Stanley Hoffmann observes, is that the global economy "is literally out of control, not subject to rules of accountability and principles of legitimacy that apply to relations between individuals and the state." No one, moreover, has even come up with a theory "that acknowledges the public aspects of such private activities across borders and establishes a kind of common government for those activities."[3]

Among the greatest intellectual hurdles Americans face in attempting to devise a response to the new rules of global capitalism is the sheer size and complexity of the international networks that presently rule the cosmos of trade and finance. Thomas Friedman describes them as "an electronic herd of anonymous stock, bond and currency traders, sitting behind computer screens. The members of this herd live everywhere there is a trading floor. . . . The electronic herd cuts no one any slack. It does not recognize anyone's unique circumstances. The herd only recognizes its own rules."[4] In the winter of 1995 the herd turned Mexico from a poster child for the International Money Fund into a basket case overnight. "Give us a truce," begged Finance Minister Guillermo Ortiz to his faceless enemy as if he were a Carthaginian general pleading for mercy from a Roman proconsul. "You have pounded us to death."[5] President Clinton responded with an emergency $50 billion loan package that included an end run around congressional objections and hence evaded any form of democratic or constitutional scrutiny until after its completion.[6] As with a potential missile launch, the speed and intensity of the global market precludes the possibility of meaningful democratic debate.

No less anachronistic than Cold War institutions in the transnational world of global capital is the idea of the "U.S. corporation." In July 1995, when Zenith, the last American-owned television manufacturer, gave up its dramatic battle for survival and sold out to South Korean industrial giant LG Electronics, it was by that point making only tubes in the United States. The largest U.S. manufacturer of television sets is Thomson of France, followed by Philips of the Netherlands and Sony, Sharp, Matsushita, and Toshiba, among others.[7] Transnational alliances are now, in the words of management guru, Peter Drucker, "the dominant form of economic integration in the world economy."[8] Their power, moreover, is growing exponentially. Foreign investment flows may make up only approximately 10 percent of annual world trade flows, but intrafirm trade (for example, sales by Honda Japan to Honda USA) account for an amazing 40 percent of all U.S. trade.[9] Such alliances have no country and no concept of patriotism.

The global reach of transnational corporations (TNCs), even those not tied to larger alliance structures, has also multiplied and diversified. According to the UN Center on Transnational Corporations, these firms are now "the most important actors in the world economy." The largest TNCs boast sales larger than the output of all but a few countries. Taken together, the top 600 companies alone account for almost a quarter of all the value added in the worldwide production of goods and services.[10] Moreover, TNCs are growing more rapidly than nation-states. The sales of the fifty largest TNCs equaled 28 percent of the U.S. gross national product in 1975; by 1989 that number had reached nearly 40 percent.[11]

While TNCs are largely beyond the control of any national government, they are particularly powerful in the United States, where they face the world's least restrictive markets.[12] This openness increases American workers' vulnerability, owing to the relatively high wages they had previously enjoyed and coupled with the minimal costs of relocating production facilities. In 1997, U.S. labor rates averaged $17.74 per hour, including benefits. This figure was considerably less than for workers in Germany and Japan, and a bit lower than in France and Italy, but more than three times that in South Korea and over thirty times that in China.[13] Any executive in a labor-intensive industry who chooses to locate a manufacturing plant in the United States rather than, say, in Malaysia or Mexico had therefore better be able to explain that decision to the stockholders. For instance, when IBM announced the transfer of its disk drive–manufacturing plants from the United States to Asia, a *Wall Street Journal* report noted, "IBM plan[ned] to establish this new site as a joint venture with an undetermined Asian partner and use non-IBM employees so that it will be easier . . . to move to an even lower-cost region when warranted."[14]

The response of the political elite, extending from Bob Dole and Newt Gingrich on one side to Bill Clinton and Al Gore on the other, to the brave new world of unfettered market power has been an unequivocal philosophical endorsement of open markets and the freest possible exchange of trade and investment funds. The bipartisan consensus on behalf of free trade is roughly analogous to the belief in anti-Communism and the necessary containment of the Soviet Union during the Cold War. It overshadows virtually all other foreign policy goals.[15] As with containment, to question the consensus from any political standpoint is to invite both ridicule and irrelevance.

To argue in favor of free trade in the American political discourse is to invoke an unbroken political, cultural, and intellectual tradition that stretches beyond the American Revolution and even beyond Adam Smith's *Wealth of Nations*. Drawing on Locke and Montesquieu, Thomas Jefferson considered "free trade with all parts of the world" to be a natural right, "unabridgeable by any law."[16] Thomas Paine went so far as to claim that "if commerce were permitted to act to the universal extent it is capable of, it would extirpate the system of war, and produce a revolution in the uncivilized state of governments."[17] Though the doctrine occasionally conflicted with nativist pride and patriotism—George Washington once declared he would "use no porter [ale] or cheese in my family but such as is made in America"—such sentiments found little support in either the republican or liberal philosophies of the Revolutionary and

Federalist eras.[18] Like contemporary politicians, the first Americans were free traders in theory but protectionists in practice. They did not believe, for instance, in free trade with nations who did not practice it themselves. To achieve free trade for American agriculture, James Madison argued for "commercial discrimination" against Britain in order to force the removal of restrictions on American commerce there.[19]

Ultimately, Americans would take Madison's pragmatic view of free trade to its logical conclusion. But when, in late 1791, Alexander Hamilton submitted his report on manufacturers to Congress calling for protective tariffs to foster American industry, Congress ignored it. Like so much of Hamilton's work, the report would prove uncannily prophetic. Congress did not begin using the tariff for protective purposes until after the War of 1812, when it sought to shelter New England's burgeoning textile mills. Rates increased steadily until 1828, when, ignoring the demands of southern cotton growers, Congress passed the so-called "Tariff of Abominations," the highest in all U.S. history. The law led South Carolina's John C. Calhoun to declare a doctrine of "nullification" that would allow a state to interpose itself between federal law and its own citizens. Lawmakers ultimately reached a compromise and the crisis was solved, but the nation had been given its first taste of the sectional conflict that would soon split it into warring halves.

Before the Civil War, tariff measures were important to individual industries and Democratic party politics, but they had little significance for the state of the overall economy owing to the relatively meager size of the foreign-trade sector. Following Reconstruction, however, as the ideological distinction between the parties dwindled, the tariff began once again to assume a central role in political debate. Economic interests lined up behind each party depending largely upon whether they believed themselves to be in need of cheap imports or domestic protection. Louisiana beet growers, Pennsylvania iron and steel manufacturers, West Virginia coal miners, and Ohio and Texas wool producers agitated for protection. New York importers, iron manufacturers dependent on imported ore, railroads seeking lower prices for steel rail, Chicago meat packers, and farmers and cattlemen with large overseas markets fought for rate reductions.[20] Free trade became an essential component of Populist ideology and was adopted by William Jennings Bryan as part of his rallying cry. Republicans, meanwhile, assimilated protectionism into their "free labor" belief system. Republican protectionist victories followed those of Grant's army. William McKinley's victorious slogan in

1896 was "Peace, Prosperity, and Protectionism." The following year, duties rose an average of 57 percent.[21]

Even with a decimated southern economy and a weak national Democratic party, extremely high tariffs provided their own self-corrective mechanism in the form of retaliation by U.S. trading partners. As American manufacturers grew more efficient and their global distribution networks more sophisticated, their own interests moved from a policy of protection to one of free trade and "open doors." Progressive reformers also agitated for freer trade, or at least a trade policy devised by experts rather than politicians. (Protection was viewed as part and parcel of the corrupt influence of big business on good government.) Protectionism earned a respite under Theodore Roosevelt, who believed that "every class of our people is benefited by the protective tariff."[22] In 1909, however, under President Taft, Congress lowered rates to a still quite respectable 38 percent.[23]

Under Woodrow Wilson, duties descended significantly when Congress passed the Underwood Tariff of 1913. No less significant was Wilson's call for an independent Tariff Commission to oversee the process in the future. Congress created the board in 1916 following the progressive blueprint it accepted with the creation of the Interstate Commerce Commission, the Federal Trade Commission, and the Federal Reserve Board. Bipartisan in composition, the commission was charged with giving Congress objective, scientific advice about constructing rate schedules. Tariffs, progressives hoped, would be removed from party politics, but these hopes proved illusory. Republican protectionists gained control of the Tariff Commission and saw to it that it accomplished nothing beyond a few dilatory investigations and equally tepid recommendations. Following the war, however, as the world financial and trading system teetered toward collapse, such ideals were forgotten. The Republicans increased tariff rates significantly, passing the protectionist Fordney-McCumber Act of 1922, which brought rates back up to an average of more than 38 percent, followed by the extremely restrictive Smoot-Hawley Tariff in 1931, which carried 1,500 separate special-interest amendments, a historic record. Under Smoot-Hawley some duties reached their highest level in American history, while others of comparable value were actually lowered. By 1939 world trade was less than it had been in 1914. The downward trend long predated Messrs. Smoot and Hawley, but the two men's historical reputations, slandered by generations of editorial writers and corporate lobbyists, have never recovered.[24]

However unfair to the legislators' place in history, Smoot-Hawley proved a turning point as the Depression opened a policy window. Beginning with the Trade Agreements Act of 1934, the executive wrested from Congress the lead in trade policy formation, setting in motion an almost unbroken half-century trend toward freer trade. Following World War II, with both Europe and Asia economically prostrate, Americans finally felt strong enough to practice the free trade they had so often preached. Manufacturers in the United States achieved a degree of pre-dominance that matched and perhaps exceeded Britain's at the dawn of the Industrial Revolution. Moral high ground plus perceived self-interest —Virtue and Commerce—proved to be an unmatchable combination. Trade liberalization became an indivisible component of the new American internationalism, a faith so widely and deeply believed that the issue of protectionism all but disappeared from the elite policy agenda. Beginning with 1934 and followed by U.S. ratification of the GATT accord during the next decade, tariffs receded in importance and were soon superseded by import quotas, variable levies, export subsidies, and the like. For most practical purposes, U.S. trade policy was turned over to administrative agencies like the International Trade Commission (ITC), the Office of the U.S. Trade Representative (USTR), the Department of Commerce's International Trade Administration (ITA), and the Court of International Trade (CIT).[25] Republican protectionism went the way of Republican isolationism until Patrick Buchanan tried to revive them both in the presidential campaigns of 1992 and 1996. Buchanan's efforts, however, were doomed to failure at the level of policy discussion. Free trade had earned itself a place just behind free speech and free elections in the canon of bedrock American beliefs.

Part of the doctrine's appeal lies in its algebraic simplicity: Free trade = lower prices = market efficiency. In the realm of contemporary economic theory, dominated in the West by neo-Classicists and neo-Keynesians, skeptical thinkers lack firm theoretical ground upon which to mount a challenge. Efficiency is the system's deity. The interests of consumers, rather than those of producers or workers, are deemed paramount. Unlike James Madison and company, however, contemporary free traders do not have much to say about a trade relationship where only one party believes in free trade, except to argue that the free-trading country's consumers continue to benefit from lower prices. (The jobs issue does not seem to arise in such calculations.) This ideological consensus has grown so powerful that it remains in force despite powerful counterexamples from both history and contemporary practice. According to Frank Taussig, a Harvard economist quite critical of protectionism, "manufactures in general grew and flourished" during the forty-five years prior to the Civil War, when U.S. tariffs were near their historical peak. After dominating the world market through the early 1960s, however, U.S. manufacturing industries began to experience a precipitous decline during a period of unilateral free trade. The history of British trade policy demonstrates a similar dynamic.[26] Free trade economist Dani Rodrik notes that "no widely accepted model attributes to postwar trade liberalization more than a very tiny fraction of the increased prosperity of the advanced industrial countries."[27] While protectionist ideology has failed to find a credible ideological foothold within the insider discourse, its practice has mushroomed in the form of special interest lobbying at the agency level. As the political parties have declined in influence, the ability of well-funded and organized special interests to achieve their aims has increased inversely. President Ronald Reagan, for instance, spoke in soaring ideological terms about the benefits of free and open trade markets; nevertheless, according to William Niskanen, a member of Reagan's Council of Economic Advisers, "In response to domestic political pressure, the administration imposed more new restraints on trade than any administration since Hoover."[28] While much of the public—Buchanan's so-called "peasants with pitchforks"—remains extremely suspicious of the effects of free trade agreements on their lives, in the elite debate such views are met with undisguised contempt. Free trade has became a kind of holy virgin of American political ideology: nearly everyone pays it homage, though few seek to follow its example.

Antonio Gramsci once observed that old orders have a habit of dying long before new orders are ready to be born. By the 1990s, the United States boasted both the world's largest current accounts deficit and its smallest tariff rates, which averaged just 4.5 percent (before NAFTA and GATT), excluding oil.[29] But Americans who believe their livelihoods and communities are threatened by the effects of unrestricted trade and investment agreements still lack a principled foundation upon which to base their appeal, to say nothing of a financial and intellectual infrastructure in the media or universities from which to launch an intellectual assault. In each of the past four presidential elections, at least one major candidate has attempted to make protectionism a centerpiece of his campaign; all such candidates were pilloried in the media until the issue was dropped. Despite the public's uneasiness with the effects of various free trade and investment treaties, giving voice to these fears remains a one-way ticket to political irrelevance within respectable political circles. In 1994, the Republican Party's "Contract with America" elected a group of forty legislators who would later vote, as a majority, to oppose giving President Clinton "fast-track" authority to negotiate trade agreements. Yet the contract did not even mention trade policy, lest it be deemed radical and irresponsible by the Washington punditocracy.

In contrast to the depoliticization of trade issues during the postwar era, the first half of the Clinton administration witnessed debates on two major national trade initiatives: the North American Free Trade Agreement (NAFTA) and the General Agreement on Tariffs and Trade (GATT). In each case, proponents of the accord portrayed the debate as about the efficacy of free trade itself. Opponents, whose minions included conservative Republicans and liberal Democrats but few denizens of the center of either party, were faced with a triple disadvantage. In being forced to oppose "free trade," they were forced to oppose a value that Mobil Corporation, at least, felt it could credibly advertise right next to motherhood and apple pie on the op-ed page of the *New York Times*.[30] (Another pro-GATT lobbyist alliance ran an advertisement in the *Washington Post* once again slandering Messrs. Hawley and Smoot. Beneath a full-page photograph of the two men, it warned Congress, "When you vote on GATT, keep these two fellas in mind.") Second, they needed to overcome the natural aversion that most Americans have toward involving themselves in any specific foreign policy issue, excluding those relating exclusively to war and peace. And third, they faced a unified front inside the political and media elite that almost uniformly defined their position as the "left fringe" or the "right fringe." The *Wall Street Journal*'s chosen epithet for NAFTA opponents Pat Buchanan, Jesse Jackson, Ross Perot, and Ralph Nader was the "Halloween Coalition."[31]

The conservative Republican attack on the treaty did not enter into the free trade debate. Nor did it focus much on the more tangible effects of its likely economic impact. Rather it sought to replace one ideology, that of free trade, with another: the protection of absolute sovereignty. Conservative opponents argued, in Buchanan's provocative phrasing, that NAFTA and GATT were "part of a skeletal structure for world government" whose "anti-freedom" tenet "insults the memory of the men of 1776."[32] Ross Perot's bizarre performance in a debate on the treaty with Vice President Al Gore, however, proved to be the opposition's last gasp. He combined anachronistic fears for U.S. sovereignty with questionable economic figures to evoke the specter of apocalyptic job losses: the "great sucking sound" he alleged to have detected emitted by low-wage Mexican factories. With the media planted firmly in Gore's camp, the debate seemed to echo the famous Clarence Darrow–William Jennings Bryan showdown over evolution, with Perot playing the barefoot simpleton and Gore the sophisticated cosmopolitan. Support for the treaty nearly doubled following the debate.[33]

Ironically, Perot and Buchanan were joined in opposing the treaty by what remained of the liberal wing of the Democratic party. The surprising breadth of this unusual coalition forced reporters to pay attention despite the contempt most held for the arguments the coalition put forth. Like the conservatives, the liberals did not take on the idea of free trade per se.[34] Rather they went after the specifics of each treaty. NAFTA, its opponents argued, would encourage TNCs to move jobs across the border and use the threat of such a move to attack the wages, benefits, and environmental protections that U.S. workers had come to enjoy.

The anti-NAFTA team was never really in the game. NAFTA proponents questioned the manliness and patriotism of those who argued that the United States had anything to fear from Mexican peasant workers. Americans, they insisted, compete with German and Japanese workers, not Mexicans. (At the time of the vote, the U.S. economy was experiencing a temporary trade surplus with Mexico owing largely to an artificially overvalued peso. Within eighteen months, following the collapse of the peso, a $350 million surplus soon became a $17.5 billion deficit, the largest in history.[35]) In addition, the most effective political argument of NAFTA's opponents—that the treaty was almost certain to increase illegal immigration—suffered from its own complexity. An immigration upturn would be the natural result of both increased imports of U.S. farm products into Mexico as well as the modernization of the Mexican agricultural industry. Both phenomena would have the effect of displacing Mexican peasants in the countryside, forcing greater internal migration towards already overcrowded cities, and hence, forcing more people toward the border in search of relief. One study predicted that NAFTA would initially increase the number of Mexicans moving permanently across the border by between 20,000 and 30,000 per year for the rest of the decade. Such arguments have no place in a debate characterized exclusively by nine-second sound bites and were easily counteracted by proponents' simplistic claims that NAFTA would mean more jobs for Mexico and hence less immigration.[36] The power of organized labor to oppose the treaty, moreover, had declined precipitously. By 1993, unions represented barely more than 10 percent of the private work force. They were further hobbled in the debate by their worries of damaging a Democratic president and by the hypercautious leadership style of then-AFL-CIO president Lane Kirkland. Support for the idea of a positive role for government in the economy had also declined precipitously. In 1964 barely one-fifth of Americans surveyed agreed with the statement that "you cannot trust the government to do what is right most of the time." This figure rose steadily until 1980 when it reached approximately three-quarters of all Americans, where it has remained ever since.[37] In the context of the trade debate, NAFTA equaled not only free trade but also less government interference.

Despite these advantages, the Clinton administration was forced to engage in an unusual amount of horse-trading and political bribery to pass both accords. To win NAFTA, for instance, it offered wavering representatives additional funds for highways, research centers, agricultural deals, and the unneeded production of C-17 cargo planes. To succeed with GATT, the administration offered special favors to the steel, automobile, wheat, lumber, cement, ball bearing, cellular telephone, civil aircraft, and apparel industries.[38] President Clinton also resorted to claims his own advisers knew were false. For instance, the president insisted that "the peso would become stronger if NAFTA passes because it would strengthen the Mexican economy," even though an (overly optimistic) internal Treasury Department estimate had already judged the currency to be overvalued by at least 10 percent. The latter claim also belied Clinton's repeated assertion that the accord "will create 200,000 jobs," since such calculations were based on the artificial exchange rates.[39]

Elite media opinion was nearly unanimous in its support for the treaty. This was perhaps a reflection of the changed socioeconomic situation of Washington journalists. No longer working-class heroes, they now tended to view politics from the same perspective as that of the political class.[40] On the bottom of the scale were the workers who would now be forced to bargain for wages and working conditions against their underpaid and underorganized counterparts in Mexico. These people had provided the electoral base for President Clinton's victory, yet this betrayal seemed too tawdry an issue even to raise for discussion. From the perspective of power politics, the working poor, like Black and gay Clinton supporters, had nowhere else to go. The question was not one of internal political conflict, *New York Times* editors insisted, but "America's appetite for global leadership after the Cold War." The *Los Angeles Times* declared a pro-NAFTA vote to be "a vote for U.S. foreign policy continuity." The *Washington Post* called the vote "a historic test of American intentions toward the rest of the world." Senator Byron Dorgan (Democrat from North Dakota) noted that the *Washington Post* had published 63 feet of pro-NAFTA editorials and columns since January compared to only 11 feet of anti-NAFTA commentary on its op-ed page. News coverage was even further tilted. Seventy-one percent of expert sources quotes in the *Post* were pro-NAFTA and only 17 percent were opposed. The *New York Times* followed with 66 percent quotes for the treaty and only 24 percent for opponents. Even a top administration official, whose job it was to sell the treaty to Congress and the public, said he could not remember a single issue in which the media coverage had been so biased in favor of the administration's position. As the pundit Mark Shields observed at the time, "It's an act of courage to support NAFTA, but if you're against NAFTA, you're voting your fears and obviously bowing to pressure from organized labor."[41]

The only drama in the GATT debate of winter 1994 derived from the *Washington Post*'s embarrassment when a competing communications conglomerate revealed that the newspaper's owners stood to gain hundreds of millions of dollars in forgiven licensing fees because of a rider that Congressman John Dingell had attached to the treaty. *Post* editorial page editor Meg Greenfield called the notion that her editorial page was secretly trying to advance the company's corporate interests was "a bit nutty," noting that the *Post* had run more than 400 editorials in favor of "free trade."

With the enthusiastic support of the Clinton administration, Congress further reduced the democratic component of the agreement's approval by abdicating a number of its constitutional charges. The treaty's approval process limited the representatives' ability to scrutinize and modify the trade agreements. According to these rules, no amendments were permitted to the implementing legislation or the trade agreement, and a "yes" or "no" floor vote needed to be taken within sixty to ninety legislative days of its submission. The Senate allowed twenty hours of debate; the House only four. Representative Marci Kaptur of New Jersey pointed out that "even the section on patents and weakening our inventors' patent protections deserves at least four hours."[42] Ultimately, because President Clinton called a special session of Congress to consider the accord after the November 1994 elections, the accord was approved by a lame-duck Congress that was unresponsive to any democratic constituency.

The approval process for GATT accord, and U.S. entry into the new institutions it created, raised other constitutional issues as well. The collaborative accord between President Clinton and the Senate to consider GATT an executive agreement rather than a treaty contravened all relevant legislative precedent as well as the clearly enumerated provisions for such matters. Although trade agreements have traditionally been approved by simple majorities of both houses of Congress, the United States has historically entered into standing international organizations through treaties, which require a two-thirds majority of the Senate for approval. The United States joined the United Nations, the World Bank, the International Monetary Fund, and NATO by treaty. Indeed, it originally joined GATT through the treaty process. In 1947 President Truman tried to submit the International Trade Organization to both houses as an executive agreement once it became clear that it would not get through the Senate as a treaty. This avoidance strategy failed, however, when crucial senators, backed up by the American Bar Association, objected, thereby preventing the accord from ever reaching the floor.

The GATT accord runs 22,000 pages, weighs 385 pounds, and required seven years of negotiations. Many of its clauses and footnotes refer both forward and backward to other clauses and footnotes. All are written in the nearly impenetrable lingua franca of international bureaucratese. Given the size and complexity of the accord, it is doubtful that anyone in the world could honestly claim to understand all of its significant implications.

Inevitably, any debate on such a document is going to be conducted in sound-bite form, with code words and rhetorical heat crowding out all but the most powerful rays of light. But while it is easy to deplore the state of American political culture, the widely held belief that America was engaged in a debate about foreign affairs rather than crucial issues of domestic policy made it impossible for Congress and the public to understand the issues at stake.

As the nonpartisan Congressional Budget Office noted at the time, Mexico's goal under NAFTA was "to attract and productively absorb foreign capital" and to make itself "more attractive for U.S. investors." At least some this investment would have to come, by definition, at the expense of investment and jobs in the United States. The fastest-growing component of U.S. investment in Mexico at the time of the accord was manufacturing. Between 1986 and 1990, manufacturing jobs in Mexican affiliates increased by 25 percent, whereas those in the U.S. domestic economy grew by barely 1 percent.[44] According to a U.S. Commerce Department survey, United States–based companies planned to spend $2.3 billion on plants and equipment in manufacturing businesses in Mexico following the treaty's passage. This figure was more than three times the amount invested five years earlier.[45] Now, one might argue that ultimately such investment could benefit American workers in the form of cheaper component prices for imports, or in the creation of a richer export market in Mexico, but certainly these numbers call for a much more concrete response than a blanket philosophical defense of free trade.

Perhaps the most significant effect of the NAFTA accord was to reduce the power of local government to exercise some form of democratic control over international capital. Among the rights the United States signed away as a result of NAFTA were the rights to require foreign investors to transfer technology, to mandate that a share of materials used in production be locally purchased, to require companies to gear production toward national markets rather than continental or world ones, to require that raw materials be processed to a certain level before export, and to require that a certain share of profits be locally invested. Nor can the federal government decide to create a public corporation, embark on new programs, or introduce new regulations that reduce the "reasonably expected" value of foreign investments. This would rule out, for instance, the creation of a single-payer health insurance corporation if it adversely affected the value of the rest of the insurance industry, regardless of its public value or democratic desire for one. Nor could Congress pass a law, for instance, requiring cigarette manufacturers to sell their wares in generic packages to discourage teen smoking. Such a law would constitute a "taking" of intellectual property under the terms of the treaty.[46]

The democratic problems raised by GATT are no less worrisome but are considerably more complex. Despite what may have been deliberate scare tactics and exaggerated fears on the part of some GATT opponents, the treaty did raise important issues about the sovereignty of American law and the efficacy of the American democratic process. Most of these issues arose from the creation of the World Trade Organization, which now arbitrates trade disputes between nations and whose criteria for decision making provide precious little room for democratic input.

Under the new GATT rules, trade disputes are heard by a three-member WTO panel of trade experts who meet in secret to decide whether a challenged domestic law constitutes a barrier to trade. Amicus briefs are not allowed, and the public has no means of access whatsoever. Under previous GATT rules, decisions put forward by the dispute panel had to be approved by consensus of all the contracting party countries. Any country could block it. Under the new rules, however, the panel's decision is automatically adopted within sixty days unless all members reject it. A unanimous rejection is impossible, however, because a country that wins a favorable ruling is not about to vote to reject. Alternately, a nation can appeal. The WTO appellate board then is made up of trade experts who also meet in secret without any public input. Appeals are limited to issues of law covered in the panel report and interpretations developed by the panel. (Thus if the panel chooses to omit relevant facts from its analysis, the Appeals Board may not consider them.) The appeals decision is also binding unless unanimously rejected by the full WTO membership within thirty days of its issuance. Again, such a rejection would require the cooperation of the winning party and hence is not going to happen. Once a final decision is approved, the country found in violation must change its laws or face automatic economic sanctions. All documents remain secret and are not subject to the U.S. Freedom of Information Act. When Representative Vic Fazio asked U.S. Special Trade Representative Mickey Kantor how the United States could bind itself to so secretive and unaccountable an organization, Kantor replied, "You have to understand, most of the signatories of this agreement, they do not believe in our system of jurisprudence. They would be very uncomfortable if we had rules of law. They are much more comfortable with secret tribunals with no conflict of interest laws."[47] Suffice it to say that these same countries—to say nothing of the companies that stand to benefit from the accord— would be even more "uncomfortable" were the WTO subject to any possible form of democratic scrutiny or accountability.

The United States' participation in the WTO causes numerous problems for American citizens who seek to exercise established constitutional and democratic rights. Here are just a few:

CHALLENGES TO THE FEDERALIST STRUCTURE OF THE U.S. GOVERNMENT

Under the GATT accord, the terms of the agreement, and hence WTO decision making, are applicable to the states as well as on the federal government. U.S. domestic courts entertaining state tax disputes will consider these rulings as binding unless formally rejected by the U.S. government. Thus, under GATT, foreign corporations can argue persuasively in U.S. courts that a state or local tax practice violates the U.S. Constitution by virtue of its inconsistency with a WTO ruling. They need not bother arguing their case under American law; WTO rulings will suffice. The WTO's Dispute Settlement Bodies are comprised of international trade experts who can hardly be expected to be sympathetic to, or even knowledgeable about, America's federalist structure. Their decisions would not be bound by U.S. court precedents or any other body of law. States have no standing before them. The federal government may defend the states' legitimate interests, or it may not. The decision is solely at its discretion.[48]

Although GATT rulings are not directly binding on the federal government—they authorize fines and trade retaliation rather than court orders—they are binding on the states. Unlike the federal government, the states are bound by the National Supremacy and Foreign Commerce Clauses of the Constitution. Thus, foreign parties could conceivably demand enforcement of a GATT ruling by bringing suit against a given state under the Foreign Commerce Clause.[49]

CHALLENGES TO GENERAL SAFETY LAWS

U.S. safety laws are also threatened by the GATT accord. Dispute panels of the World Trade Organization provide multinational corporations with an all but irresistible opportunity to challenge such laws without being required to go through Congress or the courts. At risk are workplace safety specifications, product safety and labeling rules, bans on asbestos and other dangerous substances, and literally any other law that provides standards for products or services.[50]

Even if a particular law's goals are allowable under WTO rules, the means to achieve them must also meet the WTO's test of "least trade-restrictive alternative." GATT requires the United States to ensure that safety measures "are not more trade restrictive than required to achieve their appropriate level of protection, taking into account technical and economic feasibility." A footnote provides that "a measure is not more trade restrictive than required unless there is another measure, reasonably available taking into account technical and economic feasibility, that achieves the appropriate level of protection and is significantly less restrictive to trade." What the regulation ignores, however, is that not everything that is technically and economically feasible is also feasible politically. The distinction is critical. In the GATT challenge to the U.S. "gas guzzler" tax, for instance, the European Union argued that a carbon emissions tax would be a less restrictive way to promote fuel efficiency. However, when President Clinton proposed such a tax, it was shot down immediately in Congress. Technical and economic feasibility are therefore moot points in practical terms but could easily prevent the United States from instituting any fuel economy laws at all.[51]

Challenges to Food Safety Laws

"There is a tension between the two goals of safety and trade," former Special Trade Representative Mickey Kantor admits, and it is one for which Americans' right to ensure the safety of the food they consume must be compromised. America's food-inspection system is over a hundred years old. Inspectors from the U.S. Food and Drug Administration (FDA) test an increasingly tiny fraction of the 30 billion tons of food now imported into the United States. State health departments are overburdened and underfinanced, owing in part to the expense of responding to the AIDS crisis. Twelve states have no system at all for reporting food-borne disease. In 1993, citing "enormous inefficiencies in the current food-protection system" and the "ever-increasing challenges" posed by increased food imports, the FDA petitioned the Clinton administration for the power to bar foods imported from any nation with an inferior inspection system. During the heated battle over "fast-track" free-trade authority, the administration concurred, and proposed giving the FDA the power to demand just such equivalency. By the spring of 1998, however, absolutely nothing had happened, by either presidential order or congressional legislation. Partly as a result of these weaknesses, according to the Centers for Disease Control and Prevention in Atlanta, during the 1990s U.S. consumers experienced avoidable outbreaks of infectious disease deriving from the imports of raspberries from Guatemala; carrots from Peru; strawberries, scallions, and cantaloupes from Mexico; coconut milk from Thailand; canned mushrooms from China; and many others.[52] Overall, the CDC said, domestic and imported food-borne disease kills thousands of Americans and sickens millions, perhaps tens of millions, every year. Under GATT and NAFTA these problems can only worsen, as nations that believe their food exports are subject to overly onerous inspection procedures may label such inspections as unfair trade restrictions and demand redress from the WTO. Under NAFTA, U.S. officials are forbidden to inspect food that crosses the border into the United States more thoroughly than they would inspect an "equivalent" U.S. food product, regardless of how lax the exporters' standards might be.[53]

The Codex Alimentarius Commission (Codex) was set up by 130 nations in 1963 to facilitate trade in foods and establish uniform safety standards. Under GATT, contracting parties are obliged to set standards in line with those of Codex as far as is possible. Any national food standards set more strictly than Codex standards could be challenged as a violation of GATT, and the offending country would have to prove the scientific legitimacy of its higher standard. Thus international corporations can argue that Codex standards should take precedence over tougher U.S. standards. Philip James, chair of the World Health Organization committee that produced that organization's 1990 report on diet and health, warns that should this take place, "Nutrition development would literally be stopped in its tracks," and the resulting cancer risk could increase by a factor of twelve over current rates.[54] In 1997, Codex rejected U.S. efforts to reduce the acceptable levels of lead in mineral water by 50 percent and to require dairy products to be pasteurized. These are very important issues, Kantor later explained, speaking of an analagous set of safety regulations, "but it is like they are being dealt with in a closet somewhere and no one's watching."[55]

CHALLENGES TO WILDLIFE AND ENVIRONMENTAL PROTECTION

Over the past four decades, the United States has successfully used trade measures to protect animals and guarantee their humane treatment. Over the years, the U.S. Congress has passed many laws that protect animals through the use of trade measures.[56] As with food-safety regulations, these measures are now increasingly at risk. For example, according to GATT and WTO principles, the United States no longer enjoys the right to try to protect the lives of dolphins except those living inside its borders. In a story that went largely unreported in both the *Washington Post* and the *Wall Street Journal*, the WTO ruled in the spring of 1998 that the United States did not have the right to pass a law prohibiting shrimp imports from countries that fail to protect sea turtles from deadly entrapment in the trawls of shrimping boats. The turtles are at risk of extinction, but the three-member WTO panel ruled the American law to be an unfair barrier to trade. [57] Other wildlife-protection laws now at risk include the Wild Bird Conservation Act, the African Elephant Conservation Act, and the Federal Humane Slaughter Act.[58] New technologies devised to protect the environment may also be barred under WTO sovereignty. For instance, Northern Telecom recently developed a non-ozone-depleting way of cleaning printed circuits and microchips. If, in the interest of saving the ozone layer, the United States decided to require this process for all chips purchased in this country, Northern Telecom's rivals could argue that the law had placed them at a competitive disadvantage. It would therefore qualify as discriminatory under the WTO.[59]

Most members of the political establishment consider the arguments just discussed to be purposefully alarmist and deliberately exaggerated. Perhaps they are. But similar fears appeared to be corroborated in April 1996 when the WTO reaffirmed its first decision: a final ruling that a key section of the U.S. Clean Air Act discriminated against foreign oil refineries. The panel ordered Congress to change a law regulating the emission standards of imported gasoline or else face unspecified sanctions.[60] It offered Americans the choice of either changing its regulation to allow more-contaminated gasoline to pollute its cities and highways or facing $150 million in annual trade sanctions until 1998.[61] While the issue itself may have been rather arcane and complicated, no doubt, by the differing internal standards in the nations that export gasoline to the United States, the idea of the WTO ordering the United States to relax its citizens' antipollution protection or pay hundreds of millions of dollars in fines is indeed portentous.

Clearly the issues raised by GATT and NAFTA constitute a powerful challenge to established U.S. democratic practices. To discuss them simply as "foreign policy" or "free trade" issues is to obscure the profound effects each accord is likely to have on U.S. immigration policy, working conditions, food and occupational safety practices, and ecological and wildlife protection, to say nothing of laws designed to protect small enterprises, regional cultures, or ways of life. Yet only a tiny percentage of these questions were raised during the course of debate on either agreement. Americans continued to labor under an artificial distinction between domestic policy and foreign policy. While the U.S. democratic process makes allowances for citizen and community input into domestic policy, foreign policy still operates in an environment of virtual representation. In this case, almost all elite opinion was united in favor of the two agreements. Backed by the full political resources of the White House, the nearly unanimous arguments of the mainstream media, and the fully committed economic resources of much of global capitalism along with those of the Mexican government, pro-NAFTA elites managed to spin a slim majority of the U.S. Congress into its corner.

According to pollsters for Times Mirror, the debate began with "public and elite opinion at loggerheads." While elites were unified in favor of the accord, the public, according to Times Mirror, was "largely skeptical and disengaged from the debate."[62] Through 1991, fewer than one in three Americans had heard or read anything at all about the NAFTA accord. This figure rose to about one in two just before the November 1992 election, with about 40 percent of Americans professing to follow the issue "closely" (13 percent) or "fairly closely" (27 percent). This combined figure climbed all the way to 68 percent during the congressional debate and finally to 73 percent when President Clinton signed the bill into law in December 1993.[63] By 1996, however, when election time rolled around, Clinton's advisers were telling the president to keep quiet about the administration's singular foreign policy achievement, as Americans, by a three-to-one majority, did not believe that either NAFTA or GATT had created any new jobs in the United States.[64] In contrast to the global elites who determine the parameters of debate on U.S. trade policy, Americans stubbornly continued to view themselves as producers rather than consumers. NAFTA's threat to their livelihoods carried far more weight than the promise of marginally cheaper goods.

The lack of early public interest and knowledge about the accord, however, did offer those seeking to influence public opinion a reasonably untouched tableau upon which to attempt to sketch a consensus before the congressional votes. Before the 1992 election, 72 percent of business executives polled favored the accord. A year later, this figure was still more than twice the approval rating given by members of the larger informed public. The larger public, however, did eventually come to favor the accord by a small margin once it passed, though as late as July 1993, 49 percent of those Americans surveyed said they were not sure they had ever heard of the proposed deal.[65] Exactly how this transformation came about is an extremely complex and ultimately unanswerable question. We would be foolish to discount the effects of a committed White House and an unusually unified elite articulating its message through a sympathetic mass media backed by tens of millions of dollars in lobbying fees and paid advertisements provided by the Mexican government and an alliance of transnational corporations. By autumn 1997, however, the numbers had returned to their original state: 43 percent of those polled believed NAFTA had had a negative impact, while only 28 percent considered it positive.[66]

Like NAFTA, the GATT agreement played no discernible role in the 1994 election, according to exit polls. Opponents of the treaty vowed to make supporters of the accord pay a price at the polls. By election day, however, they had lost interest in doing so. One national poll found that only 2 percent of the electorate cited "foreign trade/NAFTA" when describing the two most significant issues that had determined their vote. This was half the number that mentioned "campaign finance reform" and one-tenth of those who chose "crime."[67] (This is just as well, since fully 79 percent of those polled by the *New York Times* had no idea where their representative stood on NAFTA.) The public also remained largely detached from the insider debate on GATT. In October 1994 a Times Mirror survey found GATT was "followed closely" by 26 percent of the public (8 percent followed it "very closely"), even less than NAFTA had fared at a comparable period. Like NAFTA, GATT received negligible amounts of attention before or during the midterm elections, despite Senator Ernest Hollings's decision to force a postponement of the vote until after the election. A postelection poll found the percentage of those claiming to follow the issue up to 44 percent (16 percent "very closely"), but more than half the public (53 percent) told pollsters that they were unaware of the creation of the World Trade Organization, the accord's most prominent feature. In any event, the House approved the treaty by almost two to one, and the Senate did the same by more than three to one.[68]

In the autumn of 1997, the Clinton administration and its corporate allies attempted to repeat the NAFTA/GATT exercise in support of NAFTA's sequel: the allocation to President Clinton of the power to negotiate treaties on the basis of a "fast-track" negotiating process (meaning that such agreements cannot be amended but can only be voted up or down). This time, however, they failed miserably. Conditions had changed considerably during the three years following the original act's passage. The original treaty's effects proved disappointing to its supporters and added further fuel to the anger of its original opponents. Cheered by the victory of striking United Parcel Service workers, the labor movement revived itself under the militant leadership of John Sweeney. And Clinton himself had grown increasingly unpopular within his own party for his refusal to stand with the Democratic Congress on issues from welfare reform to education cuts. His party was looking to teach the president a lesson, and the fast-track legislation provided the perfect opportunity.

Meanwhile, the NAFTA/GATT coalition mistook its unchallenged primacy within the punditocracy for an automatic victory in Congress on the fast-track legislation. Most members did not even bother to respond to opponents' objections. President Clinton made only two appearances outside Washington to support his side and insulted his opponents in each of these. Republican Bob Dole and former Clinton treasury secretary Lloyd Bentsen joined together to caution that "given the public's general ambivalence about trade matters, it would be easy for either party to try to score political points by criticizing *responsible* [my emphasis] proponents of free and fair trade. Criticism is easy. Leadership requires hard work. Our leaders must step forward, now, to do what is right for America's future."[69] In other words, the two grand old figures of American politics were saying, Let's not allow the public's concerns to find a political vehicle for expression, lest it muck up our plans to extend NAFTA without their interference.

Shocked by the convincing rejection of fast-track, pundits of every ideological stripe treated the victors as moral midgets and intellectual idiots. From the Left, the *New York Times*'s Anthony Lewis explained, "Richard Gephardt's Democrats and their union allies want to stop the world and get off. . . . backward toward economic and political disaster."[70] From the Right, the *Washington Post*'s James Glassman suggested that the House of Representatives rename itself "the Washington chapter of the Flat Earth Society," adding, "It's hard to find a respectable economist who opposes free trade, the value of which is glaringly obvious."[71] From deep center, pundit dean David Broder condemned the victorious side for "pandering to the ideological extremes."[72] The editorial boards of the *New York Times* and the *Washington Post*—to say nothing of the *Wall Street Journal*—were equally scornful. They blamed the defeat of fast-track on "special pleaders . . . irresponsible political forces . . . fear mongering . . . and political retribution from organized labor."[73] But as a Pew Research Center poll pointed out at the time, while 82 percent of elites were still supporting NAFTA at the time of the fast-track debate, only 47 percent of the broader public concurred.[74] That three-quarters of the Democratic Party kept faith with its most loyal constituency, however, was almost never mentioned in the one-sided punditocracy debate that followed the president's defeat. Neither was the coalition's bipartisan composition, as one-quarter of Republican Congressmen voted no as well. The political elite's bedrock beliefs handicapped its ability to hear the arguments of its opponents, and hence to take seriously any challenge to its economic ideology. This inability left them deaf and blind to the anger growing among many Americans over the unfettered effects of globalization in which the security of jobs and communities was considered expendable.

The American political system continues to face threats to its traditional understanding of the world. As long as Americans continue to conceive of foreign policy as a world apart from domestic policy, they will find themselves unable to exercise their rights as enumerated in the U.S. Constitution. And as the new global economy reaches ever deeper into the lives of citizens, it circumscribes every nation's ability to act. Newly discovered challenges to the global ecology infuse issues that were once the exclusive purview of diplomats with immediate ramifications for the everyday lives of all Americans. But the legacy of the Cold War, on top of fifteen decades of increasing and unchecked executive authority, has left the American political system wholly unable to address crucial foreign policy issues in a constructive democratic context. In the United States laws are being changed and communities are being threatened with no opportunity for democratic participation whatsoever. Ross Perot's and Pat Buchanan's presidential campaigns, which combined elements of populist nativism and intolerance, might be viewed as a warning shot across the bow of the political establishment lest these antidemocratic mores continue unchecked. The fast-track debate demonstrates that the opposition is real and politically significant, though it remains unable to articulate a coherent alternative ideology. Unless Americans are willing to rethink and ultimately to reconstruct the nation's present system for dealing with foreign policy issues to allow for a far greater commitment to democratic practices than Cold War institutions allow, then the belief in democracy in America will become, in this fundamental aspect, a historical anachronism. Popular frustration will likely vent itself in means that grow ever darker and more difficult to address. But the task of democratizing U.S. foreign policy is even more daunting than it first appears. The following two chapters explain why.

Thriving on Chaos: Foreign Policy Making and Special-Interest Manipulation

> I didn't have to get permission from some old goat in the United States Congress to kick Saddam Hussein out of Kuwait.
> —George Bush, 1992

"As long as people are people," Vaclav Havel explained to a joint session of Congress in February 1989, "democracy in the full sense of the word will always be no more than an ideal; one may approach it as one would a horizon, in ways that may be better or worse, but it can never be fully attained." Havel humbly credited his hosts with the "great advantage" of having approached democracy "uninterruptedly for more than two hundred years."[1]

But the Czech president and former prisoner of conscience was overly generous. Not all movement is progressive. In recent decades, the quality of American democracy has degenerated. Democracy is hard work. It requires considerable commitment on the part of citizens above and beyond that of their daily work and family lives. It requires healthy mediating institutions where people can meet and exchange views and information. Finally, it requires a class of honest political brokers dedicated to the explication of significant political issues that face the polity and a willingness to carry out voters' wishes once expressed. American democracy today enjoys none of these crucial prerequisites. Owing largely to the legacy of the Cold War, the making of U.S. foreign and military policy, even more than domestic policy, is hostage to an ad hoc process dominated by special interests that are able to exploit the American people's ignorance to bend the nation's policies to their own benefit. Presidents play on the natural patriotic and deferential tendencies of most American citizens. Corporate power, ethnic lobbies, and self-interested bureaucracies scrap among themselves in Congress and in the media to determine the parameters of the president's choices with no input whatever from the general public. The result is less democracy than unmediated chaos and unending manipulation.

Much of the populace, while genuinely eager to participate in politics in some fashion, feels itself purposely excluded from the national political process, which it largely considers to be a shell game. In a rather remarkable news story (given its source) published in 1990, the *New York Times* reported that "an unhappy consensus has emerged that domestic politics has become . . . shallow, mean, and even meaningless."[2] "When Americans talk about who drives politics today," seconded a careful 1991 investigation by the Kettering Foundation, "their views are easy to discern: a select group of power brokers is the ultimate decision maker on policy issues—and not citizens."[3] A consistent set of polling data demonstrates that for the past three decades, Americans have voiced progressively less confidence in the honesty and competence of their political leaders. The Louis Harris poll, which has tracked the subject since 1966, recently noted the lowest level of confidence ever in our political leadership.[4] In the summer of 1995, a full 59 percent of Americans could not identify a single elected official they could honestly admire.[5]

The United States also has beyond question the weakest record of voting participation of any advanced capitalist nation. The roughly 50 percent participation rate in U.S. presidential elections is nearly 25 percent lower than the average turnout in Britain, and 35 percent lower than in most of western Europe.[6] (It is also a significantly lower number than the percentage that regularly voted in nineteenth-century America.[7]) In midyear elections these numbers fall even further, to about one in three. Much about the American political system actually discourages voting. State election laws are so easily manipulated that a crafty politician such as New York Senator Alphonse D'Amato can prevent a contested primary.[8] The voters of Kansas did not even get the chance to vote in a 1996 primary because the state's governor, a Dole supporter, decided holding the election would be too expensive. When fair elections do take place, an indecipherable miasma of state and local registration requirements can do much to obstruct even conscientious voters, particularly the poor and the less educated. Our midweek elections ensure that wage workers frequently must pay for the privilege of waiting on line to vote. As a result of these barriers, the poor and the poorly educated vote in considerably smaller numbers than do the middle class, the wealthy, and those with a college or high-school education, thereby skewing the results in favor of older, whiter, and wealthier citizens.[9] States that do allow voters to register on election day generally boast much higher turnout figures than the rest of the nation, but even their numbers lag behind most of Europe.[10] One result of this system is that nearly 80 percent of the voting-age population did not vote for their congressional representative in 1994, and fewer than one in four eligible Americans voted for Bill Clinton two years earlier.[11]

In countries with a more highly developed sense of tradition and hierarchy than the United States, patterns of history have forged stronger links between classes and a more powerful sense of mutual responsibility between the governed and the governing. Aristocracy, noted Tocqueville, "links everybody from peasant to king, in one long chain. Democracy breaks the chain and frees each link." Each man "is forever thrown back on himself alone," and "shut up in the solitude of his own heart."[12] Americans' apparent mania during this period for forming and joining associations can easily be interpreted as a means of compensation for common bonds denied this largely self-invented nation.

These bonds are important. "Networks of civic engagement," notes political scientist Robert Putnam, drawing on a twenty-year study of civic life in Italy, "powerfully affect the performance of representative government."[13] In Putnam's studies, membership in choral societies, church groups, and football clubs were not merely ancillary phenomena related to healthy democratic politics; rather, they were preconditions for it. Yet civic engagement in the United States, according to many key measurements, is in decline. Putnam's highly contested data reveal that since 1973,

> membership records of such diverse organization as the PTA, the Elks club, the League of Women Voters, the Red Cross, labor unions, and even bowling leagues show that participation in many conventional voluntary associations has declined by roughly 25 percent to 50 percent over the last two or three decades. The same decline is evident in many measures of collective political participation, including attending a rally or speech (off 36 percent between 1973 and 1993), attending a meeting on town or school affairs (off 39 percent), or working for a political party (off 56 percent.).[14]

Putnam's critics have pointed out that some voluntary organizations, such as the National Rifle Association and the American Association of

Retired People, have grown dramatically in size, but these are generally special-interest lobbying organizations with passive membership, and they rarely promote any face-to-face discussion or direct exchange of information between common citizens. As Putnam demonstrates, "Only nationality groups, hobby and garden clubs, and the catch-all category of 'other' seemed to have resisted the ebbing tide." These data were provided by the General Social Survey, which was conducted nearly every year for more than two decades.[15]

With the decline of the corner bar as a community meeting place and a precipitous fall in newspaper readership, particularly among the young, the loss of these institutions means that adult Americans no longer have the opportunities to learn what John Dewey called democracy's "vital habits." Instead, notes Putnam, we have television, which appears to increase pessimism about the possibilities of republican institutions while it consumes free time otherwise available for civic pursuit. The public loses not only the information that might have resulted from face-to-face exchanges but also the shared commitment to success that such collective enterprise can engender. Society becomes increasingly atomized and politics begins to take on a distant and bothersome hue. As a result, the connective tissue between the representative and the represented atrophies and withers away.

Instead of through caucuses, canvases, local meetings, and face-to-face local conventions, today's election campaigns are conducted almost exclusively through the media. Presidential-nominating conventions have become a form of summer camp for journalists. The political parties, once the hub of associational activity and collective commitment, function today as little more than money drops for their respective contributors, the vast majority of whom are senior citizens. Yet even by this profoundly passive measure of political participation, fewer than one in a hundred Americans believes either party is worth a dime.[16]

Two effects of the media campaign are the growth in the level of independence of individual candidates from their parties as well as the spectacular increase in the cost of running for office. In 1996, the median expenditure on a House race rose to $559,807, and on a Senate race, $3.5 million. In an expensive media market such as New York, the amount of money required can be eight times as high. By 1997, according to Federal Election Commission figures, the two parties were raising over $600 million in soft money alone, with the Republicans enjoying a nearly two-to-one advantage. That amount was more than triple the number it had been five years earlier.[17] The net result is an election system in which corporations, through their political action committees (PACs) and their executives (and sometimes their executives' wives and children) posing as individual donors, finance campaigns in exchange for favorable legislation. This process of organized, legalized bribery lies at the heart of the American democratic process and corrupts not only the representatives themselves, but also the very idea of representation. Our political districts are divided geographically, but corporate contributors have no such loyalties. The process further degrades our democracy by giving incumbents an enormous competitive advantage. In recent years, this has translated into a ten-to-one fund-raising advantage ratio for incumbents over challengers. In 1992, for instance, in the 279 races where the incumbent raised more than twice the funds of the challenger, 98 percent of the incumbents won their races.[18] Abuses go unpunished and the system runs on its own fuel. In 1997, Congress rejected a budget request from the Federal Election Commission charged with investigating alleged financial abuses of the extremely elastic system. The net result was that the commission, which was already handling a backlog of cases from 1994, would be forced to dismiss an even higher percentage of potential abuses without serious investigation. At the time of the rejection, 217 of 319 promising cases had already been abandoned for lack of funds.[19]

The current campaign finance system, created in 1974 by the incumbents who so benefit from it, makes a mockery of our claims to democracy—particularly of its foundational principle of "one person, one vote"—and costs the federal treasury hundreds of billions of dollars in favors repaid at taxpayers' expense. When Roger Tamraz, the businessman who contributed $300,000 to the Democratic Party during the 1996 election cycle, was asked why he never bothered to register to vote, he replied sardonically, "Well, I think this is a bit more than a vote."[20] But the parties who benefit from the system have no incentive to change it. In his 1996 campaign manifesto, "Putting People First," Bill Clinton bemoaned the fact that "on streets where statesmen once strolled, a never-ending stream of money now changes hands—tying the hands of those elected to lead." Following the 1994 election, the president and Newt Gingrich shook hands in New Hampshire on a promise to address the continuing scandal of campaign financing. Yet on a single night in the spring of 1996, the president and his party raised $12.5 million from these same special interests, many of whom sought and received favors from the White House and Congress.[21] Gingrich, through parliamentary maneuver, managed repeatedly to quash any hopes for such reforms once they gained strength in the Republican Congress. The amount spent on lobbying Congress, according to the Center for Responsive Politics, now exceeds $1.2 billion a year, or more than $100 million per month.[22] In electing a president and a Congress who once again promised reform and delivered only promises, the American people understandably feel powerless to intervene.

For those who do participate, the democratic content they enjoy is highly problematic. American elections are driven largely by spectacle and sound bite–sized slogans. According to the late campaign guru Lee Atwater, the main task of a candidate's top advisers is to gather round a table "every morning at seven o'clock and spend an hour and a half figuring . . . what stunt you can pull that will give you fourteen seconds of news hole."[23] Ed Rollins, Atwater's predecessor and former boss as head of the Republican Party, explains that the entire election exercise is about "one thing: to drive the other guy's negatives above fifty percent. You can talk about the issues all you want. That's all there is."[24] Despite the enormous degree of time and effort devoted to it, the process evinces precious little educative value. In an extensive study of New Jersey voters (who stand quite late in the queue of presidential primaries), Scott Keeter and Cliff Zukin point out that as the process unfolds, citizens show almost no increase in knowledge or understanding about the candidates.[25]

The U.S. election process also corrupts the quality of our governance, even when representatives attempt to appeal to their constituents rather than to the corporate PAC donors who fund them. The character of both the media and the U.S. election system forces congressional attention away from policy making toward fund-raising, effective advertising, claiming credit, and adopting popular positions. Conscientious attention to legislative matters for the sake of good policy carries no demonstrable political reward. Members of Congress have little incentive to support legislation that does not provide extremely particularized benefits for select constituencies, and no incentive whatever to mobilize support for new or unfamiliar policies.

When large numbers of people do get involved in the legislative debate, the campaign can often have all the sincerity and spontaneity of a television infomercial. In 1995, for instance, NTS Marketing, a Washington lobbying firm that specializes in generating "mass response" telegrams for corporate lobbyists seeking to create the false impression of grassroots anger, admitted that it had sent tens of thousands of telegrams to members of Congress without bothering to contact the people who allegedly signed them. "Nobody's perfect" was the explanation offered by Charles Judd, the firm's president.[26] In most cases, aside from favors done for individual corporations and industries, little attention is paid to the actual content of the laws that are passed or the success of their implementation. "Public policy," observes Morris Fiorina, "emerges from the system almost as an afterthought . . . The general, long-term welfare of the United States is no more than an incidental by-product of the [electoral] system."[27]

A strict limit on the size and character of political contributions could significantly improve the American election system. But it would hardly provide a solution to all the problems discussed here. The problem of minority rights that bedeviled James Madison continues to plague us today, but so does the problem of locating genuine majorities. Elections, notes Robert Dahl, can be "a crucial device for controlling leaders," yet "quite ineffective as indicators of majority preference."[28] True democratic participation, as Dewey explained in the 1920s and Matthew Glass argues in the 1990s, "emphasizes a flow of influence upward from the masses; and above all . . . does not involve support for pre-existing national interest, but is part of the process by which the national interest or interests are created."[29] Such interests cannot be elected; they need to be discovered, communally, through discussion and personal interaction. Alternatives to the policies outlined by the national leadership class do not come before the electorate and hence are defined outside the parameters of relevant debate. Even at its best, a mere vote is restrictive because election choices are confined to those positions already defined by the political system. They do not allow for the creation or institution of mass change from below. To begin to approach a truly democratic policy process, the public would need to involve itself not merely in ratifying the choices put before it by the political class, but in defining and refining those choices in the first place.

All of the unhappy trends discussed here are operative in the creation of American foreign policy, but they are compounded by a series of special conditions that further reduce that policy's democratic content. Max Weber observed that our times are characterized by "rationalization and intellectualization" of the problems society faces, problems that chase from public life what Weber calls the "ultimate and sublime values" the way bad money chases away good in a financial panic.[30] The very competence of people to participate democratically as citizens is called into question. Following on Weber, Jurgen Habermas notes that in contemporary political life, "Those areas of social life over which cultural institutions previously guided individual conduct and social development: family, religion, tribal and local governments, are demeaned in light of the clear need for experts who can predict and control contingencies on the basis of technical knowledge." Hence, in American politics, democratic participation tends to be neutralized in favor of what is put forth as "expertise." Citizens' "everyday consciousness" becomes "fragmented" and brings little relevant judgment to bear on those matters that require urgent policy decisions. Citizens become mere clients of public policy, even though those decisions tend to be justified in a way that nods to civil rights, democracy, and the will of the people.[31] This is a qualitative shift, Habermas argues, from the eighteenth century, in which public opinion was mediated through a true "public sphere," separate and different from the political and economic structures that govern society.[32]

Foreign policy carries this antidemocratic phenomenon nearly to its ultimate end. One problem is the perceived "foreignness" of foreign policy. The barriers are more difficult than the obvious one, that of most Americans' extremely limited knowledge of and curiosity about the mores of other cultures. ("If you understand Jackson County, you understand the world," bragged Harry Truman.[33]) Many Americans feel uncomfortable about their competence to determine their government's foreign policy and would prefer not to be consulted at all. A 1989 survey conducted for the Carnegie Council on Ethics and International Relations found that nearly half of Americans do not believe the public to be "qualified to participate in deciding on U.S. foreign policy."[34] Bob Dole spoke to this reticence during the 1996 New Hampshire primary when he told business leaders at a Nashua breakfast, "I know foreign policy is rarely considered when you walk into the voting booth. You're worried about jobs and crime, education and the environment, Medicare, whatever. . . ."[35]

What Emily R. Rosenberg has called "the discourse of national security" seems almost calculated to exclude those outside the foreign policy priesthood.[36] As historically defined since the onset of the Cold War, a "matter of national security" postulates the interrelatedness of countless political, economic, and military factors. A fair estimation of its importance appears beyond the competence of all but those few blessed with not only the intellectual ability but also the usually classified information necessary to balance these competing factors. That the implied cost of miscalculation is always a national catastrophe intimidates many people who otherwise feel competent to make personal and professional decisions that are hardly any less difficult. Citizens are thereby excluded, both practically and psychologically, from participating in the decision-making structure no matter how great the effect on their lives. In 1977, for instance, the Carter administration proposed to build a railroad system for the MX missile in the Great Basin of the American West. The rail system was so extensive that had it been built, it would have become the largest construction project in human history. The MX rail system would have forced the dislocation of people who had been settled in the area for generations—in the case of the western Shosones, for perhaps several thousand years—and it would also have caused widespread and irreparable damage to one of the country's most fragile ecosystems. Nevertheless, Carter proposed it and Congress prepared to build it. When citizens' groups sought to question government and military officials regarding the justification for this colossal operation, U.S. Air Force General Thomas Stafford told the Nevada legislature that opposition to the project indicated only strategic ignorance.[37] The Air Force then appropriated the rhetoric of democratic debate to create a veneer of participation. Undersecretary of the Air Force Antonia Chaynes wrote to the *Salt Lake City Tribune* of "making every effort to consult with the leaders and citizens of the potentially affected areas so as to devise approaches to this vital national undertaking which are compatible with local concerns and values." Just what concessions the Carter administration had in mind was never clear, as Chaynes's bottom line was that "the Air Force's mission in strategic defense, as in all other areas, is to protect our way of life."[38] The Air Force finally went down to defeat on the rail system, but like Wilson's 1919 setback on the League of Nations, the opponents' victory represented a rare confluence of left and right political forces. It left no institutional imprints or structures in its wake.

An unmistakable Cold War dynamic continues to thwart the possibility of democratic discussion of U.S. foreign policy even in the absence of a credible military threat. That point was particularly clear in George Bush's 1990–91 decision to go to war in the Persian Gulf when what remained of the Soviet Union was actually allied with the United States.[39] Within days of the Iraqi invasion of Kuwait, Bush dispatched troops to Saudi Arabia without any congressional authorization or debate. His administration's position was that as president, Bush had full authority to commit the nation to war in the Gulf on his say-so alone. Bush's view was supported by most Republicans and virtually the entire punditocracy. "The United States cannot afford to be diddled," former secretary of state Henry Kissinger insisted, "and it simply cannot afford to lose."[40] Fred Barnes, then editor of the *New Republic*, argued at the time that "Congress has no business getting involved. They would stew and whine and yap and they couldn't even pass a budget." Barnes's colleague, Morton Kondracke, added, "Congress is chicken."[41] General Colin Powell, chairman of the U.S. Joint Chiefs of Staff, reportedly advised Bush that U.S. objectives could be accomplished over time without a war, and his field commander, Norman Schwarzkopf, argued that "if the alternative to dying is sitting out in the sun for another summer, that's not a bad alternative."[42] This view was seconded by the vast majority of living ex–secretaries of defense and ex–Chairmen of the Joint Chiefs of Staff. But it soon became politically unsustainable. "Politically," George Bush allegedly explained to his top military officer, "I don't think there is time."[43] As "the unchallenged superpower . . . the center of world power" and "the apex of the Industrial West," in Charles Krauthammer's evocative phrasing, we simply *had* to do something.[44] And given the processes set in motion by Cold War democratic practices, that something had to be military. Senator Daniel Patrick Moynihan dissected this phenomenon on the Senate floor during the debate on a congressional resolution authorizing war: "What we find is a kind of time warp in which we are acting in an old mode in response to a new situation. . . . It is in that mode of which we are in a bipolar, permanent crisis with the enemy. It used to be totalitarian, Leninist Communism. Without a moment's pause almost, we shifted the enemy to this person at the head of this insignificant, flawed country whose boundaries were drawn in 1925 in a tent by an English colonial official, an artifact of the Treaty of Sevres."[45]

Congress did ultimately debate the war, but given Bush's prior commitment of U.S. troops and prestige, it was presented with a Hobson's choice of either backing the president or humiliating him before the world. Bush's close margin of victory in the Senate was provided by legislators who insisted that they opposed his chosen path but could not bring themselves to accept the implications of defying the wishes of the nation's president in a matter defined to be so central to U.S. national security.

With considerably less at stake, President Clinton demonstrated even fewer concerns with constitutional matters in 1994 when he decided to order the U.S. military into Haiti. Congress was deliberately not consulted in the decision, owing to what appeared to be majority opposition there. Preinvasion poll numbers also indicated the opposition of 66 percent of those questioned.[46] Instead, drawing on the lexicon established by Harry Truman in Korea, administration officials referred to the Haiti invasion as a "police action" rather than a war and likened it to the equally questionable U.S. invasions in Panama, Grenada, and the Dominican Republic. Assistant Attorney General Walter E. Dellinger III, who headed the Justice Department's Office of Legal Counsel, called the invasion "fully consistent with this past practice" and hence "within the president's Constitutional authority."[47] Congressional leaders may have been pleased that they were never forced to take responsibility for approving or disapproving in advance an invasion that turned out quite well, but that is hardly the intended purpose of the Constitution's war-making powers. Today, as in during the Cold War, issues of war and peace remain too delicate to allow for the niceties of democratic debate.

Throughout the Clinton administration, Congress continually registered its unambiguous disapproval of the president's policy in the Balkans, but it never succeeded in forcing a change, nor even in offering a coherent alternative. No wonder. For all the noise that Congress made about Bosnia and the collapse of the former Yugoslavia, it never once held hearings on the issue while the breakup was taking place. The numerous resolutions presented afterward were never even brought to a vote.

The Senate Foreign Relations Committee and the House Foreign Affairs Committee (later called the International Affairs Committee) frequently pilloried President Clinton's advisers over these issues but rarely if ever even suggested a constructive alternative. Public discussion of Haiti turned largely on the issues of refugees and illegal immigration while the question of military intervention to prevent the genocide in Rwanda never appeared to register at all. In each case, the president was forced to take full responsibility for all action and inaction while Congress needed only to be ready to assign blame. When confronted with the issue of whether to commit troops to Bosnia, Lee Hamilton, the Democratic chair of the Foreign Affairs Committee, argued, "The real question here is, are you prepared to send young men and women from the United States, from my own state of Indiana, to give their lives in the Balkans. I'm not prepared to do that at this point because I can't see a vital American interest."[48] From a public-opinion standpoint, this kind of statement was cost-free. For the public paid little attention to Bosnia, except when the question of troops arose. Indeed, the administration rarely focused on it either. In the Times Mirror and Pew Foundation's measurement of public attention, the percentage of people questioned who even claimed to follow the conflict "very closely" rose above 20 only once, in May 1993. Usually it hovered nearer to 12.[49] Senator Wyche Fowler, who paid dearly in Georgia for voting against war in the Persian Gulf, says he was never once asked about U.S. Bosnia policy in over sixty town meetings across the state.[50] Foreign policy mandarins in the punditocracy assumed a similarly irresponsible pose. Lawrence Eagleburger, who oversaw the Bush administration's disastrous Balkan policies, grumbled aloud that Clinton's foreign policy made the country "look like a bunch of wimps." The *New York Times* editorial page complained of "public posturing" that did nothing but "squeeze another droplet from the Administration's almost empty vial of foreign policy credibility."[51] This chaotic and irresponsible pattern of criticism-without-responsibility assumed no role whatever for the interplay of democratic forces on foreign policy, save those interested parties who had committed themselves on the basis of one or another special interest.

Other problems abound. Americans are considerably less informed about "foreign affairs" than about what they consider to be domestic policy. The oft-repeated horror stories regarding popular ignorance are by now well known, but suffice it to say that a nation where majorities do not know on whose side their government is intervening, as with the Reagan administration in Central America, or whom the NATO alliance was formed to oppose, cannot be expected to contribute intelligently to the details of policy formulation. Bruce Russett estimates that a mere 5 percent of the population is active on any given foreign policy issue at any one time, save issues of war and peace.[52] The lack of both information and attention leaves the public vulnerable to a government whose commitment to truth is often less aggressive than it is to its own ideological preconceptions or political well-being. Virtually every president elected in the postwar century has felt free to deliberately mislead the American public about crucial foreign and military issues.[53] Lyndon Johnson could promise voters just weeks before the 1964 election, "We are not about to send American boys nine or ten thousand miles away from home to do what Asian boys ought to be doing for themselves," when in fact his administration was planning to do just that.[54] Candidates also feel free to treat foreign policy as a political football. After accusing the Republicans of having "lost Cuba" during the Eisenhower administration, one of John Kennedy's campaign strategists pretended to ask his boss just how "we would have saved Cuba if we had had the power." JFK responded, in good humor, "What the hell, they never told us how they would have saved China."[55] In a more serious vein, in 1969, then–national security adviser Henry Kissinger told the Soviets not to pay attention to "separate critical statements by the president on one Eastern European country or another, since this is only tribute to some layers of the U.S. population which play a role in American elections."[56] Apparently, Kissinger also helped candidate Richard Nixon manipulate the Paris peace talks over Vietnam to prevent a preelection agreement for the Democrats in 1968, and then again to give a false impression of imminent peace four years later.[57] Given the significance of these issues, such deception amounts to an end run around democracy itself.

Another defect of our election system in the realm of foreign policy originates with Americans' admirable tendency to rally around their leadership during times of perceived crisis.[58] Politicians are hardly above exploiting this characteristic for personal gain. Bruce Russett argues that leaders' incentive to channel hostility toward a foreign adversary is unusually high in democracies, where internal dissent cannot be legally suppressed.[59] Military actions are therefore more likely to take place immediately before and after elections. Indeed, it may have been the upcoming congressional election that helped to trap John Kennedy into raising the issue of Soviet missiles in Cuba from a manageable diplomatic problem—the missiles did nothing to affect U.S. deterrence policy or the mutual balance of terror—into a potential trigger for a nuclear Armageddon. In the weeks before the missiles were discovered, congressional Republicans had warned that Cuba would be "the dominant issue of the 1962 campaign." Whatever the diplomatically prudent course may have been, the president recognized, in the words of top adviser Roger Hilsman, that "the United States might not [have been] in mortal danger but the administration most certainly was."[60] Kennedy's calculations, while unusually dramatic, were hardly unique. Politicians, notes Russett, "are unlikely to engage in full-scale conflicts before elections (when memories will linger) but will sometimes initiate "crowd-pleasing" limited actions just to boost their popularity."[61]

That such efforts enjoyed little popular support in principle becomes irrelevant once they are under way. Support for the use of military force against foreign adversaries, notes Russett, is almost always lower in the abstract than in concrete situations. Americans are not a particularly warlike people. When asked in opinion surveys about the hypothetical use of force, they generally disapprove. But Americans' invariable *immediate* reaction to its use is favorable, as demonstrated in the cases of Lebanon, the Dominican Republic, Vietnam, the Mayaguez affair, Grenada, the bombing of Libya, the invasion of Panama, and the war in the Persian Gulf. This tendency holds for popular presidents as well as unpopular ones. Before President Johnson sent U.S. troops to Vietnam following the Tonkin Gulf incident, only 42 percent of those polled said they supported U.S. involvement in the war in Vietnam; immediately afterward, 72 percent approved. Similarly, only 7 percent endorsed the *idea* of an American invasion of neighboring Cambodia; following Nixon's decision to do so, the number rose to 50 percent.[62]

Protest movements, it should be added, are not entirely irrelevant to the political calculations involved in foreign policy, but their influence is tremendously difficult to gauge since politicians rarely credit them. Clearly protests against U.S. South African policy in the 1980s made a difference. Frequent demonstrations against President Reagan's Central American policies may have given his administration pause there as well. Regarding the Vietnam protests, widely credited with having ended U.S. participation in that war, the evidence is mixed. It is certain that presidents Johnson and Nixon did not relish the domestic unrest the war was causing and may have rejected arguments in favor of escalation on behalf of domestic peace. But both presidents—Nixon in particular— derived great sympathy from large majorities of the country on Vietnam- related issues owing to the unpopularity of the protesters themselves. It was not until important establishment figures joined the ranks of the antiwar cause that either Johnson or Nixon seemed even to take it seri- ously.[63] In either case, protest movements are no more or less democratic than other special-interest movements, except to the degree that they represent genuine majorities. More often than not, their demands are co- opted by politicians who learn how to speak their language but finesse the substance of their complaints. In what Robert M. Entman and Andrew Rojecki call "a classic example of symbolic gratification," fol- lowing years of lobbying and mass protests, the House of Representa- tives voted to endorse a resolution supporting a nuclear freeze in the summer of 1983 only to appropriate $2.6 billion to fund a land-based version of the MX missile two months later.[64] Far more effective than protesters on a day-to-day-basis are the interest groups, including pro- military concerns such as the defense contractor lobby; the elite Cold Warrior organization, the Committee on the Present Danger; and well- funded public-policy foundations such as the Heritage Foundation, the American Enterprise Institute, and the Hoover Institution at Stanford University.

To say that U.S. foreign policy is not democratically conceived or exe- cuted is hardly to say that it is made in isolation of domestic considera- tions and constituencies. In most cases, when foreign policy specialists speak of democratizing U.S. foreign policy, what they have in mind is expanding the number and character of these groups. If in the 1950s it was bankers, oil companies, United Fruit, and the Council on Foreign Relations who privately helped shape the direction of foreign policy, today that list should include newly emerging ethnic groups, some environmental organizations, new regional groupings, a smattering of human-rights groups, and perhaps a few women's associations.[65] But such a model does little to attempt to elicit the true feelings of the American electorate; it merely seeks to include a higher number of individuals from that tiny number of Americans who are already active.

The model, moreover, has problems, since it assumes passivity on the part of the uninvolved. This is both unfair and untrue. Americans without access to the levers of foreign policy power have the same rights to democratic representation as those who do. By appealing only to the politically active, no matter how expansive a view one wishes to take of their composition, one must inevitably fail in seeking to construct a democratic foundation for the nation's foreign policies. The result is foreign policy by active minority rule. George Kennan has complained, with some justification, that "our actions in foreign affairs are the convulsive reactions of politicians to an internal political life dominated by vocal minorities." With considerable less justice, Kennan blamed "maladjusted groups: in our country, Jews, Negroes, immigrants—all those who feel handicapped in the framework of a national society. . . ."[66]

Minority domination is a problem in all regimes, but it takes on a special character in the making of a democracy's foreign policy. Elections, notes Robert Dahl, spur minorities into action. Since the preferences of vocal minorities must be at least considered, if only to be co-opted, Dahl describes the difference between dictatorships and democracies as one of "minority rule vs. minorities rule." The majority rarely has the opportunity to weigh in on any specific policy, but concerned minorities frequently do. So the de facto functioning of democracy is one where particular issues are hashed out by those small groups particularly concerned with them. "Thus the making of governmental policy is not a majestic march of great majorities united upon certain matters of basic policy," he notes. "It is the steady appeasement of relatively small groups."[67]

The politics of American foreign policy requires the appeasement of any number of groups—some small, some not so small. The influence of U.S. corporations on the foreign policy process has historically been so powerful, so prevalent, and so unembarrassed that a considerable (and no doubt reductionist) body of work argues that no other influences need be considered. "Trade," broadly defined, has always been at the center of U.S. foreign policy goals and, America being America, this trade is almost always conducted by private concerns. These interests, some stronger and more influential than others, work in tandem with U.S. diplomats and military strategists to shape official policy in their areas of concern. In the case of Latin America, the U.S. government has offered its military forces to individual companies for the purpose of achieving an individual corporation or industry's goals. This was frequently the case in the nineteenth century, when Americans first became aware of Latin America, and has continued, indisputably, through the CIA's 1954 overthrow of the elected government of Guatemala, inspired in large measure by the United Fruit Company.[68] The Nixon administration's ultimately successful plan to destabilize the legitimately elected Allende regime in Chile in the early 1970s was also hardly independent of ITT's concerted campaign to do the same.[69] Chase Manhattan's David Rockefeller and John J. McCloy were instrumental in convincing Jimmy Carter to allow the Shah of Iran into the United States for medical treatment in 1979, though Carter had been warned that it might inspire the taking of American hostages.[70] One does not require a conspiracy theory, moreover, to understand that U.S. foreign policy in the Persian Gulf is heavily influenced by the interests of U.S. oil companies. Nor should anyone be shocked by the surmise that the United States did not become the world's largest supplier of weaponry by a considerable margin without a concerted effort by U.S. arms manufacturers to convince Congress and the president that such weapons sales were an important component of U.S. foreign policy. In 1996 and 1997, America's six biggest military contractors spent $51 million on lobbying Congress, according to the Campaign Study Group. If lobbying costs from all companies involved in military-related businesses were included, such as computer and technology firms, the number would dwarf all other industries.[71] Perhaps the Senate would have voted overwhelmingly to expand NATO without these contributions; of course, we will never know. Indeed, given the sympathy accorded commercial pursuits in American ideology, coupled with the power of corporate lobbyists, one could compose a nearly endless list of direct interventions in U.S. foreign policy by powerful economic interests. In foreign as well as domestic politics, democracy works quite nicely from the standpoint of United States–based corporations.

The U.S. foreign policy process also does quite well for the interests of pro-Israel American Jews. The multicultural makeup of American society is one of its most distinctive characteristics, and the degree of ethnic and minority group influence on the making of U.S. foreign policy may be unique among the nations of the world. That the Council on Foreign Relations, the historic bastion of the foreign policy establishment, recently cosponsored a supportive conference on the role of "minorities and U.S. Foreign Policy" offers impressive testimony for Nathan Glazer's claim that "We Are All Multiculturalists Now."[72] While all ethnic groups seek to influence the making of U.S. foreign policy to favor the interests of their respective homelands, until recently most have had to make do with fiery election-year speeches and the occasional congressional solidarity resolution. Consider American-born and naturalized Poles, Czechs, Hungarians, Armenians, Lithuanians, Latvians, Croats, Serbs, and so on. During the Cold War, all had the complete rhetorical support of the U.S. government. None, however, received much in the way of significant aid, even in the case of open rebellion, lest it conflict with the larger purposes of U.S. Cold War policy. With the significant exception of Anglo-Americans—who are so effective they have convinced themselves and the rest of us that they do not even constitute an ethnic group—no racial or ethnic minority can even begin to approach the effectiveness of the contemporary American Jewish community.

Because American Jews feel so intimately connected to their frequently endangered brethren overseas, they have gone to extraordinary lengths to attempt to influence U.S. foreign policy in matters that have had little bearing on their own well-being. That the pro-Israel position may have been morally correct in most or even all of these interventions is beside the point. At the highest levels, U.S. foreign policy is not made with morality uppermost in the minds of decision makers. That so tiny a minority as American Jews have been so successful, with one tragic exception, in shaping U.S. foreign policy despite a considerable history of anti-Semitism at nearly every level of American society demonstrates just how open the U.S. foreign policy process is to such manipulation, given the right circumstances.

The history of American Jewish intervention in foreign policy began with an effort during the Russo-Japanese War to restrict loans to the Russian czar. Following the reignition of violent anti-Semitic pogroms in the Russian Pale in the early 1900s, the wealthy German Jewish banker Jacob H. Schiff organized Jewish and other banking firms to block the extension of credit to Russia. His avowed goal was "to make the Russian government feel that it cannot continue forever with immunity its shameful policy towards its Jewish subjects."[73] Later, noting the importance of the Jewish vote in New York, prominent Jews lobbied President Theodore Roosevelt to protest enforcement of a provision of an 1832 commercial treaty that permitted the czar to bar U.S. Jews from entering Russia. Six years later, in December 1912, Roosevelt's successor, William Howard Taft, terminated the treaty.[74]

Despite initial successes and the continued persecution of European Jews, the community continued to press its case with extreme delicacy. Many Jews felt themselves to be guests in this country and were fearful of awakening anti-Semitic animosities. Their insecurity, coupled with profound anti-Jewish feelings at the highest levels of the State Department—along with what can only be termed the indifference of President Franklin Roosevelt—would combine to create one of the most shameful episodes in the history of American foreign policy: the United States' nonresponse to the Nazi genocide of European Jewry. After November 1942, when the horrible reports were finally confirmed, American Jews repeatedly entreated President Roosevelt to intervene, somehow, against Hitler's killing machine. But the president and his advisers refused to consider any such measures, including those that would simply have forced the State Department merely to allow its legal quota of Jewish refugees to enter the United States.[75]

The combination of the shock of the discovery of the Holocaust and the efforts of Jewish Zionists to found the state of Israel transformed American Jews' self-image and willingness to operate within the American political arena. Organized Jewish lobbying efforts, far less timid than those seeking the safety of European refugees, were instrumental in convincing President Truman to support and immediately recognize the State of Israel in 1948, despite the nearly unanimous opposition of the upper reaches of the State Department.[76] In a pattern to be repeated over time, the 1948 election found Truman and Republican candidate Thomas Dewey battling over whose presidency would be more supportive of Israel, with each seeking to outdo the other by calling for a larger portion of the Negev desert to be incorporated into the new state's border following its war of independence.[77]

Following this historic victory, American Jews remained only one voice in the cacophony of those fighting to influence U.S. Middle East policy during the 1950s and 1960s. That both State Department specialists and the enormously influential "Seven Sisters" oil companies viewed the region from a quite different perspective served as a considerable counterweight. President Eisenhower could therefore chastise Israel just moments before an election for its invasion (in tandem with

Britain and France) of Egypt's Sinai desert without worrying about political consequences. Despite John Foster Dulles's complaint that "the Jewish influence here is completely dominating the scene and making it almost impossible to get Congress to do anything they don't approve of," his own president avowedly proved him wrong.[78]

The turning point in U.S. Middle East policy came during the war of 1967 when American Jews, who had previously evinced an ambivalent though ultimately supportive relationship with the state of Israel, transmuted the embattled democracy into the focus of their collective identity. Israel's stunning victory in 1967 gave American Jews a new confidence and coincided with their almost complete assimilation into the American elite.[79]

Israel did not really need the United States to defeat its Arab neighbors in 1967, but it did six years later. In October 1973, when Israeli leaders feared "the crumbling of the third temple," American Jews organized a furious lobbying effort in which business, labor, religious, and congressional leaders bombarded the White House on Israel's behalf.[80] Though obsessed by Watergate, President Nixon promised he would "not let Israel go down the tubes."[81] Nixon then authorized the largest U.S. military airlift since World War II for Israel, providing more than $2.2 billion worth of equipment during the course of 566 separate flights.

The power of America's Jews in the making of U.S. foreign policy continued to grow after the near-debacle of 1973. Some politically active Jews had formed the American Zionist Council of Public Affairs in 1954 (soon renamed the American Israel Political Affairs Committee [AIPAC]) to aid Israel in its battles on Capitol Hill and (though they would never own up to it) guide American Jewish contributions to congressional candidates.[82] The effort took quite a while to gear up, but by the late 1970s it had become an important influence on both congressional decision making and fund-raising. Early in 1981 AIPAC lost a major battle with Ronald Reagan over the president's decision to sell Saudi Arabia sophisticated military aircraft; the president objected to "representatives of a foreign country . . . trying to interfere with what I regarded as our domestic political process."[83] It was the last battle the lobby would lose for more than a decade. When Reagan defeated AIPAC, the organization had 8,000 members, a staff of 24, and a budget of $1.8 million. Within a decade, it boasted nearly 50,000 members, a staff of 150, and a budget of $15 million.[84] Its membership constituted a virtual army of energetic lobbyists and campaign donors. Soon Israel was receiving one-fifth of all U.S. development, economic, and military aid. Between 1981 and 1991, no president dared to take on AIPAC in open political combat. Arms sales to Arab nations were canceled before they were announced. Candidacies for public office were undermined before they had a chance to buy a single commercial. Any senator or congressional representative who contravened the AIPAC line even as it related to, say, El Salvador or Zaire found himself risking a ferocious battle for reelection against a well-funded opponent. Many, including former Senate Foreign Relations Committee chair Charles Percy, owed their defeat to AIPAC's efforts to raise funds and organize on behalf of their opponents.[85] Not until George Bush and James Baker decided that American Jews were themselves sufficiently divided over the nature of the Israeli government's intransigence toward the Palestinians did the American government even attempt to maintain a position in the Middle East that did not have at least the tacit support of AIPAC. In the aftermath of AIPAC's defeat by the Bush administration, some observers were ready to write the organization's epitaph. The lobby's ability to finesse a unanimous Senate vote in mid-1996 for a bill that penalized foreign companies who did business with Iran put an end to such musings. According to a *Wall Street Journal* report, to raise the issue's profile, AIPAC orchestrated threats against foreign companies considering commercial ventures with Tehran. The bill caused no end of consternation to U.S. allies and resulted in an extraordinary breach of diplomatic protocol. The European Union's top executive turned to President Clinton during a joint news conference to complain that it wasn't "justifiable or effective for one country to impose its tactics on another."[86] With AIPAC foursquare behind the measure, however, President Clinton was hardly in a position to help.

American Jews have a number of advantages over other ethnic groups that makes their power to influence U.S. foreign policy difficult to imitate. Because of their extraordinary social and economic success, American Jews are able to contribute enormous sums of early money to political candidates. This allows them to make demands on the winners just like any corporate giver. American Jews also enjoy tremendous access to the highest reaches of the punditocracy, where, in tandem with the White House and Congress, insider opinion is shaped and debated. Martin Peretz owns the *New Republic*. Mortimer Zuckerman owns *U.S. News and World Report*, the *Atlantic Monthly*, and the *New York Daily News*. The American Jewish Committee publishes *Commentary*. Australian press magnate Rupert Murdoch owns the Fox TV network, the Fox News Channel, the *New York Post*, and the *Weekly Standard*. All are passionate, unashamed partisans of the Israeli cause. Among the most influential pundits in America, including most particularly William Safire and A. M. Rosenthal of the *New York Times;* Charles Krauthammer of *Time* and the *Washington Post;* Lally Weymouth, also of the *Post* and daughter of its majority owner; and (gentile) George Will of the *Washington Post* and *Newsweek,* and many, many others, Israel can do virtually no wrong. This sympathy extends itself to the lower ranks of the profession as well. According to Seymour Martin Lipset and Earl Raab, 26 percent of reporters, editors, and executives at major print and broadcast media are Jewish and therefore, one may fairly speculate, likely to be sympathetic to Israel.[87] The Israelis themselves are also extremely savvy and frequently eloquent politicians and are adept at exploiting the American political process. Americans' admiration for Israel, as well as some people's continuing guilt over American inaction during the Holocaust, further greases the skids for a one-sided policy on matters of crucial concern. Arab Americans have almost none of these advantages and must contend with powerful negative racial stereotypes deriving from the media's sensational coverage of Middle Eastern terrorism and Arab oil wealth. The "Arab lobby"—the National Association of Arab Americans—had a staff of exactly three in 1995. Its director conceded that once the peace process had begun, Israel's late prime minister Yitzhak Rabin proved a far more effective advocate for the PLO than his organization had ever been.[88]

The only ethnic lobby that has come close to rivaling American Jews' success is Miami's Cuban-American community. Like the Jews, the Cubans are geographically concentrated, extremely wealthy, and politically savvy. Their cause, moreover, is perfectly consistent with American anti-Communist ideology. The Cubans have therefore been able to bend the political process to their own purposes, even when these have a questionable relationship to U.S. interests. Like the Jews, the Cubans have allowed the most hawkish elements of their community—in the form of the National Cuban American Foundation—to dictate their policy, despite the fact that poll data consistently demonstrate a wide variety of views within the larger community. Thus, because of the vagaries of the political system, foreign policy is not democratically representative, even when it kowtows to a particular democratic constituency.[89]

Most American ethnic minorities would, like the Cubans, gladly emulate the Jews' tactics if they could, but none can boast even a fraction of their advantages. In 1985, when then Mexican foreign minister Lopez Portillo met with leaders of the Mexican-American community, they offered to work with him against proposed legislation in Washington affecting Latino immigration. The chairman of the League of United Latin American Citizens told reporters, "We feel that in the future Mexico can use us as Israel uses American Jews. . . ."[90] The National Council of La Raza, a Hispanic American organization founded in 1968, was able to demonstrate some influence in the defeat of certain immigration legislation during the 1980s, and Mexico's efforts in the NAFTA battle demonstrated discernible AIPAC-like savvy, though in both cases far more powerful forces were at work to influence the outcome.

Greek Americans also frequently compare their efforts to those of American Jews. They too suffer from the comparison. They frequently lobby Congress and the administration to address more energetically the problem of Cyprus and of what Greece considers to be Turkey's illegal occupation of the island. Working through the American Hellenic Education Progressive Association (AHEPA) and the American Hellenic Institute (AHI), in 1975 they were successful in convincing Congress to embargo arms to Turkey, but this was overturned three years later. In reaction to their lobbying defeat, Turkish Americans organized themselves and went a step further than the Greeks by enlisting prominent American Jews, including Morris Amitay, the founder of AIPAC, to argue their cause. The Turks have long been concerned with congressional efforts to memorialize the slaughter and forced repatriation by Turkey of perhaps 1.5 million Armenians in 1918. Lacking a significant Turkish-American community, they fell back on a pro-Israel lobbyist to make their case.

Until the Clinton administration, Irish-American ethnic groups in the twentieth century had been largely ineffective in convincing American presidents to take a harder line with Britain over the Irish question. In 1993 they achieved a stunning success, however, paving the way for the first real peace talks between the two sides since the bloody conflict began. Irish-American politicking inside the Clinton administration on behalf of U.S. recognition of the Irish Republican Army, and the granting of a visa for Gerry Adams, president of Sinn Fein, the IRA's political arm, demonstrated a new AIPAC-like self-confidence and sophistication. The net result was, in the words of one observer, "the strongest Irish-American influence on policy" since the presidency of Andrew Johnson.[91]

African Americans have met with mixed success, owing perhaps to their lack of political cohesiveness as well as the multiplicity of causes that might attract their energy. In the summer of 1974, Martin Weil authored an article in *Foreign Policy* that asked, "Can the Blacks Do for

Africa What the Jews Did for Israel?" Organized efforts by the community began around 1976, when then congressman Andrew Young brought together 130 black leaders to challenge Henry Kissinger's coddling of the racist regime of what was then Rhodesia. Two years later, African Americans launched TransAfrica, an attempt to create an AIPAC-like organization to influence policy toward Africa and the Caribbean. Ironically, it was the insistence of AIPAC and other prominent American Jews that Young be fired from his position as the United States' UN representative following his meeting with the UN PLO Observer that galvanized the Black community into becoming more organized and assertive about its interests. (It also became considerably more resentful of—and perhaps a bit paranoid about—Jewish political power.) Soon, TransAfrica became the focal point for opposition to the Reagan and Bush administration's policies toward South Africa, helping to create a mass movement in America to boycott the perpetrators of apartheid. By the time the Clinton administration came to power, TransAfrica was extremely influential in dictating not only African policy, but also U.S. policy in Haiti, where a hunger strike by the organization's head, Randall Robinson, was praised by President Clinton and widely credited with helping to force the 1994 U.S. invasion.

Asian Americans had much to overcome as an ethnic lobby. In addition to ingrained American racism, they had their own internal differences, the legacy of Pearl Harbor, the victory of the Chinese Communist revolution, and later the enormous success of Japan and other East Asian nation's exports in penetrating American markets. The power of the conservative "China lobby" in supporting the corrupt regime and later preventing recognition of the People's Republic was legendary, though it was not spearheaded by Chinese Americans themselves. By 1989, however, this group did assert themselves in seeking to prevent the return of 40,000 Chinese students in American universities following the uprising (and ensuing political repression) in Tiananmen Square. President Bush opposed the bill, but it passed Congress nevertheless.

But none of these organized ethnic groups—not even AIPAC—can compare with the power of Anglo Americans. In "Federalist Two," John Jay explained the genealogical basis of the nation's good fortune: "Providence has been pleased to give this one connected country to one united people; a people descended from the same ancestors, speaking the same language, professing the same religion, attached to the same principles of government, very similar in their manner and customs."[92] The description bore a distant relation to reality when Jay offered it in 1789. It bears none whatever more than two hundred years later, when Americans of British stock had become less than half the country's population. Still, had Jay merely been referring to the upper echelons of the U.S. foreign policy establishment, his description would not require much adjustment. Despite avowed efforts to recruit minorities for the foreign service, the Council on Foreign Relations, and the rest of the establishment organizations, the very top positions generally remain under the purview of the old Anglo-American elite. The ethnic background of America's foreign policy decision makers retains a significant influence on both the tone and the direction of U.S. foreign policy. In the spring of 1982, for instance, when the United States offered England secret military support, including both intelligence and materiel, during the Malvinas/Falklands War, it did not act on the basis of strategic calculation.[93] Rather, the driving force appeared to be ethnic solidarity. Top U.S. officials viewed England as a kind of extension of the United States. Secretary of Defense Caspar Weinberger was even knighted by Queen Elizabeth for his "fraternal role in the Falklands crisis." Despite various inroads made by other regions and ethnic and racial minorities, the Atlanticist franchise over U.S. foreign policy remained only marginally less complete in 1980 than it did in 1780. The Anglo Americans, as Alexander DeConde dryly notes, "seldom faced such charges, because they had created the national ideology."[94]

The final set of Americans for whom U.S. foreign policy may appear relatively democratic are those working in what are termed nongovernmental organizations (NGOs.) These are groups whose international concerns derive from their expertise or passionate interest in a particular issue that has clear international ramifications. They include environmental groups, conservation organizations, world hunger associations, human rights lobbyists, free trade enthusiasts, women's rights groups, pro- and antiabortion fighters, religious fraternities, revolutionary solidarity societies, and various United Nations support groups. The people who work in these groups are often the most dedicated, expert, and selfless individuals involved in any given issue. Many have experience making U.S. foreign policy in their areas of expertise and can be expected to assume such positions in future administrations. Many have either advised Congress or served in Congress themselves. Their causes, moreover, are frequently just as well as in the interest of the people of the United States. The International Campaign to Ban Landmines, recipient of the 1996 Nobel Peace Prize, constitute one such inspirational example. But NGOs are interested parties only because they choose to act as such.

When they make policy, they do so simply because they care enough and no one else is sufficiently organized to stop them. Strictly speaking, they represent only themselves. Their legitimacy hence rests on an extremely tenuous relationship to democratic theory, involving a rather extravagant interpretation of Madison's theory of factional representation as enunciated in "Federalist Ten." Writing in 1935, Walter Lippmann proposed just such a system of government as a means of avoiding any democratic participation in policy making. "The burden of carrying on the world," he wrote, "lies not upon public opinion and not upon government but on those who are reasonably concerned as agents in the affair. Where the problems arise, the ideal is a settlement by the particular interests involved. They alone know what the trouble really is."[95] As with the corporate lobbyists with whom they must work, much of an NGO's ability to succeed on any given issue depends quite frequently on the ability of all parties to shield the policy-negotiation process from the light of democratic debate, except on those rare occasions when victory requires the stimulation of the appearance of a public outcry.

The politics of American foreign policy are ultimately rather chaotic. Little democratic input is requested or offered unless for some reason Congress or the media decide to take an interest. The reasons that some area or issue might be raised from the backwater of an assistant secretary's desk to a televised congressional hearing or an evening on *Nightline* are often highly capricious. A dignitary's plane might crash, an earthquake may hit, some freelancing congressional representative may decide to create an international incident, or the expertise of a particularly influential congressional staffer may lead his or her boss to raise the profile of some country that most Americans cannot name or place. A network producer might receive a hot news tip from an interested party. A particularly influential pundit, such as Thomas Friedman or William Safire of the *New York Times*, may force an otherwise obscure issue into the forefront of high politics simply by riding a particular hobbyhorse until an administration is forced to respond. Sometimes the White House will choose to make a particular country a showcase of the administration's ideological virtue, as Reagan did with El Salvador and Nicaragua in the early 1980s. (Though these two besieged Central American nations all but dominated foreign policy reporting and discussion for much of the Reagan years, the words "El Salvador" and "Nicaragua" do not appear in the index of either one of Henry Kissinger's two volumes of memoirs covering a period that ended less than a decade earlier.)

Sometimes, a politician in trouble with home-state voters will attempt to force a showdown with a particular nation to remake himself before the national spotlight. This was the case in 1980 when Senate Foreign Relations Committee chair Frank Church chose to go public with the knowledge that the Soviets had troops stationed in Cuba. Even though the U.S. government had been fully aware of their presence and the Soviets were not in technical violation of any agreements, the Carter administration was forced to deal with an invented political crisis that mesmerized the national media and further crippled Carter's foreign policy apparatus for weeks. While the prestige and power of the Senate Foreign Relations Committee has declined precipitously for nearly two decades in a row, any number of congressional committees, subcommittees, caucuses, and lone experts have arisen to take its place. Working together with reporters and television producers and following Church's example, these groups and individuals can combine to create what seems to be an endless series of crises for U.S. foreign policy, despite the relative arcania of any of the particular issues in question. In the case of such crises, all players become extremely worked up and occasionally even talk of war. The public, however, remains unmoved and uninvolved—at least until the bombs actually begin to fall.

Six of the eighteen powers delegated to Congress by the Founders relate to foreign affairs, but as an institution, Congress has ceded its de facto constitutional powers to the president. It has not managed to pass a foreign aid authorization bill, its primary vehicle for making foreign policy, since 1985. The previous one passed in 1981. Congress, moreover, has no institutionalized process for making foreign policy. Former senator Dick Clark, author of the famous Clark amendment (later overturned) that prevented Richard Nixon from sending troops to southern Africa, noted, "Unless you've worked or served in Congress, it's difficult on the outside to imagine how disorganized, chaotic and incomplete it can be." "We don't even scratch the surface," adds former House Foreign Affairs Committee chair Dante Fascell.[96] According to Stephan Weissman, longtime staff director of the House Foreign Affairs Subcommittee on Africa, excluding just a few exceptions, "it is not too much to say that Congress has substantially ceded its fundamental Constitutional role in foreign policy." Weissman cites the executive as the main beneficiary of Congress's default but notes that "narrow-based special interests have also gained."[97] Regarding intelligence-related matters, particularly covert action, the congressional record has been even less impressive.[98] Presidents have taken advantage of Congress's reluctance to involve itself in substantive matters by concluding nearly 13,000 executive agreements without congressional sanction.[99]

Were Congress to play a more active role, one would be hard-pressed to argue that its intervention represented a more democratic response to the crisis than that proffered by the administration. Exactly the same antidemocratic influences that operate on the making of administration foreign policy can also be found in Congress, though the proliferation of influential bodies there makes their dominion appear more diffuse. Congress, too, is responsive only to active minority interests. To the degree that AIPAC influenced U.S. policy during the 1980s, it did so largely through Congress—by virtue of its ability to help fund candidates, intimidate legislators, and control debate rather than by educating and mobilizing voters.

Given the failings enumerated here, one is forced to conclude that, in foreign policy at least, the promise of democracy goes largely unfulfilled in the United States today. What we have instead is what Robert Dahl calls "pseudo-democratization," a process that takes place when a system purports to be democratic and retains many of the trappings of democracy, most particularly elections, but functions to exploit the fruits of democratic legitimacy without sufficient attendant substance.[100] The problems, moreover, cannot easily be repaired because the people served by the system are the same people upon whom the prospect of such reforms must rely. Elected representatives have little incentive to change a system that so heavily favors incumbents. Neither are corporate chieftains and ethnic lobbies likely to support a weakening of their own influence. To effect a national campaign of reform, the American people would first need to understand the problems caused by our ad hoc, antidemocratic, and ultimately chaotic foreign policy process. Given the nation's current structure for the communication of information, the only conceivable educative instrument for such a lesson is the national media. This is hardly an optimistic conclusion, however, for reasons that I explain in the next chapter.

The Media Cacophony:
Ain't Nobody Here But Us Chickens

> Should big corporations use their power to influence public opinion?
> You bet.
> —*Herb Schmerz, a Mobil Corporation public relations executive,*
> *in a quarter-page advertisement on the* New York Times *op-ed page*

"Why are not republics plunged into war," Tom Paine wondered, "but because the nature of their government does not admit of an interest distinct from that of the nation?"[1] Paine's assertion strikes one as hopelessly naive today, though this may be a reflection less of its accuracy than of the degeneration of our republican institutions. In an ideal republic, citizens would have perfect access to their official representatives, perfect information about their actions, and perfect understanding of the issues involved. But we live in an imperfect world and a profoundly imperfect republic. The population is too large and the government too complex for even Ralph Nader to keep track of everything. Given the daily scramble between jobs and families that most Americans undergo each day, the political ideal bears little resemblance to our reality.

Enter the media. Protected by the First Amendment and inspired by both personal ethics and professional competition, the journalist provides the metaphorical bridge between the representatives and the represented. Almost by definition, any attempt to improve the system's accountability therefore requires the cooperation of the media as its messenger. Whenever any organization, be it the White House National Security Council or the neighborhood committee for aluminum recycling, seeks to gain support for a particular viewpoint, its first strategic question is always the same: how to manage the press? In foreign policy, where events take place well beyond the eyes and ears of everyday citizens, it is particularly difficult to imagine an alternative. The media, explains Jurgen Habermas, provides the political stage.[2] This stage is perceived through what V. O. Key called an "echo chamber," made up in part by the media and in part by the citizens' own preconceptions and prejudices.[3]

Judged exclusively on the basis of individuals' access to information, the system works pretty well. The proliferation of new avenues and forms of communication, including new electronic and interactive media, offers just about anyone Andy Warhol's fifteen minutes of media attention. Certainly, Donald Trump gets more media face time than the rest of us, but most imaginative and intelligent Americans can, if sufficiently dedicated, find a place to publicize their stories. (Lazy reporters love to republish press releases; local TV stations love good "visuals.") On the consumer side, moreover, it's hard to argue that one cannot find the kind of information one desires *somewhere* in the American media, particularly if one includes the widely available British press as well. Between the *Weekly Star,* Rush Limbaugh, *Hard Copy,* and Jerry Springer on the one hand, and the *Economist,* the *New York Review of Books,* the *Nation,* and the *New Republic* on the other, the media does offer literally something for just about everyone. The problem is not that the media does not serve consumers well; rather it is that it does not, collectively, serve the republic.

Ever since Walter Lippmann launched his blistering critique of the failings of "news" and "public opinion" back in 1919, democratic theorists and reformers have attempted to come up with ways to reshape the media to address the many problems he identified. Simply stated, Lippmann's argument was that the media was not up to the task of providing Americans with the relevant, unbiased, and sophisticated understanding of problems and issues they required to make intelligent decisions about their government. The problem was compounded in foreign policy, where good information was even scarcer and citizens' experience even more limited and less relevant than on domestic issues. As discussed in chapter 2, John Dewey raised important questions about Lippmann's analysis and provided both an alternative diagnosis and a prescription for the sickness that ailed American democracy. But Dewey's vision of democratic culture has proven utopian in a nation where half the population declines even to vote once every four years, where most forms of associational activity (not including prison) are declining, and where the media grows increasingly less concerned with the commons and tends, for commercial as well as cultural reasons, toward both balkanization and sensationalism. A great deal has changed in America since the Lippmann-Dewey debate of the mid-1920s, but the late 1990s finds the media no better suited to carrying democracy's heavy burden. Despite the explosion in available information in the last half century, Americans on average are no better informed about their government than they were in the 1940s, and they are considerably less civic-minded.[4] The "public's right to know" has become a catchphrase justifying all manner of ethical misfeasance in intrusion into people's private lives, and yet the "public" for most practical purposes has disappeared. As James M. Carey observes with alarm, "If one looks at voting statistics and other evidence of participation in politics, or examines the knowledge people have of public affairs, or the declining attention to news on television or in print, one must conclude that the political constituency has disappeared altogether. Out there, there is no there there."[5] "The only sober response to an empirical analysis of how the system is actually working for many people," laments Jurgen Habermas, is to say "forget about democracy."[6]

The media's responsibility for this state of affairs is considerable and multifaceted. In the first place, the media is not structured to provide citizens with the information they need; it is designed to supply consumers with the information they want. To blame journalists or even publishers and producers for this situation is both pointless and counterproductive. The dilemma for even the most conscientious journalistic enterprise is inescapable. As Robert Entman notes in his important study, *Democracy Without Citizens*:

> To become sophisticated citizens, Americans would need high-quality, independent journalism; but news organizations, to stay in business while producing such journalism, would need an audience of sophisticated citizens. . . . Because most members of the public know and care relatively little about government, they neither seek nor understand high-quality political reporting and analysis. With limited demand for first-rate journalism, most news organizations cannot afford to supply it, and because they do not supply it, most Americans have no practical source of the information necessary to become politically sophisticated. Yet it would take an informed and interested citizenry to create enough demand to support top-flight journalism. The nature of both demand and supply

cements interdependence and diminishes the press's autonomy. On the demand side, news organizations have to respond to public tastes. They cannot stay in business if they produce a diverse assortment of richly textured ideas and information that nobody sees. To become informed and hold government accountable, the general public needs to obtain news that is comprehensive yet interesting and understandable, that conveys facts and outcomes, not cosmetic images and airy promises. But that is not what the public demands.[7]

Even more so than in the past, the primary purpose of media today is profit, extremely unsentimentally defined. Owing to a recent wave of mergers and acquisitions among communications companies, information providers are operating from a position of almost de facto conflict of interest. The communications industry was the sixth-largest contributor to the candidates in the 1994 election, ponying up nearly $10 million directly to political action committees. As they seek to buy favorable treatment in law, rules, and regulations and to win government contracts, these corporations become suppliants of the very institutions whose behavior they must monitor if their work is to be of any value to American citizens. Helping to inspire what Dewey termed "democracy's vital habits" could hardly be further from their collective minds.

The media is profoundly corrupted by its own economic interests, and this corruption shows up in both large and small matters. In the case of media conglomerates, this power *can* easily include influencing what is published or broadcast. For instance, it may have been a coincidence when the *Washington Post* coverage of the $1.4 million sale of the *Minneapolis Star-Tribune* failed to mention the newspaper's 28 percent interest in the deal. And perhaps it was just another coincidence when the Washington Post Company, whose 1994 revenues totaled nearly $1.2 billion, saw its newspaper run repeated editorials and op-eds in favor of the GATT accord as it simultaneously lobbied for a special rider to the bill designed to save the company millions of dollars. (The *Post*, to its credit, printed these facts in a paid advertisement placed in its pages by one of its competitors.) The *Post* editorial pages also said not a word about a Republican-sponsored telecommunications bill that even *Wall Street Journal* editors called a "giveaway" to communications companies like the *Post*.[8] Television networks, too, according to the *Wall Street Journal*, "tune[d] out the airwaves-auction battle" of 1996.[9]

At the beginning of the 1980s, Reagan administration officials decided that the public no longer had an interest in broadcasting specifically or the media in general, save having their community obscenity standards observed. The Fairness Doctrine, which had previously attempted to force network broadcasts to reflect competing sides of a political issue, was abolished. To the Reagan administration, a television, in the words of Reagan-appointed Federal Communications Commission (FCC) chair Mark Fowler, was "just another household appliance, a toaster with a picture."[10] The results were swift. According to Ben Bagdikian, between 1983 and 1992, the number of companies that, together, controlled half or more of the media business shrank from fifty to twenty, with only eleven newspaper corporations, two magazine publishers, three television networks, and five book-publishing corporations controlling a majority of what was published or broadcast in the U.S. media.[11] These trends turned out to be mere prologue to the summer of 1995, when Disney purchased Capital Cities/ABC, thereby creating a $16.4 billion communications behemoth. Time Warner then responded by merging with CNN, giving birth to a $19.8 billion conglomerate. In between, the Westinghouse Electric Corporation bought CBS for $5.4 billion.

"The liberties protected by the principle of participation lose much of their value whenever those who have greater private means are permitted to use their advantage to control the course of public debate," John Rawls noted in his 1971 masterwork, *A Theory of Justice*. Because of the decline in the number of media corporations and the concentration of power in the hands of so few, the attitudes of the corporate masters to their civic responsibility has significant implications for the quality of American democracy. The dangers to democratic debate in such concentrated media power are manifest. On ABC's *Good Morning America*, Charles Gibson interviewed Thomas S. Murphy, chairman of Capital Cities/ABC and Disney's Michael D. Eisner upon the announcement of the deal. "Where's the little guy in the business anymore?" asked Gibson. "Is this just a giant that forces everybody else out?" Murphy, Gibson's boss, replied, "Charlie, let me ask you a question. Wouldn't you be proud to be associated with Disney? . . . I'm quite serious about this."[12]

Upon taking control of ABC, Eisner promised to make the new conglomerate reflect "what this country stands for."[13] Just what this implies, perhaps even Eisner does not know. But were he to decide that ABC News would, for instance, no longer report stories likely to reflect badly on Disney or even on the entertainment industry, he would be fully within his legal rights and hardly without precedent. If the *Village*

Voice is to be believed, when the stock market experienced a near melt-down in October 1987, with the Dow Jones average dropping 509 points in a single day, John Welch, chair of NBC's parent company, General Electric, called the network's president, Lawrence K. Grossman, to insist that "newsmen stop using phrases like 'Black Monday,' 'alarming plunge,' and 'precipitous drop' to describe the day's events." Such phrases, Welch allegedly explained, were scaring stockholders and further depressing the corporation's stock price. "NBC," Welch explained, "should stop fouling its own nest."[14] Marc Gunther reported in the *American Journalism Review* a 1989 incident in which a segment on the *Today* show concerning defective bolts failed to mention GE, which used exactly these bolts for its nuclear reactors; GE was mentioned only in a damage-controlling follow-up. A 1990 *Today* segment on consumer boycotts, Gunther adds, also omitted any mention of a campaign against GE itself, and one guest insists that a producer cautioned him not to bring it up. (NBC said the producer acted independently in this incident.)[15] Within weeks of the announced merger between ABC and Disney, the ABC Radio Network canceled "Hightower Radio," the country's only nationally syndicated left-wing populist talk-radio show. Jim Hightower, its host, had previously devoted segments of his shows to Disneyland's exploitation of homeless workers while "that Michael Eisner, Disney's 'Big Cheese,' " took home "$78,000 an hour" in 1993.[16] Later in the year, CBS's √50

Minutes canceled a planned segment on the tobacco industry to avoid a costly lawsuit despite its conviction that the information it contained was completely true.[17] Though it is the only network to accept so called "advocacy advertising," CNN also pulled an ad during 1997 because it objected to its content. The network later offered to reinstate the ad once certain factual assertions were corrected.[18] During this same period, an executive at Time Inc. instructed then-editor Steven Brill to kill a story critical of William J. Bauer, the director of the Federal Trade Commission's Bureau of Competition, while the conglomerate was still waiting for approval of its merger with Warner Brothers. Brill told *Vanity Fair* that Time's chief financial officer called him and said, "We are working hard on Bauer and anything that gets him nervous or makes him think we don't appreciate him could hurt us."[19]

Even without the rare direct intervention of a corporate censor into the content of the news, any number of everyday phenomena interpose themselves between what a citizen's representatives actually say and do, and what the elite Washington media chooses to report. Perhaps the most obvious problem is one of sources. The governing class that makes up most of the national news consists of the same people who control policy outcomes in Washington: top officials in the White House and executive-branch agencies; members of Congress and powerful congressional staffers; representatives of important interest groups; and members of the punditocracy, including think-tank experts, former officials, and would-be journalist/philosophers. These are all people with a powerful stake in the manner in which any given story is reported.

Reporters' dependence on these highly self-interested parties leaves them severely vulnerable to political manipulation. It is a devil's bargain in which each side peddles something the other needs. One has newsworthy political information; the other, the forum to express it. Journalists can burn their sources if they wish, but they can do so only once and at great cost to their ability to do their jobs effectively (as the profession defines it) ever again. The idea that the press is somehow "free" to report whatever it believes to be true therefore obscures more than it reveals.

Like most people, governing elites have little interest in putting "truth" above self-interest. With some significant exceptions, they believe they serve a higher interest than a temporary truth or democratic principle. They do not believe in the ultimate victory of virtue in the marketplace of ideas because, excluding universities and small-circulation opinion magazines, there is no such marketplace. There is only the news, which has little time or patience for a complex or subtle rendering of any public policy program. Any unnecessary admission of imperfection by a public official carries with it the real risk of attack and purposeful (or even purposeless) distortion. The job is to manage the news, not simply to provide it. The power of "truth" in this calculation is roughly akin to that of the military forces controlled by the Pope.

Former secretary of state Dean Acheson put the case for untruth quite elegantly in his memoirs:

> The task of a public officer seeking to explain and gain support for a major policy is not that of the writer of a doctoral thesis. Qualification must give way to simplicity of statement, nicety and nuance to bluntness, almost brutality, in carrying home a point. . . . In the State Department, we used to discuss how much time that mythical "average American citizen" put in each day listening, reading, and arguing about the world outside his country. Assuming a man or woman with a fair education, a family, and a job in or out of the house, it seemed to U.S. that ten minutes a day would be a high average. If this were anywhere near right, points to be under-

standable had to be clear. If we did make our points clearer than truth, we did not differ from most other educators and could hardly do otherwise.[20]

From Dean Acheson and Harry Truman, it is only a short road to Richard Nixon and Ollie North.

Conventional wisdom holds that events like Watergate and the Iran-Contra scandal demonstrate the media's unfailing ability to hold the government accountable, no matter what the obstacles. But Entman argues, "The point of a free press is to prevent rulers from damaging the nation and destroying themselves, not to let them plunge the country into disaster now and make them pay with their political fortunes later. The press certainly provided retrospective accountability in each of these cases, which was far better than nothing, but far inferior to what free press ideals presume."[21] In each of these cases, the media allowed the government to frame its reporting about events until events literally overwhelmed them. By the time a scandal reaches the proportions of, say, a president selling missiles to the Ayatollah, lying about it, and encouraging his aides to conduct a secret foreign policy that Congress has explicitly outlawed, the top media personalities are also invested in the government's version of events and find it difficult to report and process information that so profoundly contradicts their own world-views. The Reagan administration's secret arms sales were revealed not in the U.S. media but in the Lebanese weekly *Al-Shiraa*, although much of the evidence was, in retrospect, readily available.

Part of the problem is that, as Senator Joe McCarthy certainly understood, the rules of objective journalistic reporting do not permit journalists to point out when a politician is lying. The best an objective journalist can usually do is to highlight differing perceptions of truth between opposing parties. When mistakes or lies are particularly egregious, newspapers (though rarely television) may examine the veracity of a public figure's claims. Such scrutiny has little impact, however, either as prophylactic or punishment. While top government officials conduct their business exclusively with the most prestigious reporters of the networks and the top metropolitan dailies, this reporting reaches only a small fraction of the American people. As Peter Teeley, press secretary to vice presidential candidate George Bush, explained after the 1984 Bush-Ferraro debate, "You can say anything you want during a debate, and 80 million people hear it." If the press then points out an error, "So what? Maybe 200 people read it, or 2,000 or 20,000."[22] Even so, once a lie has been corrected, journalists generally believe the job is done and then move on from there. This gives politicians license to continue to mislead without sanction.

According to a detailed 1984 national survey by the University of Michigan Center for Political Studies (CPS), only about one in six Americans reports regularly reading two or three newspapers, a figure that is likely inflated given survey respondents' tendency to wish to sound more civic-minded than they really are.[23] These people can claim to participate actively in what remains of the American marketplace of ideas, getting more than one perspective on events in a format that can do justice to the complexity of the issues that make up our politics. It is a tiny percentage, however, and it has been dropping rapidly since 1984, as has the number of cities served by more than one newspaper.[24]

Television news, which provides the majority of Americans with literally all the political news they actively seek, does not begin to give citizens a sound basis for political decision making. Even the most conscientious of viewers would have trouble making sense of American politics based purely on television coverage. The average sound bite or bloc of uninterrupted speech fell from 42.3 seconds for presidential candidates in 1968 to only 9.8 seconds in 1988. In 1968 almost half of all sound bites lasted 40 seconds or longer, compared to less than 1 percent in 1988. In 1968, candidates' sound bites frequently lasted for over a minute on the evening news. Twenty years later, such moments had disappeared entirely.[25] What coverage the television media does provide frequently has little to do with the issues themselves. According to a study by Michael Robinson and Margaret Sheehan, in its entire preconvention period from January to June 1980, CBS offered a total of 450 minutes of campaign coverage, 307.8 minutes of which could be classified as horse race coverage. Hence, only a bit more than two of the seven and one-half hours were devoted to covering either candidates' views during the entire election.[26] These observations were made, lest we forget, before the rush to tabloidization that overtook the mass media in the early 1990s. This coverage was the best the top television networks had to offer in an era that evokes nostalgia in today's O. J.- and Diana-soaked media veterans. It was, however, wholly insufficient regarding what a citizen needs to make an intelligent decision about which politicians should pursue what policies.

Nothing is more important to an understanding of political issues than historical context, yet nothing is considered more foreign to the idea of "news" as currently practiced. The word "history" is considered a powerful pejorative in the news business, often given as a sufficient reason to kill a story. Standards of evidence, moreover, can be notoriously elastic. Despite a repeatedly asserted Joe Friday–like devotion to "the facts," many news reports are based on evidence that is lighter than air. The media frequently reports on fictional "crime-waves" and pretends to divine the "mood" of entire nations, or even continents.[27] Because of its lack of social scientific or even simple intellectual rigor, the media is profoundly easy to manipulate by dedicated interests with sophisticated public-relations capabilities. Concerted letter-writing campaigns contrived to pressure public officials, for instance, often lead the media to speak of the "force of public opinion," even when the letter writers' views remain deeply at odds with those of the majority. In the case of Oliver North and the Iran-Contra scandal, Seymour M. Hersh charged in the *New York Times* that the members of the congressional investigating committee were "intimidated by the public reaction to the immunized testimony of Marine Lieut. Col. Oliver L. North."[28] The irony of this situation is that the reported reaction to North's testimony in no way reflected most Americans' profound disapproval of both his methods and his aims, as Amy Fried's thorough examination of the subject has demonstrated.[29] If Hersh is correct, therefore, the committee was reacting not to the genuine beliefs of the American public, but to a fictional public created by the concerted efforts of a vocal pro-North minority and duly reported as fact by the U.S. media.

"Facts" like North's phony approval ratings begin to take on a life of their own, thereby further corrupting efforts to report the "truth" of any given situation. *Time*, for instance, reported that "the Boy Scout and the Patriot had the nation rooting for him," while *Newsweek* subtitled its cover story, "The Fall Guy becomes a Folk Hero." Its attendant coverage argued that North "somehow embodied Jimmy Stewart, Gary Cooper and John Wayne in one bemedaled uniform."[30] Both magazines' reporting was directly contradicted by the polls published alongside them. On July 9, 1987, *CBS Evening News* with Dan Rather reported, wholly inexplicably, that "ninety-six percent of you back North up, saying you approve of his actions." The broadcast went on to compare North to Rambo and Dirty Harry.[31] In truth, the number of Americans questioned who considered North a hero ranged from 4 percent in a *Los Angeles Times* poll taken July 10, 1987, which was far fewer than the number who believed that North "could be bought," to 19 percent in an ABC News poll taken the next day. Overall, in four separate polls taken in June and July 1987, between 68 and 81 percent of Americans questioned disagreed with the appellation "hero" when applied to Oliver North. The appellations "villain," "victim," dangerous," and "fanatic," proved considerably more popular.[32]

Once again, these problems are compounded by the foreignness of foreign policy. In my own experience as a journalist, I was once censored in the pre-Iran-Contra period by a liberal Washington magazine editor with an unmatched reputation for independence for reporting that the human rights situation in U.S.-supported El Salvador seemed to me to be far worse than in U.S.-opposed Nicaragua. The editor did not contest my reporting, undertaken during a one-month trip to the region. Nor did he pretend to any particular expertise in the region. He merely explained to me, "Our readers have been hearing everywhere how awful Nicaragua is and how much better El Salvador is. It will hurt our credibility to tell them otherwise."

Even so, the 1990s also saw a significant drop in the degree of foreign reporting offered in the media regardless of its quality. Between 1989 and 1997, foreign-news coverage on the three networks dropped by roughly 50 percent.[33] A four-month analysis of over 7,000 international news stories reported in the first half of 1995 found that newspaper and network reporting focused most often on international news with a distinct American orientation, while local television (from which one-quarter of Americans get most of their news) pretty much ignored the world beyond our borders entirely. Fewer than 10 percent of what international news was broadcast dealt with stories other than fast-breaking "crises."[34] In a 1993 survey, several scholars found that American television news rated "the lowest in information value of any TV news" among eight countries polled.[35] The public, however, is hardly clamoring for more.

Without a solution to the media's Catch-22, described by Robert Entman, any hope of constructing a democratic foreign policy based on the contemporary views and mass participation of the American people is doomed to failure. But no solution is likely to arise. Efforts to replace the current competitive, capitalistic ethic with one of "public" or "civic"-minded journalism are currently under way in a handful of communities but have proven extremely controversial within the profession. While these efforts may be worthy and may have positive results in those communities that are their focus, they can hardly be expected to counteract the trends that have fed the industry's profit-driven frenzy of conglomeration, commercialization, and tabloidization. In the summer of 1995, the same season that saw the fevered consolidation of broadcast media, a significant proportion of America's most respected and venerable journalistic institutions began a process of downsizing their news operations and dumbing down their coverage. The *Los Angeles Times* abolished 800 jobs and shut down its weekly "World Report" section. The *Baltimore Sun* cut 125 jobs. The *Miami Herald* killed its Sunday feature section and promised to concentrate on the nine subjects deemed most important in reader surveys; national and world news were not among them. The *Buffalo News*, with a front page slimmed down to just three stories, chose one day to feature the marriage rumors about O. J. Simpson and Paula Barbieri and the marriage-counselor consultations of comics characters Dagwood and Blondie Bumstead. The *Houston Post*, the *Baltimore Evening Sun*, and *New York Newsday* shut down entirely, with one columnist from that much-admired tabloid complaining of too many stories "on nuclear nonproliferation so nobody can read it or understand it." With fewer Americans reading newspapers and television news programs fighting their way downmarket, to believe that the media will be able to provide a sufficiently sophisticated understanding of the news to masses of Americans while simultaneously helping to revitalize democracy's vital habits is to believe in tooth fairies and Easter bunnies.

"A people's capacity to govern itself democratically," Arthur Koestler once wrote, "is proportionate to the degree of its understanding of the structure and functioning of the whole social body."[36] Yet Americans have little proclivity to educate themselves about the political structure that underlies their nation's foreign policy, and the people who are entrusted with its conduct have no great desire to muck up the process with the intrusive complications of democratic discourse.

Ironically, the only place where the media begins at least to imitate the constitutional role that traditional democratic theory defines for it is in the wilds of talk radio. Rush Limbaugh's listeners take politics as seriously as anyone in the policy-making elite. They argue excitedly about the details of policy and frequently, after hearing about some issue that excites their ire, call or write their representatives in protest. Unfortunately, the involvement of this one segment of the public has the effect of further perverting the democratic content of foreign policy rather than expanding it. While the talk-radio audience does, in important ways, emulate Deweyite notions of cultural conversation, because of the ignorance of both the callers and the interlocutors, anger and resentment feed upon themselves irrespective of the actual events that have inspired them. Limbaugh and his imitators see their role as stoking the fires of their listeners' prejudices and ignorance rather than seeking to use conversation to elevate the discourse and introduce new levels of complexity into the conversation. Here, for instance, is Limbaugh's October 23, 1995, disquisition on the U.S. Congress's unwillingness to make good on the country's debts to the United Nations:

> It's ridiculous to hear that we don't have any credibility to the rest of the world, but if that's truly the case, then to hell with the rest of the world; those nations should be worried about their credibility with us, not the other way around. If America is this generous and giving, and if all the rest of the world can do is complain about our life-style or other parts of our prosperity, then forget them until they start thanking us and appreciating us. I see no reason to bend over and grab the ankles for a bunch of little nations whom nobody has heard of.[37]

The extreme right-wing bias of almost all talk-radio hosts, along with Limbaugh's own vision of himself as a sort of unofficial pitchman for the Republican Party, further constricts the already narrow band of respectable political discourse and further increases the penalties for any public official who seeks to introduce a note of complexity or unorthodox thinking into a controversial issue. The power and immediacy of many listeners' reactions to congressional votes brings with it almost all the foibles of direct democracy with none of its virtues. Political discourse ends up a cruel parody of Deweyite democracy rather than its realization.

Given these circumstances, those who profess to care about democratic input into foreign policy generally have little to rely upon save polling data. Currently, such advocates are compelled to argue for a vastly reduced American role in addressing global political and military issues. On October 3, 1993, upon seeing television film of an American soldier being dragged through the streets of Mogadishu, Americans witnessed the mission of the 28,000 U.S. troops stationed there being extended from peacekeeping to building the nation and arresting warlords. Support for the operation naturally dropped, as the nation had not been consulted about the transformation of the mission from one of rescue into a futile exercise in nation building. Neither did they support President Clinton's efforts to restore Father Aristide to power in Haiti, despite its apparent success. Americans also spoke consistently against U.S. military intervention in Bosnia. They didn't much like foreign aid or immigration, either. According to the pollsters, the "mood" of American "public opinion" regarding foreign policy during the mid-1990s was increasingly one of "isolationism."[38] Yet in the cases of Haiti and Bosnia, the Clinton administration ultimately went ahead with its cautious multilateral military interventions and ended up paying no discernible price for either one. To the contrary, the price the administration paid within the establishment for not intervening seemed, in retrospect, far more costly to its reputation than did the interventions themselves. Incredibly, the administration achieved this despite the opposition to both missions of the military hierarchy itself, a hierarchy that has hardly been shy in asserting its will in the political arena.[39] In fact, the American people's much-vaunted isolation seemed far less pronounced by every conceivable measure—including voting, polling, and the dearth of large-scale protests—than did the establishment's fear of said animal.[40] Perceived success, or the absence of widely predicted failure, in both Haiti and Bosnia helped the president project an image of decisiveness and political courage. By the same token, however, Clinton's willingness to sit by and allow genocide to occur unimpeded in Rwanda caused no public outcry whatever. Clearly, information provided by the polling data tells us only a small part of the story of public opinion on these issues.

Polls do not help much in these matters because, as one-time American Political Science Association president Sidney Verba explains, polls provide "low-grade information" that fails to "capture the richness of individuals' views."[41] Polling data is restricted to those questions that politicians and interested parties want answered; it allows them, Benjamin Ginsberg argues, to tame public views by co-opting or isolating fundamental objections before they have time to develop a mass following.[42] A close look at the methodology of modern-day polling, moreover, demonstrates that even the largest majorities on behalf of one foreign policy position or another can be politically meaningless. The science of polling, at least the type that is routinely reported in the media, is notoriously unscientific and unreliable. The very term "public opinion," notes David Matthews of the Kettering Foundation, "implies the existence of developed public attitudes. Yet when attitudes are measured in an opinion poll, they may represent little more than the aggregation of hundreds of off-hand, unreflective responses to a pollster's suggestions."[43] When a pollster calls to ask a person questions about his or her views, most people feel obliged to have an opinion in order to be helpful. But as many as 80 percent of such people do not have stable, nonrandom opinions. Instead, they have what psychologists call "nonattitudes" or "pseudo-opinions" and hence invent their answers on the spot.[44] These nonviews, superficially held and frequently based on no knowledge whatever, are then aggregated with the views of those whose beliefs are strongly held. The results therefore have almost no predictive value. In 1995, the *Washington Post* even went to the trouble of commissioning a poll on the "twentieth anniversary" of a nonexistent act of legislation to determine whether it should be repealed. Almost everyone interviewed had an opinion, and most could be predicted by a cue in the questioner's language that indicated the act was supported by either President Clinton or the Republican Congress.[45]

The unwillingness of the government to own up to its actions and the inability of the media to hold the government accountable can cause a degree of ignorance on the part of even the most conscientious citizens that makes it difficult for them to judge the wisdom of a given policy. As Benjamin I. Page and Robert Y. Shapiro demonstrate in their survey of nearly half a century of public opinion data, "Concerning a number of foreign policy matters over the last five or six decades, presidents, government officials, and others have attempted to mislead the public often (as best we can tell) deliberately, and often with considerable success. In many cases misinformation from official sources has been accepted by experts and commentators (who are largely dependent on the official word) and then transmitted more or less intact through mass media reports of what the experts, commentators, and officials have to say."[46] The government does this despite the repeatedly stated belief on the part of large majorities of the public that the government is "never" justified in lying to the people it represents.[47]

The government's willingness to mislead the public for political purposes, coupled with the public's own well-documented ignorance about even the broadest outlines of major foreign policy issues, makes polling data on these issues particularly suspect. Governing elites believed themselves justified in ignoring the professed desires of large majorities of the American people because, lacking both information and access to relevant levers of power, those majorities have no means of sanction. Page and Shapiro's research indicates that approximately one-third of the time, U.S. foreign policy fails to reflect what the public says it wants.[48] But those who argue that the government should follow the lead of public opinion find themselves unable to respond to the retort that the public is both ignorant and confused regarding much of U.S. foreign policy, that small wording changes in a single polling question can often elicit a completely contradictory response.[49] (This is, after all, a country where more than three times as many people can name the

Three Stooges than can name three Supreme Court justices.[50]) And anyway, the argument continues, if the American people were so keen to have their own views represented in foreign policy issues, they would demand better media coverage of those issues and greater honesty about U.S. actions abroad from relevant officials, and would force candidates to outline their specific foreign policy views more clearly in national elections. When President Clinton signed the NATO expansion treaty in Madrid in July 1997, the level of public support for his position fluctuated by as much as 15 percent depending upon whether the questioner mentioned the economic costs involved. Roughly one-quarter of Americans polled at the time, however, were under the impression that Russia was already a member.[51] In one 1997 poll, 63 percent of Americans questioned told pollsters they favored NATO expansion, though only 10 percent could name a single country under consideration for invitation.[52] Game, set, match for the antidemocratic status quo.

Or perhaps not. To address these criticisms while simultaneously transforming the foreign policy process into one that truly embodies democratic principles, we will have to reconsider both the form and the content of that process. What follows is an immodest proposal to do just that.

Reviving the Liberal Republic:
An Immodest Proposal

It is the [citizen's] sweat which is to earn all the expenses of the war,
and their blood which is to flow in expiation of the causes of it.
—Thomas Jefferson

Direct mass democracy is only one interpretation of our constitutional order and not, I would argue, the most accurate one. The Founders envisioned a republican order based on a deliberative model of politics. By recreating deliberative politics, based on the examples of the Athenian assembly and the modern-day jury system, Americans can reproduce a republican democratic order that would be both more responsive and less corrupt than present political practice. Such a system—briefly sketched in this chapter—could simultaneously democratize and depoliticize U.S. foreign policy while helping to restore a sense of continuity to it. It would furthermore provide an institutionalized voice to the vast majority of citizens who today go unheard and whose concerns therefore go unheeded.

Clearly, mass direct democracy is unlikely to take hold in the United States today. The Deweyite dream of a vital, vibrant culture of communication recedes further with each new corporate PAC contribution, media megamerger, shrunken news hole, nine-second sound bite, negative commercial, shuttered corner bar, and failed public school. Indeed, Richard Rorty, America's foremost Deweyite, judges it to be impossible.[1] But direct democracy is not the only nor even the most desirable form of democracy. Republicanism, as is evidenced by the Founders' arguments for the Constitution, posits another way. The problem today is that we have allowed the executive to expropriate the power that the constitutional system allocated to Congress while simultaneously allowing the power that remains in Congress to be corrupted by money. This corruption has made the body unreformable for the purposes of democracy. The current election-funding system of organized influence peddling gives those who already own the office a near monopoly on raising funds. Congress has proven itself both unwilling and unable to practice self-reform, for good reason. Congressional fund-raising and vote selling is a true perpetual-motion machine. The Supreme Court, moreover, has ruled that money equals speech, and hence fundamental change would require a constitutional amendment, something a determined political minority could easily block. To create a truly republican foreign policy, we must find a way to transcend Congress while simultaneously forcing the executive to respond to legitimate democratic currents rather than simply to a conglomeration of active and vocal minorities as is presently the case.

To democratize U.S. foreign policy intelligently, we must first remove it from the corrupt practices of American money politics. We have ample precedent for this course. Monetary policy has been depoliticized; so has much of the judiciary. So, too, has the enormously quarrelsome problem of setting tariffs. These are hardly trivial examples. But depoliticization without democratization—as was undertaken in these cases—is hardly a suitable solution to the problem at hand. What is required instead is a means to expand the democratic content of our foreign policy as we simultaneously protect it from the corrupting influences of everyday money-driven politics. This requires expanding our operating assumptions about the types of representation that best serve democracy and a willingness to consider ideas that sound implicitly unlikely and even, at first blush, impossible.

The removal of foreign policy from the hurly-burly of everyday politicking would be more consistent with the intent of the Constitution's primary author, James Madison, and its primary explicator, Alexander Hamilton, than is current practice. (Jefferson, one is compelled to admit, was a far greater optimist and hence more of a Deweyite.) Madison argues in "Federalist Ten" that a republic need not process raw public opinion directly into policy. The job of the representative is instead "to refine and enlarge the public views by passing them through the medium of a chosen body of citizens." Madison reasons that such deliberations may represent a more thoughtful form of democracy. "It may well happen that the public voice, pronounced by the representatives of the people, will be more consonant to the public good than if pronounced by the people themselves, convened for the purpose."[2]

Speaking of the proposed senate in "Federalist 63," Madison further insists:

> Such an institution may be sometimes necessary as a defense to the people against their own temporary errors and delusions. As the cool and deliberate sense of the community ought, in all governments and actually will, in all free governments, ultimately prevail over the views of its rulers; so there are particular moments in public affairs when the people, stimulated by some irregular passion, or some illicit advantage, or misled by the artful misrepresentations of interested men, may call for measures which they themselves will afterwards be the most ready to lament and condemn. In these critical moments, how salutary will be the interference of some temperate and respectable body of citizens, in order to check the misguided career and to suspend the blow mediated by the people against themselves, until reason, justice and truth can regain their authority over the public mind.[3]

Yet as the Founders understood it, when deliberation checks democracy it does so to serve a deeper democratic—and republican—principle: the rule of deliberative majorities. When, as a result of passion, interest, or the demagogic appeals of ambitious men, the people fall prey to "temporary errors or delusions," their immediate desires, their unwise and possibly unjust inclinations must be resisted by those in positions of public trust while these temporary errors give way to better information, and more deliberate reaction, so that "reason, justice, and truth can regain their authority over the public mind." The point is not that citizens cannot know their own interests or that public judgments ought to supersede the greater wisdom and objectivity of elected officials, but rather that the ruling force ought to be "the cool and deliberate sense of the community" and not every immediate desire or inclination.

In the framers' minds, the crucial distinction was between passion and reason. The theory of deliberative democracy that undergirds the American constitutional order rests on the central proposition that there are two types of democratic voices: a spontaneous, emotional, reactive voice and one that is deliberative, reasoned, and fully informed. This is one reason that the power to declare war is so clearly vested in Congress rather than the executive. Wise rulers, according to the framers' lights, will ignore the emotional and encourage the development of the deliberative. Passions were to be controlled so that reason might emerge as the people came to understand their true interests. In "Federalist 71" Alexander Hamilton defended the Constitution on the grounds that it allowed time to encourage "cool and sedate" reflection to overcome the "temporary delusion . . . of transient impulse."[4] In his classic nineteenth-century defense of democracy, John Stuart Mill argued that "the steady habit of correcting and completing [one's] own opinion by collating it with others, so far from causing doubt and hesitation in carrying it into practice, is the only stable foundation for a just reliance on it."[5] It therefore follows, Joseph M. Bessette argues, that the true standard for evaluating the democratic character of a democracy is "how well the institutions of government foster the rule of informed and reasoning majorities rather than the rule of uninformed, passionate or prejudiced majorities."[6] The ultimate goal would be the democratic rule of what Robert Dahl terms "enlightened understanding." According to Dahl: "In order to express his or her preferences accurately, each citizen ought to have adequate and equal opportunities for discovering and validating, in the time permitted by the need for a decision, what his or her preferences are on the matter to be decided."[7]

The "Great Community" that Dewey sought appears to be much the same thing as Jurgen Habermas's "public sphere," in which "all citizens may confer in an unrestricted fashion about matters of general interest, with specific means for transmitting information."[8] Both concepts draw strength from Jeremy Bentham's original conception of a "public opinion tribunal." The United States already has such a system, made up of public and private research institutes, specialized journals, advocacy groups, and individual experts. But collective deliberation rarely if ever takes place because, for all the reasons discussed up to this point, the public sphere that helped create the American Revolution has disappeared. We must seek to repair it. To do that, we must look back to the framers' example as we simultaneously raise and reduce our demands for practical democracy.

James Fishkin notes that the electoral college had originally been intended to constitute a deliberative body. Alexander Hamilton argued that "the immediate election should be made by men most capable of analyzing the qualities adapted to the station and acting under circumstances favorable to deliberation."[9] At one point, he notes, the framers seriously considered using a lottery to create a special body drawn from the legislature to deliberate on the most qualified individual. The lottery would have permitted a smaller deliberative body to discern the best-qualified candidate. This would have been a far less direct form of democratic election than what was eventually adopted, but it would also have lent itself to far more effective deliberation. Historians have speculated that this proposal was influenced by the example of Athenian lotteries.[10]

In ancient Athens, any adult citizen was eligible and could expect to serve, for a day, in one of a number of roles: as head of the official executive body of the Athenian state, in the council, receiving and conferring with foreign envoys as the representative of Athens, or preparing the agenda for formal meetings of the council or assembly. Every Athenian citizen who reached the age of thirty was eligible (and expected) to staff one of the multitude of official positions and to sit in the courts. By the fourth century many of these activities were paid positions, ensuring that all Athenians could participate regardless of wealth. Later, Athens began to elect a small number of more permanent public officials, but these were seen to be compromises with unpleasant realities—necessary but hardly the soul of democratic life.[11]

The proposal I have in mind, inspired by Habermas and Fishkin, is based on the framers' beliefs drawn from the Athenian example, and on our own jury system. It combines the face-to-face discussion and deliberation so crucial to Dewey's notions of democracy with Lippmann's insistence on untrammeled access to insider information, without suffering the inadequacies of the contemporary media or polling system. It addresses the weaknesses of our current system by placing less emphasis on poll-driven policymaking and attempts instead to value deliberation, discussion, public education, and republican rather than consumerist notions of civic engagement. While it may appear unlikely as an alternative to the current system, I would argue that unless we are willing to consider such unlikely alternatives, what remains of the vital habits of the American democracy will continue to degenerate and may possibly disappear entirely. (I would also argue that simply because a political program seems unlikely to come to fruition in the near future is hardly a sufficient reason to dismiss it out of hand, as Nelson Mandela, Vaclav Havel, and Boris Yeltsin, among many others, would be happy to explain.) The plan is admittedly quite rough and would be subject to reform as problems arose. I am offering it not as a detailed blueprint, but rather as a suggestive road map. The body I am proposing would be made up of ordinary people "hired" by the American public to be full-time citizens and foreign policy jurors for a one-time period of, say, six years. Working together, these people would pursue the Deweyite deliberative ideal: "to cultivate the habit of suspended judgment, of skepticism, of desire for evidence, or appeal to observation rather than sentiment, discussion rather than bias, inquiry rather than conventional idealizations."[12] And they would do so in a newly created, nationally available "public sphere."

Fishkin calls his plan a deliberative opinion poll. Ned Crosby of the Jefferson Center for New Democratic Processes in Minnesota proposes "electoral juries of twelve to eighteen persons who would monitor the U.S. presidential campaign in various parts of the country, weigh testimony from competing witnesses or experts, and make public recommendations." His organization has already successfully experimented with "policy juries" on questions like organ transplants and water policy. These bodies are broadly representative, in a flexible, jurylike way, of the population. Both of these proposals echo that of Robert Dahl, who has put forth the idea of statistically representative panels of citizens who could make recommendations on specific policy issues.[13] They also recall Lippmann's ill-fated solution, proposed seven decades ago in *Public Opinion*, of a "specialized class of men," though the men and women of the new foreign policy body would be common people, democratically chosen. More recently, Dahl has extended his panel notion to the extremely ambitious idea of creating a "minipopulous" of as many as a thousand people.[14] To be statistically meaningful, the citizens jury for foreign policy would need at least four hundred to five hundred members. Given numbers like these, the body would obviously do much of its work by committee.

The jury notion is crucial to retain the democratic character of this proposal. Juries are bodies of deliberation where citizens undertake, for a brief time, to educate themselves with regard to all available relevant information before coming to judgment. They then discuss the question in a room where everyone present has had the same access to the same information and where each person's vote counts equally. The questions before each juror often turn on the most esoteric points of law and legal history and require extremely specialized knowledge and a sophisticated ability to weigh counterevidence and extenuating circumstances. These decisions can sometimes involve matters of life and death. If we are willing to trust the common citizen to decide whether a man or woman should spend life in prison, or even be executed, how can we argue that the same citizen is not capable of understanding the decisions involved in mapping the nation's foreign policy, once that citizen has had had ample opportunity for education and deliberation? Writing in the *New York Review of Books*, Andrew Hacker describes his own experiences as a New York City juror:

> No one, at least in my experience, tried to dominate the discussions, and jurors listened to what the others were saying. After the first hour, the foreman usually becomes just another juror. . . . In my first murder trial, the initial balloting—which we decided to take before we started talking—tied 6–6. Nor did this surprise me. As is usually the case, most of us had in effect been watching different trials. We then sought to move from twelve

different versions to one, or at least to sufficient consensus for a unanimous verdict. By the fourth hour, three of us changed our votes, now making it 9–3. We were reminded of certain faces we had ignored, or felt were unimportant, or we were shown that other interpretations were possible. At one point in writing about the General Will, Jean-Jacques Rousseau said that for democracy to work, citizens must be willing to say, "I was mistaken." This is not something most of us are willing to do; yet it must happen if juries are to function and I have observed more than a few of my fellow New Yorkers make that admission. About two hours later, we were down to 10–2, and then it took another four to arrive at 12–0. At no point were the divisions along racial or other social lines. And as we moved toward unanimity, it became evident that each of us was gaining a broader perspective. That twelve minds can take in more than one is the epistemological rationale for the jury system. But the rationale only works when bond traders are willing to listen to bus drivers and learn from them. Thus far the only place I have found that happening is inside the jury room.[15]

Hacker's experience may not be universal. Not all juries in American history have yielded fair-minded, intelligent decisions based on the evidence presented to them. For instance, many Americans found the juries' decisions in the O. J. Simpson trials objectionable. Nevertheless, I would still argue that the American jury system's record for fair-mindedness, intelligence, and honesty is a great deal more impressive than that of the U.S. Congress. Juries carry on true debates; Congress does not. Juries require genuine and respectful efforts to persuade; Congress does not. Juries require everyone present to focus their attention on reaching some resolution of the problem at hand; Congress does not. And finally, juries do not usually sell their votes to the highest bidder while spending the balance of their working days searching for potentially higher bidders.

The most effective manner in which to choose a foreign policy jury would be to invite a statistically representative body of the population— to simply reproduce America in miniature. This was the method used by Fishkin in each of the brief trial runs undertaken in Manchester, England, in 1993 and in Austin, Texas, in January 1996. But a statistical sampling is representation without democracy. Ultimately, for the foreign policy jury to be simultaneously democratic and republican, the jury must be elected by the population at large. In our current system, politics reflects both economic class and power inequalities between people. Because the system is answerable to money long before it is answerable to votes, both parties compete for the patronage of the wealthier and more powerful segments of the population and leave the poor and the powerless to fend for themselves. This vastly reduces the choices offered to the populace and prevents the electorate from engaging candidates across a broad array of issues rather than just "character" or "the economy." Voting would be undertaken strictly on the basis of biographies and short statements provided by the potential jurors. Once elected, the jurors would be paid a decent middle-class salary for their efforts. Any attempt to supplement that salary would be punishable by a mandatory jail sentence equivalent to the person's term of office, for both the bribe taker and the bribe maker. After serving out their terms, the jurors would, having signed a contract to do so, return to their former lives and hold seminars in local schools, libraries, and public-access cable-television stations explaining how they came to hold their current beliefs. Their salary would continue under the same restrictions. Reelection would be prohibited, and so would any form of lobbying.

Instead of our current winner-take-all system, citizens would be given the opportunity to divide their votes into percentages, in a manner proposed by the unfairly maligned Lani Guinier, so that the democratic process might reflect a broad array of citizen concerns rather than the one or two oversimplified election issues that now dominate the process. When, in 1988, Chilton County, Alabama, the self-proclaimed "Peach Capital of the World," experimented with a cumulative voting system in order to comply with a court order demanding a more effective enfranchisement of its poor, black minority, the results proved dramatic and edifying. Not only did a black candidate win with the largest plurarlity of all, but Republicans and women—no less rare in previous winning tickets—also found themselves elected to office. In 1992, Bobby Agee, who won his seat on the County Commission with just 1.5 percent of the white vote four years earlier, won twice as many white votes as black votes. According to Agee, "people in Chilton county started to get away from race, creed, and color" and looked instead at the ability of the person.[16]

Were such a system to be tried nationally, "single-issue" candidates would receive only the proportion of votes that voters truly wished to devote to the issue in question, rather than allowing, say, abortion or taxes to dominate all other political problems in any given election. Thus, voters might be able to vote for candidates who reflected a wide array of their concerns, say AIDS research, aid to Israel, and ballistic missile defense, rather than being forced to chose between the lesser of two political evils. Candidates could choose to run as a group or a "list," as politicians do in most of western Europe, much of the former Soviet bloc, Latin America, Israel, New Zealand, and South Africa. Voters who wished to see their class, religious, sexual, ethnic, and/or philosophical interests represented could apportion their votes proportionately. Gay supporters of ballistic missile defense, for instance, would no longer be forced to vote for a person who profoundly disagrees with them on a core political value. Such a system would significantly increase the number of women and minorities making foreign policy decisions without resorting to racial, ethnic, or sexual quotas. This change would prevent the problem of so-called "dummy" stockholders in elections: voters whose collective interests on a given issue are always outvoted and are not useful to the creation of a majority coalition. (This is why many U.S. corporations use a similar system to protect the rights of minority shareholders.) The conservative political analyst Kevin Phillips has already suggested that we convert elections to the House of Representatives to such a system as a means of reducing the disruptive power of special interests and eliminating the flagrant racial gerrymandering that characterizes so many U.S. congressional districts.[17]

Such a system would be far more representative than our current corrupt system and far more democratic than the pseudodemocratic conceit of Ross Perot's proposed "electronic town halls." It would also be more prudent and less given to political pandering. At the January 1996 National Issues Convention in Austin, Texas, for example, many delegates found themselves learning about the "gray areas" of public policy for the first time, following extensive conversations with other Americans as well as access to chosen experts, four presidential candidates, and one vice president. Craig Fitzharris, a 39-year-old Austin contractor who hated the federal government, met single mothers who could not survive without help from Washington and "changed a lot of [his] views." Fitzharris said he planned to "look at things differently because what [he] learned was to listen to others."[18] Donna Oliver, a pro-life Southern Baptist Republican from Lithonia, Georgia, had a similar experience. Now that she had been exposed to "horrendous tales about child abuse," she had become "pro-life, with a footnote." Mrs. Oliver also said she found it was possible for citizens to have thoughtful, in-depth conversations about issues without political posturing or partisan sniping.[19] The same can hardly be said about the United States Congress.

As with the National Issues Convention, citizen-jurors would not be self-selected. They would not fall into a single economic subgroup that is already overrepresented in the country's most powerful institutions and decision-making bodies. And they would be fully informed on the issues upon which they chose to focus, with unmediated access to the nation's leading writers, thinkers, and journalistic reports. The citizens' jury would invite whatever experts it chose to help educate its members on the intricacies of foreign policy questions. The State Department, Defense Department, Special Trade Representative, and National Security Council would be compelled to address its questions under oath. For educative purposes, all of the jury's deliberations would be available to Americans via cable television, live radio, and the Internet. Dean Acheson once explained that he dismissed popular opinion "not because people do not know the facts—the facts are not necessary to form opinion—but because they do not know the issues exist."[20] But seeing and hearing people who look, speak, and sound like themselves master issues like trade policy and multilateral intervention in Bosnia or Rwanda may inspire more Americans to take an interest in these questions themselves—if not for their own sake, then perhaps to a degree sufficient to determine their potential impact at home. They might form groups to replicate the jury discussions in local communities. Walter Lippmann to the contrary, information itself is not and will never be enough. We don't know what we think, as E. M. Forster once remarked, until we hear what we say. A republican foreign policy requires the recovery of the lost art of public conversation. Such conversation needs to be informed, of course, a value that would be served by the jury's debate. But it needs to be participatory as well. Democracy, at its best, after all, is highly educational. It requires us, in Christopher Lasch's words, "to extend the circle of debate as widely as possible and thus asks us all to articulate our views, to put them at risk, and to cultivate the virtues of clarity of thought, of eloquence, of sound judgment."[21] The net result might be the creation of a true "public" rather than the abstraction to which we refer today, when what we really mean is "a group of people sitting at home watching television or privately and invisibly reading a newspaper or numbers collected in a public opinion poll."[22] Even if none of these ambitious transformations were to take place, Americans would nevertheless find themselves better represented by a foreign policy jury than they are today by Congress.

Initially, the foreign policy jury would operate on an experimental basis as a means of strengthening democratic discourse and focusing debate on the concerns of the American people. It would have the power to compel public officials to meet and discuss policy with its members, but it would not replace the Congress or the executive as the nation's final authority. Over time, however, once the jury proved its ability to function coherently, the system could gradually transfer key components of the making of U.S.

foreign policy to the jury. I do not expect Congress or the president to agree to cede power voluntarily any time soon. Both branches of government currently derive too much benefit from the system's spoils, both political and economic. But over time, both parties could come to see that they would be better off ceding this responsibility and removing foreign policy from politics, just as they have done in the realm of monetary and tariff policies. Perhaps the question of whether to go to war might require majority votes of both bodies to maintain continuity with the current constitutional system. But "police actions" and the like, which characterized almost all deployment of armed force by the United States in this century, would no longer be undertaken on the word of the president alone.

Such a system would do wonders for the quality of both American democracy and U.S. foreign policy. While initially expensive, it would save trillions of dollars over the long haul by eliminating needless special-interest spending that is presently built into the system via special-interest corruption. It would also eliminate the phenomenon of self-interested organizations appropriating the foreign policy process on a given issue because no one cared enough to oppose them. It would end the process of selling some policies to the highest bidders, whether they be oil companies or ethnic lobbies. It would decrease a presidential candidate's incentive to manipulate the public on foreign policy issues or to lie to them for the purpose of deceiving foreign powers. It would make the world a safer place by eliminating the incentive presidents now have for fomenting crises at election time to improve their political prospects. Presidents and their lieutenants would also lose their incentive to curtail the civil liberties of those Americans who opposed their policies; the system would vastly reduce the political enticement to classify so much of what the government does as "secret." Congress, meanwhile, would no longer be forced to vote for trade agreements, weapons systems, and arms sales that benefit only campaign contributors and local contractors while impoverishing the taxpayer. These issues would be decided on merits by well-informed common men and women. The ultimate result might be a cleanup of the election process that extends well beyond any measures that have been proposed by the members of any major political party.

Finally, a citizens' foreign policy jury would improve enormously both the continuity and stability of U.S. foreign policy. West German chancellor Helmut Schmidt once complained, "As Chancellor, I worked under four presidents, and it is quite an experience, I can tell you . . . . First Carter sends his Vice-President to tell us almost everything done under his predecessors was wrong. Then along comes Reagan and tells us the same thing."[23] This unhealthy dynamic would end automatically. Because its foreign policy would be rooted in the values of its people, democratically debated and defined, America would again become a trustworthy partner in matters of foreign policy.

Republicanism, as E. J. Dionne argues, insists that "self-government is not a drab necessity but a joy to be treasured."[24] Under such a scheme, American democracy might very well experience a rebirth in domestic as well as foreign policy. With the creation of a national televised, interactive, and instructional "public sphere," America might solve its two-hundred-year-old Tocqueville problem and water the roots of a new democratic renaissance from the seeds of the Founders' republican faith.

Needless to say, the proposals described here appear rather improbable at present. I imagine that most readers will have trouble imagining them ever coming to fruition. Indeed, this is less a comment on the nature of the reforms, I fear, than on the paucity of political imagination in contemporary American politics. The political revolutions that undid the Soviet Union and remade Eastern Europe, giving birth to a whole new spectrum of possibility in those nations, have no corollary in the United States. Some American politicians have a hard time even admitting that the Cold War is over. Given the current context of U.S. foreign policy debate, republican democracy is so radical a notion it does not even appear on the agenda. Moreover, this state of affairs suits those who control it just fine. Everyone else seems to have given up. The current system, with declining participation and increased anger and alienation on the part of those who believe themselves shut out can probably continue indefinitely. Like western civilization and the modern novel, reports of the imminent demise of the American political system have been frequently exaggerated. It is a machine that goes by itself.

The system is not wholly impervious to change from without. But the angry apathy it engenders on the part of the citizenry helps to fortify it and casts even the mere suggestion of significant democratic reform as utopian and somehow childish. Tocqueville observed in Americans a tendency to "enclose thought within a formidable fence. A writer is free inside that area, but woe to the man who goes beyond it." True, he allowed, no one issues explicit instructions, like those of the medieval Catholic Church or the former Soviet Union, reading "Think like me or die." The writ reads instead:

You are free not to think as I do; you can keep your life and property and all, but from this day you are a stranger among us. You can keep your privileges in the township, but they will be useless to you for if you solicit your fellow citizens' votes, they will not give them to you, and if you only ask for their esteem, they will make excuses for refusing that. You will remain among men, but you will lose your rights to count as one. When you approach your fellows, they will shun you as an impure being, and even those who believe in your innocence will abandon you too, lest they in turn be shunned. Go in peace, I have given you your life, but it is a life worse than death.[25]

Before we can begin to restore democratic control to the making of our country's foreign policy, we must first overcome the psychological hurdle that prevents us from thinking, institutionally, beyond essentially meaningless tinkering with a system that has fundamentally broken down. Any society willing to consider a person as obviously bizarre as Ross Perot to be a serious presidential candidate is clearly ready to consider radical change, though it may not yet be ready to admit it. Perot's 1992 performance, and his hold on the popular political imagination ever since, demonstrates a hunger and yearning in America for new political approaches to the problems of trade policy and political corruption. The excitement stirred by the even more alarming Pat Buchanan offers further corroborative evidence that Americans are growing increasingly impatient with a political system that takes their interests, and their acquiescence, for granted. America's corporate and political elites, including most particularly the foreign policy establishment, has so far proven resistant to the changes blowing in the political winds, but they cannot resist forever. The longer they try, the less democratic and tolerant those responses are likely to be.

To transform American politics into a truly democratic endeavor, all that is necessary is for people to accept their own competence to decide for themselves where their interests lie and to force the system to respond. Simply put, no doubt, but hardly easily accomplished. The problem, in my view, is ultimately psychological. Common Americans regularly call into sports-radio talk shows and conduct long, intricate conversations with a high degree of thought and analysis, involving all manner of complicated details and virtually no deference to experts or professionals. Why can't these same people approach the life-or-death decisions of foreign or domestic political trade-offs with the same passion and sophistication that they bring to Monday-morning quarterbacking? Therein lies the key to the transformation of American politics.

A Democratic Foreign Policy Today

Do I contradict myself?
Very well then, I contradict myself.
(I am large, I contain multitudes.)

—Walt Whitman

Despite more than two centuries of economic growth, technological innovation, physical expansion, and ethnic and racial transformation, the underlying political values of the American people have remained remarkably stable over time.[1] While their leaders have, at various times, become infatuated with various crusades on behalf of democracy, free markets, and anti-Communist counterinsurgency, among a few others, common American men and women continue to see the world in much the same terms as the country's founders. Like the framers, they believe the separation between the foreign and domestic realms is, in Walter LaFeber's words, "artificial and perilous."[2] Americans believe first and foremost in preserving peace. They believe in the doctrine of free trade but are not willing to pursue it at the cost of their own well-being as workers and producers.[3] They prefer to avoid political entanglements in the affairs of other nations and wish to promote the values of democratic capitalism by example rather than compulsion.[4] They are, like Tom Paine, George Washington, Alexander Hamilton, John Adams, Thomas Jefferson, James Madison, and John Quincy Adams, liberal republicans, with all the philosophical conflicts and contradictions those two labels imply.

A liberal republican foreign policy would reverse the present priorities of the foreign policy establishment. Such a policy would be relatively minimalist in politico-military terms, but activist in support of American jobs and prosperity. The historic American yearning for unceasing expansion—the ghost in the machine of revolutionary republicanism—has ceased to imply physical control and now manifests itself exclusively in terms of commercial conquest, a much healthier and ultimately more rewarding pursuit. American racism, another snake in the Founders' garden, remains persistent in our society. But it need not infect our foreign policy once we denounce the right to order nonwhite societies as we see fit.

Briefly sketched, a liberal republican foreign policy would seek to achieve the following goals.

A STABLE PEACE ENFORCED BY THE UNITED NATIONS, THE NORTH ATLANTIC TREATY ORGANIZATION, AND UNILATERAL AMERICAN POWER AS ITS EXTREME LAST RESORT

Across the political spectrum, the foreign policy establishment believes that the United States bears a moral responsibility to maintain global peace and world order whenever possible and to do so unilaterally. The American people, however, do not agree. Like Washington, Jefferson, and the Adamses, they have no interest in empire for its own sake. Nor do they believe it their responsibility to reorder the world in their own image. If a less interventionist United States means a less tidy world, with greater instability in some areas and unfortunate ethnic strife in others, so be it. The American people prefer it to a policy of indiscriminate intervention based on values and priorities they do not share.[5] Should intervention prove necessary, Americans, by overwhelming majorities, prefer that the United States use force as part of a multilateral alliance, through either the NATO alliance or the United Nations.[6]

From George Washington's farewell address through Bill Clinton's attempts to excite support for U.S. intervention in Bosnia, the American people have viewed the commitment of blood and treasure as an extreme last resort. Presidents, empowered by historical precedent and a deferential Congress, have felt free to ignore both the constitutional strictures on their power to commit this country to war as well as the majority sentiments of the American people. These unconstitutional and anti-democratic adventures need to be terminated if U.S. foreign policy is to reflect the values of its people. If a president believes the nation or its vital interests are sufficiently threatened to necessitate war, let him make the case honestly and forthrightly. If that support is not forthcoming, he will be much better off discovering this sooner rather than later.

Those instances that may require the commitment of troops but do not justify a declaration of war should be left in the hands of a volunteer UN army, supported financially by the United States but without the power or prestige of the U.S. military. As is done presently, U.S. troops could be committed to UN peacekeeping operations if no such volunteer force is created, but the threshold for involvement would automatically be raised and the difficulties of deployment would undoubtedly multiply. Because Americans are generally so uncomfortable making genuine compromises, particularly the kind that involve bowing to the leadership of others, we would be better off detailing in advance exactly to which kinds of operations we would be willing to commit troops. While we all do bear some responsibility for alleviating the suffering of all humankind by virtue of our wealth and good fortune, the United Nations, along with other regional organizations, can, with proper support, take responsibility for global peacekeeping and peacemaking with considerable confidence on the part of the American people.[7] A modified balance-of-power arrangement, where the United States takes the lead in its own hemisphere while Europe and Russia tend to their neighborhoods and Japan and China to theirs, makes a great deal more sense than America's presently undefined and, apparently, infinite set of commitments across virtually every land mass on the globe.

The policy described here is far more congruent with present-day American values as well as the historic foundation of liberal republicanism than is the current policy. Following the American failure in Somalia, President Clinton issued PD 25, which restricted U.S. participation in collective security operations and declared that "the United States does not support a standing UN Army, nor will we earmark specific U.S. military units for participation in UN operations." Newt Gingrich nevertheless accused Clinton of harboring a "multinational fantasy" and attempting "to subordinate the United States to the United Nations." Senator Bob Dole said that international organizations often "reflect a consensus that opposes American interests or does not reflect American principles and ideals."[8] Despite a false impression conveyed by the press coverage of these issues, all of these statements are at odds with the American people's values. The public's attitude toward the UN, excluding a core unyielding minority, is overwhelmingly favorable, particularly when compared to the use of unilateral American force—a fact almost wholly lost in the context of elite public-policy debate.[9] Americans are particularly supportive of U.S. action, in tandem with UN forces, to prevent genocide, and are even willing to support American troops serving under foreign commanders as long as those troops do not constitute a majority in the unit in question.[10]

SUPPORT FOR RECIPROCAL FREE TRADE FORTIFIED BY A CRUSADE ON BEHALF OF A GLOBAL WORKER'S BILL OF RIGHTS, BACKED BY THE POWER OF THE AMERICAN MARKET

Americans believe in free trade; about this fact there can be little confusion. But as John Quincy Adams observed at the dawn of the nineteenth century, though the philosophy of free trade may be "congenial to the spirit of our institutions . . . the fairness of the operation depends upon its being admitted universally." Today Americans are being asked by the makers of their foreign policy to pursue a free-trade policy vis-à-vis nations whose workers are paid a fraction of what ours earn, and that erect any number of complex barriers to our products. This is a recipe for the gradual but inexorable impoverishment of our citizens. Thomas Jefferson believed that commerce could serve as a "messenger of American republicanism" but that it had to be kept in balance. He said, "Should any nation . . . suppose it may better find its advantage by continuing its system of prohibitions, duties and regulations, it behooves us to protect our citizens, their commerce, and navigation, by counter prohibitions, duties and regulations." Warning against unilateral concessions, Jefferson added, "Free commerce and navigations are not to be given in exchange for restrictions and vexations; nor are they likely to produce a relaxation of them."[11]

Following the Revolution, John Adams, assisted by Benjamin Franklin, drafted a model plan for commercial treaties to guide U.S. negotiators. The Continental Congress approved it with only minor changes. As adopted, the treaty plan proposed two options: reciprocal national treatment in commercial matters, or unconditional most-favored-nation policy. Free trade was preferred, but only on the condition of reciprocity. This fundamental principle of liberal republicanism remains a bedrock American value today and a useful guide to the problems we currently face. The foreign policy establishment believes in free trade pretty much regardless of the practice of other nations, however. It therefore treats the defense of lower-middle-class American jobs and community health with a disregard bordering on contempt.[12]

The answer to America's trade problems is not protectionism per se. Trade wars inevitably cause exactly the type of economic dislocation and hardship we seek to avoid. But, as Jefferson argued, because other nations are dependent on our commerce, trade policy can be used to force them to respect American rights.[13] The American market, the world's largest and most diverse, can be a powerful tool to demand fairness from the rest of the world and reciprocity for our own workers and products. Americans do not view themselves exclusively as consumers, as economists and corporate CEOs see them. Rather, they believe they are workers first and are willing to pay a premium if necessary to safeguard their living standards and economic security. The global assault on their living standards by stateless corporations is the single greatest threat to Americans' well-being, and resisting it is therefore the most important foreign policy priority, save preserving peace, that flows from their values.[14] Nowhere is the distinction between "foreign" and domestic policy less meaningful. Instead of simply surrendering to the global economic forces that have rent their lives and emasculated their earning power, American workers would be far better served by a policy that allocated access to our markets on the basis of a set of agreed-upon international workers' rights and employer norms—a Worker's Bill of Rights. The United States could set an example by passing such a law and then demanding that exporters make a good-faith effort to live up to its terms lest they sacrifice the privilege of selling in our markets. A Worker's Bill of Rights might include the following:

1. The right to collective bargaining and collective action in support of fellow workers without risk of firings
2. Reasonable work hours
3. A safe and healthy workplace
4. A fair minimum wage
5. A voice in workplace issues
6. A ban on all forced labor, including that of prisoners and children

Under such a policy, Americans would have the advantage of raising global living standards and creating new markets for our own products instead of racing other nations to the bottom of the worker-protection scale as promised by the GATT and NAFTA accords. Initial steps in this direction have already had positive results. Beginning in 1984, U.S. trade law has conditioned trade preferences to developing countries' respect for workers' rights. Threats to withdraw these preferences have resulted in important reforms abroad. El Salvador cooperated with the International Labor Organization to adopt an extensive labor code, Sri Lanka agreed to open its garment industry to collective bargaining, and Indonesia increased its minimum wage by 29 percent. Some U.S. firms, moreover, such as Levi Strauss and Sears, have agreed to voluntary codes for work they subcontract to Third World companies.[15] Americans regularly tell pollsters that they would be willing to support companies who treat their workers fairly, if only they had access to the necessary information.[16] Why not test this response by providing it? A crusade on behalf of a Worker's Bill of Rights, backed up by the power of the American market, would appeal to Americans' republican yearnings to make the world a better place while simultaneously serving their liberal interests as workers and producers.

A market-allocation strategy could also improve Americans' ecological security, since production processes that threaten the world's commons, including the oceans and the ozonosphere, could be similarly sanctioned. Such a policy would allow Americans to pursue the ultimate liberal republican values: Virtue and Commerce. Put in more contemporary terms, it addresses the two most powerful yearnings in the American heart: doing good while doing well.

A REALISTIC STRATEGY TO CONTROL IMMIGRATION

Americans remain divided about immigration. Historically, the nation has thrown up anti-immigrant barriers whenever economic insecurity appears on the horizon. Given the harsh impact of unfettered global capitalism on all nations, we can expect a sustained period of anti-immigrant fervor for many years to come. Anti-immigrant anger can reach a fevered pitch when combined with racism, and hence non-European immigration of the type we have been experiencing for the past two decades can be particularly problematic. Sixty-three percent of Americans questioned agreed, when asked by pollsters in 1994, that "Immigrants today are a burden on our country because they take our jobs, housing and health care."[17] Nearly three-quarters of those polled in the 1995 Chicago Council on Foreign Relations report saw "immigrants and refugees as a critical threat," and chose "controlling illegal immigration" as a "very important goal."[18]

Immigration, once the foundation for economic growth and cultural maturity, has become extremely difficult to sustain in times of economic insecurity and ethnic and cultural destabilization. A steady flow of immigrants willing to work below minimum wage and without any health or pension benefits reduces the wages of some categories of native-born Americans by increasing supply at the expense of demand. It can also give unscrupulous politicians an irresistible scapegoat for economic problems that demand structural economic and political change to address in earnest. The anger, tension, and, frequently, violence that can result from uncontrolled immigration overwhelms the positive contributions that further immigration can make to this country at present. As the grandson of three immigrants, I would prefer that none of this were true. I would also prefer it as a matter of personal political philosophy because, unlike most Americans, I believe that immigrants contribute far more to our economic and cultural life than they cost us. The current rate of immigration is just one-third that at the beginning of the century. Per-capita government spending is far lower for immigrants than for natives; and the majority of workers, including most minority, female, and low-skilled workers, do not experience an increase in unemployment rates as the result of immigration.[19] But my own preferences and beliefs are not at issue here. The American people want a carefully controlled, extremely limited policy of immigration based on the country's domestic needs. If politicians want to inspire them to place a greater emphasis on issues of political asylum and the problems of the world's "wretched refuse, yearning to breathe free," they must do a better job of making their case.

The Immediate Termination of All U.S. Covert Action Abroad and an End to U.S. Support for Repressive Dictatorships

Nothing could be more at odds with the concept of a democratic foreign policy than covert action. The very concept is at odds with the democratic ethos. Secret armies, unaccountable acts of war, paramilitary attacks, and policies of assassination have no place in the foreign policy of a democratic nation. Neither does deliberate disinformation or the interference in the electoral processes of other nations. The very ethos of secrecy necessary to make such policies effective is itself corrosive to democratic politics. Because presidents and their advisers become addicted to secrecy, such policies inevitably mushroom into morally questionable areas that have the effect of implicating Americans in actions they would not wish to defend.[20] Americans do not share the realpolitik arguments that insist upon the need to arm and support foreign dictators who regularly violate the rights of their own citizens for murky reasons of "national security." Such arguments may have enjoyed some persuasive power during the Cold War, but when the CIA admits to paying the murderers and torturers of American citizens and then deliberately concealing this from Congress and the American people, clearly the nation's democratic fabric has been torn beyond repair. America certainly requires a clandestine intelligence service to defend against acts of international terrorism and the spread of weapons of mass destruction. It does not require, and its people do not want, an agency with the power to conduct a secret, uncontrolled foreign policy. The destruction and replacement of the CIA with a true *intelligence* agency, moreover, is supported not only by the public, but also by every category of "influentials" polled by the Pew Center for People and the Press in 1997, save congressional staff members.[21]

A GLOBAL EFFORT TO REDUCE THE WORLDWIDE FLOW OF ARMS

By the mid-1990s, the United States accounted for between 50 and 60 percent of worldwide arms exports, and this percentage was on the rise. In 1995, the Clinton administration issued an arms-transfer policy that paid lip service to the idea of restraint but also, for the first time, explicitly supported arms exports as a way to shore up U.S. military interests. A principal goal of PD 41 was "to enhance the ability of the U.S. defense industrial base to meet U.S. defense requirements . . . at lower costs." Moreover, U.S. officials were instructed to consider "the [sale's] impact on U.S. industry and the defense industrial base" as a criterion for decision making.[22] Regardless of whether such policy makes political sense in a world where these arms can end up in the hands of a Saddam Hussein or a Mu'ammar Ghadhafi, the policy itself is directly contrary to the values of the American people. In 1995, 77 percent of those polled by the Chicago Council on Foreign Relations opposed such arms sales, up from 59 percent four years earlier.[23] The U.S. government should embark on a top-priority program to negotiate strict and enforceable limitations on global arms sales—up to and including automatic economic sanctions. To protect the workers in the defense industry, as well as the soldiers in the military who will no longer be needed, from bearing the brunt of the transformation of U.S. foreign policy, the nation should also embark on a concerted program of defense conversion, involving reschooling, retooling, and retraining. The money to pay for this policy should come from further reductions in the size and cost of the military and in the global network necessary to support it, as the American people do not desire the expensive global interventionary capacity considered to be essential by the foreign policy establishment.

"The American people," the *New York Times* reported in late 1997, "are far more willing than their government to take early, unilateral steps" to "counter the threat of global warming." While the Clinton administration publicly hemmed and hawed with regard to asking businesses and consumers to make the necessary changes, a full 65 percent of those questioned told pollsters that the country should significantly reduce its own responsibility for creating so-called "greenhouse" gases, "no matter what other countries do."[24] No wonder. "Protecting the global environment" is among the public's top priorities, placing just behind protecting American jobs and preventing the spread of nuclear weapons in one recent poll, and controlling immigration and the flow of drugs into our borders in another.[25] The Montreal Protocol, designed to rid the world of ozone-destroying chlorofluorocarbon gasses, is a favorable step in the direction of a democratic foreign policy and an important precedent for further measures. The trade-offs between economic growth and environmental protection are among the most difficult decisions that face a democratic policy maker, since both goals are strongly supported by the public. (Elite values tend to place "insuring adequate energy supplies" far higher than "protecting the environment."[26]) This potential conflict is one more reason to use the U.S. market as a lever to try to promote environmentally sustainable manufacturing processes in the rest of the world, so that the two goals might be pursued in tandem. The Worker's Bill of Rights discussed previously should therefore include strict provisions for the protection of rain forests, local ecosystems, and natural resources upon which the global commons depend; as well as a commitment to scale back the production of greenhouse gases that heat up the global atmosphere.

Reconstitute U.S. Foreign-Aid Policies

Foreign aid is one area that suffers enormously from public ignorance. Most Americans believe that spending on foreign aid constitutes more than 25 percent of the federal budget. Nearly 60 percent of those questioned in 1995 told pollsters that we spend more money on foreign aid than we do on Medicare.[27] (They were off by a factor of more than 25,000 percent.) In surveys Americans say that they would consider 5 percent acceptable. In fact, U.S. foreign-aid spending amounts to less than 1 percent of the budget, compared with 18 percent for the military. The United States already ranks last among donor nations in the percentage of its GNP it devotes to foreign assistance, and Congress plans to cut U.S. aid another 11 percent.[28]

Americans do support the principle of foreign aid, but their extreme ignorance of its size, stoked by isolationist politicians, have created a dynamic to reduce it. Were this misimpression corrected, Americans might even be willing to increase foreign aid considerably, as long as specific conditions were met, though this is hardly assured. They are particularly enamored of emergency disaster relief and would likely enthusiastically the creation of a peaceful rapid-deployment force for this purpose. Among these conditions, according to a 1995 survey by the Program on Public Attitudes, are a greater emphasis on helping the needy rather than strategic allies, promoting self-reliance rather than relief, ensuring that aid goes to the needy rather than to corrupt governments, and placing a higher priority on whether recipient countries are democratic and have good human-rights records.[29] According to one 1997 poll, Americans respond favorably by enormous majorities to questions about aid when the questioner ensures that it will be devoted to providing food and medical assistance to needy peoples (86 percent); development aid to needy countries (76 percent) and family planning and birth control (68 percent).[30] Of course, such talk is remarkably cheap. Whether people are willing to pay the bill when the time comes is a separate question and a challenge for those who believe that the world's richest economy should also be its most generous.

☆

NOTES

INTRODUCTION

1. Tom Clancy, "Know the Answers Before Going to War," *New York Times*, February 13, 1998, op-ed page.
2. Questions and answers from the Ohio State meeting can be found in "Excerpts from the Discussion on Iraq at Ohio State University," *New York Times*, February 19, 1998.
3. Cited in James Bennet, "Bad Vibes From the Heartland Launch Fleet of Finger-Pointers," *New York Times*, February 19, 1998.
4. *CBS Evening News with Dan Rather*, February 18, 1998.
5. Andrew Ferguson, *Time*, March 2, 1998.
6. Cited in James Bennet, "Clinton Tries to Repair Damage to Support on Iraq," *New York Times*, February 20, 1998.
7. See *America's Place in the World*, vol. 2 (Washington, D.C.: Pew Research Center for the People and the Press, 1997), 15.
8. See, for instance, Miroslav Nincic, *Democracy and Foreign Policy: The Fallacy of Political Realism* (New York: Columbia University Press, 1992); Eugene R. Wittkopf, *Faces of Internationalism: Public Opinion and American Foreign Policy* (Durham, N.C.: Duke University Press, 1990); Benjamin Page and Robert Y. Shapiro, *The Rational Public: Fifty Years of Trends in American Policy Preferences* (Chicago: University of Chicago Press, 1992); *The New Politics of American Foreign Policy*, ed. David A. Deese (New York: St. Martin's Press, 1994); Bruce Russett, *Controlling the Sword: The Democratic Governance of National Security* (Cambridge: Harvard University Press, 1990); Richard J. Barnet, *The Rockets' Red Glare: When America Goes to War, The Presidents and the People* (New York: Simon and Schuster, 1990); Barry B. Hughes, *The Domestic Context of American Foreign Policy* (San Francisco: W. H. Freeman, 1978); John E. Mueller, *War, Presidents and Public Opinion* (New York: John Wiley and Sons, 1973); Melvin Small, *Democ-*

191

racy and Diplomacy: The Impact of Domestic Politics on U.S. Foreign Policy, 1789–1994 (Baltimore: Johns Hopkins University Press, 1996); Alexander DeConde, Ethnicity, Race and American Foreign Policy: A History (Boston: Northeastern University Press, 1990); and Ole K. Holsti, Public Opinion and American Foreign Policy (Ann Arbor: University of Michigan Press, 1996). Also invaluable are the quadrennial surveys of American "opinion leaders" and the general public on foreign policy questions conducted by the Chicago Council on Foreign Relations and overseen by John E. Rielly and the survey material collected in Steven Kull, I. M. Destler, and Clay Ramsay, The Foreign Policy Gap: How Policymakers Misread the Public (College Park: University of Maryland Center for International and Security Studies, 1997).

9. Alexis de Tocqueville, Democracy in America (Garden City, N.Y.: Doubleday, 1969), 228–29.

10. Walter LaFeber, "Jefferson and American Foreign Policy," Jeffersonian Legacies, ed. Peter S. Onuf (Charlottesville: University of Virginia Press, 1993), 376–77.

11. See Sidney Verba, "The Citizen as Respondent: Sample Surveys and American Democracy" (Presidential Address, American Political Science Association, 1995), American Political Science Review 90, no. 1 (1996): 1.

12. Wirthlin Group, "Ideals and U.S. Foreign Policy" (New York: Carnegie Council on Ethics and International Affairs, 1989), 25.

13. Bentham and Mill are cited in Edward Hallett Carr, The Twenty Years Crisis, 1919–1939 (London: Macmillan, 1940), 33–34.

14. Locke wrote, "What is to be in reference to foreigners, depending much upon their actions, and the variations of designs and interests, must be left in great part to the prudence of those who have this power commanded to them, to be managed to the best of their skill for the advantage of the commonwealth." See John Locke, An Essay Concerning the True Origins, Extent, and End of Civil Government (New York: Harper, 1947), 195–96. Rousseau is quoted in Carl J. Friedrich, Foreign Policy in the Making (New York: W. W. Norton, 1938), 47.

15. Cited in Ted Gaylen Carpenter, The Captive Press: Foreign Policy Crises and the First Amendment (Washington, D.C.: Cato Institute, 1995), 69.

16. See Walter Lippmann, Essays in the Public Philosophy (Boston: Little, Brown, 1955), 20.

17. George F. Kennan, The Cloud of Danger: Current Realities of American Foreign Policy (Boston: Little, Brown, 1977), 6.

18. Michael H. Hunt, Ideology and U.S. Foreign Policy (New Haven: Yale University Press, 1987), 7.

19. See John Lewis Gaddis, The United States and the Origins of the Cold War, 1941–1947 (New York: Columbia University Press, 1972), 360–61.

20. Adam Ulam cited in Nincic, Democracy and Foreign Policy, 29.

21. McHenry appeared as one of two foreign policy experts to answer participants' questions. His comments were made on January 20, 1996, in response to a question from a female landlord from Indiana concerning the U.S. policy on Bosnia.

22. Zbigniew Brzezinski and Samuel Huntington, Political Power: USA/USSR (New York: Viking, 1968), 382.

23. See Richard N. Haass, *Intervention* (Washington, D.C.: Carnegie Endowment for International Peace, 1994).

24. Cited in Nincic, *Democracy and Foreign Policy* (New York: Columbia University Press, 1992), 79.

25. Maxwell Taylor made this statement to Bernard Kalb in a CBS broadcast on June 17, 1971.

26. Craig R. Whitney, "Expand NATO? Yes, Say Most Experts, But What Does the Public Think?" *New York Times*, February 10, 1995.

27. See Samuel Huntington, "The United States," in Michael J. Crozier, Samuel Huntington, and Joo Watanuki, *The Crisis of Democracy* (New York: Trilateral Commission, 1975), 113–14.

28. Gabriel Almond, *The American People and Foreign Policy* (New Haven: Yale University Press, 1960), 54, 85.

29. Dexter Perkins, *Foreign Policy and the American System* (Ithaca, N.Y.: Cornell University Press, 1952), 3. Note that this is the opening sentence of the book.

30. Hans Morgenthau, *Politics Among Nations*, 6th ed. (New York: Knopf, 1985), 168.

31. See *Mixed Messages about Press Freedom on Both Sides of the Atlantic* (Washington, D.C.: Times Mirror Center for the People and the Press, 1994). The other nations were Canada, Mexico, Britain, France, Germany, Italy, and Spain.

32. Wittkopf, *Faces of Internationalism*, 1.

33. See Pew Research Center for the People and the Press, "Washington Leaders Wary of Public Opinion," April 17, 1998, p. 1.

34. Cyrus Vance, *Hard Choices: Critical Years in America's Foreign Policy* (New York: Simon and Schuster, 1983), 28.

35. Michael Clough, "Grass-Roots Policymaking: Say Good-Bye to the Wise Men," *Foreign Affairs* 72, no. 1 (1994): 7.

36. This figure of 5 to 10 percent can be found in Wittkopf, *Faces of Internationalism*, 142.

37. In addition to Page and Shapiro, see the essays in Thomas W. Graham, "Public Opinion and U.S. Foreign Policy Decision Making" in *The New Politics of American Foreign Policy*. For related arguments, see Stephen Earl Bennett, "Trends in American's Political Information, 1967–1987," *American Politics Quarterly* 17 (1989): 422–35; Russell W. Neuman, *The Paradox of Mass Politics: Knowledge and Opinion in the American Electorate* (Cambridge: Harvard University Press, 1986); Thomas W. Graham, "The Pattern of Importance of Public Knowledge in the Nuclear Age," *Journal of Conflict Resolution* 32 (1988): 319–34; Wittkopf, *Faces of Internationalism*.

38. See Harwood Group, *Citizens and Politics: A View from Main Street America* (Dayton, Ohio: Kettering Foundation, 1991), and David Matthews, *Politics for People: Finding a Responsible Public Voice* (Urbana: University of Illinois Press, 1994). See also National Issues Forum, "A Public Voice . . . '92: America's Role in the World; Energy Options; The Boundaries of Free Speech," Fall and Winter, Dayton, Ohio, 1991/92, The National Issues Forum, "Mission Uncertain: Reassessing America's Global Role," (Dayton, Ohio: 1996) and "The Portland Agenda: Principles and

Practices for Reconnecting Citizens and the Political Process," National Commission for the Renewal of American Democracy, (Dayton, Ohio, December 1993).

39. For instance, the $27 billion to $35 billion figure that the administration reports is described as "purely illustrative and designed to provide an approximate estimate of the costs of enlargement. . . . The Congressional Budget Office study had five options, ranging in total cost from $21 billion to $125 billion through 2010." See Steven Erlanger, "Debate Raging Over Cost of NATO Expansion," *New York Times*, October 13, 1997.

40. Hector St. John de Crèvecoeur, *Letters from an American Farmer* (London, 1912, originally published in 1782), p. 43.

41. The construction is George Kennan's.

42. Times Mirror Center for the People and the Press, news release, November 2, 1993.

43. Wirthlin Group, "Ideals and U.S. Foreign Policy," National Issues Forum, "Mission Uncertain: Reassessing America's Global Role," 1996, 1–3.

44. See Richard Morin, "Influencing Opinion With Information," *Washington Post*, February 12–18, 1996, national weekly edition, p.34.

45. See, most recently, *America's Place in the World*, vol. 2, 38–39.

46. Eugene R. Wittkopf, *Faces of Internationalism*, 163.

47. "Mission Uncertain: Reassessing America's Global Role," 15.

48. John E. Rielly, ed., *American Public Opinion and U.S. Foreign Policy 1995* (Chicago: Chicago Council on Foreign Relations, 1995), 39.

49. See Andrew Kohut and Robert C. Toth, "Arms and the People," *Foreign Affairs* 73, no. 6 (1994): 55. The gaps are apparently increasing. In 1997, according to one extensive poll, "All Influential groups overwhelmingly support the use of American military forces if Iraq invades Saudi Arabia. All strongly favor its use if South Korea is invaded by the North or if Israel is invaded by Arab states. In many states, the support is greater than four years earlier. . . . The public, however, approves of committing U.S. forces only in support of Saudi Arabia (54%). A majority oppose sending American troops to help South Korea (58%), and narrow pluralities oppose sending them to Israel (47%)." These numbers show little change since 1993. See *America's Place in the World*, vol. 2, 29.

50. See, for instance, the polls cited by Kull et al., *The Foreign Policy Gap*, 26.

51. See James Sterngold, "NAFTA Trade-Off: Some Jobs Lost, Others Gained," *New York Times*, October 9, 1995.

52. *American Public Opinion and U.S. Foreign Policy, 1995*, 39.

53. See Subcommittee on Terrorism, Narcotics and International Operations, Senate Committee on Foreign Relations, *Drugs, Law Enforcement and Foreign Policy* (Washington, D.C.: U.S. Senate, 1988), and Tim Golden, "To Help Keep Mexico Stable, The U.S. Soft-Peddled Drug War," *New York Times*, July 31, 1995.

54. Think of Richard Nixon warning of the United States becoming a "pitiful, helpless giant." Think of Ronald Reagan and the dangers of Sandinista rule "just two days' driving time" from Texas. Think of George Bush calling Saddam Hussein a greater threat to the United States than Hitler. For myriad examples,

see Eric Alterman, *Sound and Fury: The Washington Punditocracy and the Collapse of American Politics* (New York: HarperCollins, 1992).

55. Cited in Sara Rimer, "Bosnia War Bewilders a Midwestern Town," *New York Times,* July 23, 1995.

CHAPTER 1

1. See Dexter Perkins, "The Department of State and American Public Opinion," in *The Diplomats 1919–1939,* ed. Gordon Craig and Felix Gilbert (Princeton: Princeton University Press, 1953), 298–300.

2. See Melvin Small, "Historians Look at Public Opinion," in *Public Opinion and Historians: Interdisciplinary Perspectives,* ed. Melvin Small (Detroit: Wayne State University, 1970), 16.

3. In another example, Bailey wrote, "But in general the rank and file of the American people were so little concerned with diplomacy that the *New York Sun* could declare in 1889. . . ."See Thomas A. Bailey, *A Diplomatic History of the American People* (New York, 1964), cited in Small, "Historians Look at Public Opinion," 17.

4. See Small, "Historians Look at Public Opinion," 17.

5. See John Tebbel and Sarah Miles Watts, *The Press and the Presidency* (New York: Oxford University Press, 1985), 80.

6. See Bernard C. Cohen, "The Relationship Between Public Opinion and Foreign Policy Maker," in Small, *Public Opinion and Historians,* 76–77.

7. At the war's end, the eligible electorate numbered 60 to 90 percent of free males, with most states edging close to the high end of that range. See Marc W. Kruman, "Suffrage," in *The Reader's Companion to American History,* ed. Eric Foner and John Garraty (Boston: Little, Brown, 1991), 1043–47.

8. See Gordon S. Wood, "Democracy and the American Revolution," in *Democracy: The Unfinished Journey, 508 B.C. to A.D. 1993,* ed. John Dunn (New York: Oxford University Press, 1992), 91–92. See also Gordon S. Wood, *The Creation of the American Republic, 1776–1787* (New York: W. W. Norton, 1969), and *The Radicalism of the American Revolution* (New York: Knopf, 1991).

9. See Richard J. Barnet, *The Rockets' Red Glare: When America Goes to War* (New York: Simon and Schuster, 1990), 25.

10. See Richard D. Brown, *The Strength of the People: The Idea of an Informed Citizenry in America, 1650–1870* (Chapel Hill: University of North Carolina Press, 1997), 64. My calculation is based on average population figures for the colonies in both 1770 and 1780, not including slaves, as published in *Historical Statistics from Colonial Times Through the 1970s* (Washington, D.C.: U.S. Department of Commerce, 1975), 1168.

11. The 1995 edition of the *Oxford Companion to Philosophy* does not even contain an entry for it.

12. John Adams to Mercy Otis Warren, August 8, 1807, cited in Daniel T. Rodgers, "Republicanism: The Career of a Concept," *Journal of American History* 79, no. 1 (1992): 38.

13. See J. G. A. Pocock, *The Machiavellian Moment: Florentine Political Thought and the Atlantic Republican Tradition* (New York: Alfred A. Knopf, 1975), 548.

14. See Barnet, *Rockets' Red Glare,* 50.

15. Quoted in Doris A. Graber, *Public Opinion, the President and Foreign Policy: Four Case Studies from the Formative Years* (New York: Holt, Reinhart and Winston, 1968), 168.

16. Samuel Adams to James Warren, Philadelphia, November 4, 1775, in Warren-Adams Letters: Being chiefly a correspondence among John Adams, Samuel Adams, and James Warren," vol. 72 of *Massachusetts Historical Society Collections* (Boston, 1917), 171–72.

17. See Gordon S. Wood, "Faux Populism," *New Republic,* October 23, 1995, pp. 39–43, and Linda K. Kerber, "The Republican Ideology of the Revolutionary Generation," *American Quarterly* 37 (1985): 474–95.

18. See Joyce Appleby, *Capitalism and a New Social Order: The Republican Vision of the 1790s* (New York: New York University Press, 1984), 16, 21.

19. Quotes are from John Locke, *Second Treatise of Civil Government and a Letter Concerning Toleration,* pp. 123 and 131. See also Kate Caffrey, *The Mayflower* (New York: Stein and Day, 1974), 114–15 and 340–41, and Louis Hartz, *The Liberal Tradition in America* (New York: Harcourt Brace Jovanovich, 1955), chapter 1.

20. Appleby, *Capitalism and a New Social Order,* 3, 16.

21. See Michael J. Sandel, *Democracy's Discontent: America in Search of a Public Philosophy* (Cambridge: Harvard University Press, 1996), 5.

22. Isaac Kramnick's categories work for Hamilton, the Federalist, and Jefferson, the anti-Federalist, but come apart in the more complicated case of Madison. Wood poses an almost equally neat split between the (republican) rulers and the (liberal) ruled. Wood cannot possibly fit Hamilton into his republican mold and so by and large ignores him. Garry Wills would insist on the primacy of the thinkers of the Scottish enlightenment, most notably Francis Hutcheson, over either one. See Garry Wills, *Inventing America: Jefferson's Declaration of Independence* (Garden City, N.Y.: 1978). See also Isaac Kramnick, *Republicanism and Bourgeois Radicalism: Political Ideology in Late Eighteenth Century England and America* (Ithaca, N.Y.: Cornell University Press, 1990), chapter 8; Wood, *Creation of the American Republic;* and Pauline Maier, *From Resistance to Revolution* (New York: Alfred A. Knopf, 1974) for an argument that charts its course along Woodian lines.

23. See Pocock, *The Machiavellian Moment.* See also Kramnick, *Republicanism and Bourgeois Radicalism;* John Patrick Diggins, *The Lost Soul of American Politics: Virtue, Self-Interest and the Foundations of Liberalism* (New York: Basic Books, 1984), chapter 1; and Linda K. Kerber, "Republican Ideology," 474–95.

24. Cited in Wood, "Democracy and the American Revolution," 97.

25. Adams cited in Kramnick, *Republicanism and Bourgeois Radicalism,* 274.

26. Hamilton, from *Federalist 12,* cited in Kramnick, *Republicanism and Bourgeois Radicalism,* 267.

27. Cited in Alfred E. Eckes Jr., *Opening America's Market: U.S. Foreign Trade Policy Since 1776* (Chapel Hill: University of North Carolina Press, 1995), 3.

28. Thomas Paine cited in David M. Fitzsimons, "Tom Paine's New World Order: Idealistic Internationalism in the Ideology of Early American Foreign Relations," *Diplomatic History* 19, no. 4 (1995): 576.

29. Madison to Jefferson, cited in Wood, *Creation of the American Republic*, 424.

30. Jefferson to Joseph Priestley, March 21, 1801, in *The Works of Thomas Jefferson*, vol. 9, ed. Paul Leicester Ford (New York, G. P. Putnam's Sons, 1905), 218.

31. Paine and Reagan are cited in Arthur Schlesinger Jr., "Foreign Policy and the American Character: The Cyril Foster Lecture" in *The Cycles of American History* (Boston: Houghton Mifflin, 1986), 51–68. For Hamilton, see Alexander Hamilton, John Jay, and James Madison, *The Federalist*, ed. Jacob E. Cooke (Middletown, Conn.: Wesleyan University Press, 1961), 3. For Paine's influence, see Fitzsimons, "Tom Paine's New World Order." See also Michael Howard, *War and the Liberal Conscience* (New Brunswick: Transaction, 1977); and Felix Gilbert, *To the Farewell Address: Ideas of Early American Foreign Policy* (Princeton, N.J.: Princeton University Press, 1961). For Franklin, see Benjamin Franklin to Samuel Cooper, May 1, 1777, *The Works of Benjamin Franklin*, ed. John Bigelow (New York: G. P. Putnam's Sons, 1904), 215–16.

32. "I can see no necessity but great inconveniences in sending Ministers abroad and receiving them at home," Elbridge Gerry explained to John Adams in 1783. "The inconveniences of being entangled with European politics, of being the puppets of European statesmen, of being gradually divested of our virtues and republican principles, of being a divided, influenced and dissipated people; of being induced to prefer the splendor of a court to the happiness of our citizens; and finally of changing our form of government from vile Aristocracy or an arbitrary Monarchy." See James H. Huston, "Intellectual Foundations of Early American Diplomacy," *Diplomatic History* 1, no. 1 (1977): 8.

33. *7 Annals of Congress 1798*, 5th Cong., 1119–32; Gerry quoted in Huston, "Intellectual Foundations of Early America, Diplomacy," 8. See also Robert David Johnson, *The Peace Progressives and America Foreign Relations* (Cambridge: Harvard University Press, 1995), 15.

34. George Washington, farewell address, September 17, 1796.

35. See Edward Pessen, *Losing Our Souls* (Chicago: Ivan R. Dee, 1995), 32.

36. James Madison to Thomas Jefferson, April 2, 1798, in *The Writings of James Madison*, 6th ed. (New York: G. P. Putnam's Sons, 1900–1910), 312–13.

37. See Julian Boyd, ed., *The Papers of Thomas Jefferson*, vol. 15 (Princeton, N.J.: Princeton University Press, 1958), p. 397. The conduct of war was antithetical to everything in which the Jeffersonians believed. As Henry Adams phrased it, "The party of Jefferson and Gallatin was founded on the dislike of every function of government necessary in a military system." See Henry Adams, *History of the United States, 1801–1809* (New York: Library of America edition, originally published 1889–91), 648.

38. See Alexander Hamilton, "The Examination, No. 1," December 17, 1801, in *The Papers of Alexander Hamilton*, vol. 25, ed. Henry C. Syrett et. al. (New York: Columbia University Press, 1977), p. 455.

39. See John Hart Ely, *War and Responsibility: Constitutional Lessons of Vietnam and Its Aftermath* (Princeton: Princeton University Press, 1993), 3–4.

40. See Alexander Hamilton, "Federalist Number 6," in Hamilton, John Jay, and James Madison, *The Federalist Papers*, ed. Benjamin Fletcher Wright (Cambridge: Harvard University Press, Belknap Press, 1966), 113.

41. The phrase is taken from Winthrop D. Jordan, *The White Man's Burden* (New York: Oxford University Press, 1974), 132–33.

42. Barnet, *Rockets' Red Glare*, 34.

43. Ibid., 31.

44. Small, *Democracy and Diplomacy*, 5.

45. See Jack N. Rakove, "John Jay," in Foner and Garraty, *Reader's Companion to American History*, 589–90.

46. See Stanley Elkins and Eric McKitrick, *The Age of Federalism: The Early American Republic, 1780–1800* (New York: Oxford University Press), 55.

47. George Washington, farewell address.

48. John M. Orman, *Presidential Secrecy and Deception* (Westport, Conn.: Greenwood Press, 1980), 4.

49. See Sissela Bok, *Secrets: On the Ethics of Concealment and Revelation* (New York: Vintage Books, 1983), 21.

50. See *The Works of John Adams*, vol. 10 (Boston: Little, Brown, 1855–1856), 113. See also Barnet, *Rockets' Red Glare*, 51.

51. See for instance the account in John Patrick Diggins, *The Promise of Pragmatism: Modernism and the Crisis of Knowledge and Authority* (Chicago: University of Chicago Press, 1994), 74.

52. Tom Paine cited in Fitzsimons, "Tom Paine's New World Order," 577–78.

53. See particularly Drew R. McCoy, *The Elusive Republic: Political Economy in Jeffersonian America* (Chapel Hill: University of North Carolina Press, 1980). See also Robert H. Wiebe, *The Opening of American Society: From the Adoption of the Constitution to the Era of Disunion* (New York: Knopf, 1984), chapter 7; and Elkins and McKitrick, *Age of Federalism*, 19.

54. Thomas Jefferson, *Notes on the State of Virginia 1781–85* (Boston: H. Sprague, 1802), 226.

55. Kramnick, *Republicanism and Bourgeois Radicalism*, 179.

56. Jefferson cited in Sandel, *Democracy's Discontent*, 139–40. See also Robert W. Tucker and David C. Hendrickson, *The Empire of Liberty: The Statecraft of Thomas Jefferson* (New York: Oxford University Press, 1990).

57. See Walter LaFeber, "Jefferson and American Foreign Policy," in *Jeffersonian Legacies*, ed. Peter S. Onuf (Charlottesville: University of Virginia Press, 1993), 378–79.

58. Ibid., 374.

59. James Madison cited in William Appleman Williams, "Expansion, Continental and Overseas," in Foner and Garraty, *Reader's Companion to American History*, 365.

60. Quoted in Walter LaFeber, *The American Age: United States Foreign Policy at Home and Abroad since 1750* (New York: W. W. Norton, 1989), 58.

61. Merrill D. Peterson, *Thomas Jefferson and the New Nation: A Biography* (New York: Oxford University Press, 1970), 754.

62. Joyce Appleby, "Introduction: Jefferson and His Complex Legacy," in Onuf, *Jeffersonian Legacies*, 10.
63. See Roger D. Masters, "The Lockean Tradition in American Foreign Policy," *Journal of International Affairs* 21 (1967): 262–63.
64. The term "imagined communities" is Benedict Anderson's. For a further discussion of this point, see Eric Foner, "Liberalism's Discontent," *Nation*, May 6, 1996, 35.
65. For a good discussion of Madison's war message see Graber, *Public Opinion, the President and Foreign Policy*.
66. For a full discussion of these events and their domestic context, see Ernest R. May, *The Making of the Monroe Doctrine* (Cambridge: Harvard University Press, 1975).
67. See Gaddis Smith, *The Last Years of the Monroe Doctrine* (New York: Hill and Wang, 1994), 24.
68. Quoted in Benjamin Schwarz, "The Diversity Myth: America's Leading Export," *Atlantic*, May 1995, 64.
69. See William Earl Weeks, *John Quincy Adams and American Global Empire* (Lexington: University Press of Kentucky, 1992), 3.
70. Adams quoted in William Appleman Williams, "The Age of Mercantilism, 1740–1828," in *William Appleman Williams Reader*, ed. Henry W. Berger (Chicago: Ivan R. Dee, 1992), 215. For Locke's comments, see Masters, "Lockean Tradition in American Foreign Policy," 260.
71. See Williams, "Age of Mercantilism," 216.
72. See Weeks, *John Quincy Adams and American Global Empire*, pp.99, 144, 145.
73. Robert H. Wiebe, *Self-Rule: A Cultural History of American Democracy* (Chicago: University of Chicago Press, 1995), 66.
74. Cited in Barnet, *Rockets' Red Glare*, 78.
75. Tocqueville, *Democracy in America*, 506.
76. Dewey, *The Public and Its Problems* (1927), is cited in Sandel, *Democracy's Discontent*, pp. 204–05.
77. Julius W. Pratt, "The Ideology of American Expansion," in *Essays in Honor of William E. Dodd*, ed. Avery Craven (Chicago: University of Chicago, 1935), 342.
78. LaFeber, *American Age*, 92.
79. Small, *Democracy and Diplomacy*, 16.
80. Cited in Schwarz, "Diversity Myth," 64.
81. Pratt, "Ideology of American Expansion," 344.
82. Tocqueville, *Democracy in America*, 126.
83. See Robert Scigliano, "Politics, the Constitution, and the President's War Power," in *The New Politics of American Foreign Policy*, ed. David A. Deese (New York: St. Martin's Press, 1994), p. 151.
84. John Quincy Adams and the House resolution are both cited in Small, *Democracy and Diplomacy*, 18.
85. Barnet, *Rockets' Red Glare*, 98.
86. See *The Political Thought of Lincoln*, ed. Richard N. Current (Indianapolis: Bobbs-Merril, 1976), 43–44, cited in LaFeber, *American Age*, 118.

87. Weeks, *John Quincy Adams and American Global Empire,* 196. Adams died the day after Polk submitted the Treaty of Guadeloupe Hidalgo to the Senate.

88. Georg Wilhelm Friedrich Hegel, *The Philosophy of History,* trans. J. Sibree (New York: Colonial Press, 1956), 84–87.

89. Cited in Wiebe, *Self-Rule,* 69.

90. See Theodore J. Lowi, *The End of the Republican Era* (Norman: University of Oklahoma Press), 6–7.

91. Bruce D. Porter, *War and the Rise of the State* (New York: Free Press, 1994), 262.

92. Ronald Steel reminds me that Americans do not even have a word for amoral foreign policy behavior. Most use the German "Realpolitik," while the German-born Kissinger prefers the French.

93. Mahan is cited in Anders Stephanson, *Manifest Destiny: American Expansion and the Empire of Right* (New York: Hill and Wang, 1995), 85.

94. The "Open Door" policy, it should be noted, applied only where it applied. In 1914, when the German government insisted on the right to participate in the collection of Haitian customs duties in order to protect German investments, the Wilson administration forgot about the open door and invoked the Monroe Doctrine to preclude not merely military intervention but also "foreign influence or interest proceeding from outside the American hemisphere." See David Steigerwald, *Wilsonian Idealism in America* (Ithaca, N.Y.: Cornell University Press, 1994), 32.

95. David M. Potter, "Economic Abundance and the Formation of American Character," in *The Character of Americans: A Book of Readings,* ed. Michael McGiffert (Homewood, Ill.: Dorsey Press, 1964), 164.

96. Richard Hofstadter noted that the following aspects of western expansion somehow escaped Turner's attention: "the careless, wasteful and exploitative methods of American agriculture . . . the general waste of resources and the desecration of natural beauty; the failure of free lands to produce a society free of landless laborers and tenants . . . the rapacity and meanness so often to be found in the petty capitalism of the new towns . . . the crudeness and disorder, the readiness to commit and willingness to tolerate violence; the frequent ruthlessness of the frontier mind, to which Indians, Spaniards, and Mexicans could testify and which had repeated reverberations in national policies . . . the arrogant, flimsy, and self-righteous justifications of Manifest Destiny engendered by American expansionism." See Richard Hofstadter, *The Progressive Historians: Turner, Beard, Parrington* (New York: Alfred A. Knopf, 1968), 147–48.

97. See William Appleman Williams, "The Frontier Thesis and American Foreign Policy," in *William Appleman Williams Reader,* 93.

98. Emily S. Rosenberg, *Spreading the American Dream: American Economic Expansion, 1890–1945* (New York: Hill and Wang, 1981), 7.

99. Quoted in LaFeber, *American Age,* 200.

100. Tocqueville, *Democracy in America,* 182.

101. See Alfred M. Lee, *The Daily Newspaper in America* (New York: MacMillan, 1937), 80–81.

102. Nearly eighty years later, a thorough investigation of the explosion determined that it had probably been caused by internal combustion, most likely in the

boiler room, rather than deliberate sabotage. See *Washington Post*, July 21, 1983, sec. A, p. 23.

103. See W. David Sloan and James D. Startt, *The Media in America: A History* (Northport, Ala.: Vision Press, 1996), 292.

104. On February 25, a few days later, the same paper contained the headlines, "Sections Widely Apart Welded by Common Impulse to Avenge Heroes of the Maine"; "Wherever Americans Gather with Patriotism—Every State Ready to Spring to Arms at a Moment's Notice." See Charles H. Brown, *The Correspondents' War: Journalists in the Spanish-American War* (New York: Charles Scribner's Sons, 1967), 129–30.

105. See Ernest R. May, *Imperial Democracy: The Emergence of America as a Great Power* (New York: Harcourt, Brace, 1961), 118. See also Walter LaFeber, *The New Empire: An Interpretation of American Expansion, 1860–1898* (Ithaca, N.Y.: Cornell University Press, 1967).

106. In fact, a 1976 U.S. naval report concluded that the battleship was probably destroyed by heat from a fire in a coal bunker adjacent to the reserve magazine. See H. G. Rickover, *How the Battleship* Maine *Was Destroyed* (Naval History Division/Department of the Navy, 1976). See also Hugh Thomas, "Remember the Maine?" *New York Review of Books*, April 23, 1998, 12.

107. Barnet, *Rockets' Red Glare*, 129.

108. The quotes are taken from Small, *Democracy and Diplomacy*, 29. The full story of the various economic pressures leading to war can be found in LaFeber, *New Empire*.

109. See Stephanson, *Manifest Destiny*, 77.

110. Roosevelt quoted in LaFeber, *American Age*, 190.

111. See Brown, *Correspondents' War*, 144.

112. Barnet, *Rockets' Red Glare*, 134.

113. William James quoted in Robert Beisner, *Twelve Against Empire* (Chicago: University of Chicago Press, 1986), 41.

114. See Stephanson, *Manifest Destiny*, 75–80.

115. Quoted in Rosenberg, *Spreading the American Dream*, 41.

CHAPTER 2

1. His successors, William Howard Taft and Woodrow Wilson, continued this practice at an accelerated rate.

2. See John Milton Cooper, *The Warrior and the Priest: Woodrow Wilson and Theodore Roosevelt* (Cambridge: Harvard University Press, 1983), 286.

3. For a useful discussion of Roosevelt's thought, see Stephanson, *Manifest Destiny*, 86–88.

4. Woodrow Wilson, *The Public Papers of Woodrow Wilson*, vol. 7, ed. Arthur S. Link et al. (Princeton, N.J.: Princeton University Press, 1966) 352.

5. See, particularly, Thomas J. Knock, *To End All Wars: Woodrow Wilson and the Quest for a New World Order* (New York: Oxford University Press, 1992).

6. See Stephanson, *Manifest Destiny*, 104–111
7. Woodrow Wilson, an address in the Princess Theater, Cheyenne, Wyoming, September 24, 1919, in Link, *Public Papers of Woodrow Wilson*, vol. 63, 474.
8. Arthur Schlesinger Jr., "Foreign Policy and the American Character," in *The Cycles of American History* (Boston: Houghton Mifflin, 1986), 54. See also Lawrence E. Gelfand, "Where Ideals Confront Self-Interest: Wilsonian Foreign Policy," *Diplomatic History* 18, no. 1 (1994): 127–31.
9. See Tony Smith, *America's Mission: The United States and the Worldwide Struggle for Democracy in the Twentieth Century* (Princeton, N.J.: Princeton University Press, 1994), 60.
10. On his return from Paris in 1919, Wilson told an audience of supporters that the League of Nations was closely related to Washington's "utterance about entangling alliances. . . . And the thing that [Washington] . . . longed for was just what we are about to supply: an arrangement which will disentangle all the alliances in the world." See Lloyd C. Gardner, "Ideology and American Foreign Policy," in *Ideology and Foreign Policy: A Global Perspective*, ed. George Schwab (New York: Cyrco Press, 1978), 135.
11. See Henry A. Kissinger, *Diplomacy* (New York: Simon and Schuster, 1994), 45.
12. See Perry Miller, *Errand into the Wilderness* (Cambridge: Harvard University Press, Belknap Press, 1956), and Sacvan Baercovitch, *The American Jeremiad* (Madison: University of Wisconsin Press, 1978), chapter 6 See also Michael Paul Rogin, *The Intellectuals and McCarthy* (Cambridge: MIT Press, 1967), 276. Melville is quoted in Stephanson, *Manifest Destiny*, 129.
13. See Roger D. Masters, "The Lockean Tradition in American Foreign Policy," *Journal of International Affairs* 21 (1967): 260.
14. John Adams cited in Fitzsimons, "Tom Paine's New World Order," 574.
15. On this point see Hans J. Morgenthau, "The Organic Relationship between Ideology and Political Reality," in Schwab, *Ideology and Foreign Policy*, 118–22.
16. Woodrow Wilson cited in Williams, "Expansion, Continental and Overseas," 366.
17. See Robert Wiebe, *The Search for Order, 1877–1920* (New York: Hill and Wang, 1967). See also Gabriel Kolko, *The Triumph of Conservatism* (Glencoe, Ill.: Free Press of Glencoe, 1963); Samuel Hays, "The Politics of Reform in Municipal Government in the Progressive Era," *Pacific Northwest Quarterly* 55 (1964): 157–69;, James Weinstein, *The Decline of American Socialism 1912–1925* (New York: Monthly Review Press, 1967); Christopher Lasch, *The New Radicalism in America, 1889–1963: The Intellectual as Social Type* (New York: Random House, 1965); and Robert M. Crunden, "Progressivism," in Foner and Garraty, *Reader's Companion*, 868–70.
18. Barnet, *Rockets' Red Glare*, 145.
19. DeConde, *Ethnicity, Race and American Foreign Policy*, 53.
20. Barnet, *Rockets' Red Glare*, 145.
21. Wilson cited in Gardner, "Ideology and American Foreign Policy," in Schwab, *Ideology and Foreign Policy*, 139.

22. Robert Dallek, *The American Style of Foreign Policy: Cultural Politics and Foreign Affairs* (New York: Alfred A. Knopf, 1983), 29.

23. See John Patrick Diggins, "Republicanism and Progressivism," *American Quarterly* 37 (1985): 581.

24. Herbert Croly, *The Promise of American Life* (Hamden, Conn.: Archon, 1963), 23. See also David Levy, *Herbert Croly of the* New Republic (Princeton: Princeton University Press, 1985).

25. Croly, *Promise of American Life*, 414.

26. Cited in Wiebe, *Self-Rule*, 172.

27. Cited in Christopher Caldwell, "The Nationals vs. The Locals," in *Wall Street Journal*, June 20, 1995, sec. A, p. 22.

28. Croly is quoted in Walter A. McDougall, *Promised Land, Crusader State: The American Encounter with the World Since 1776* (New York: Houghton-Mifflin, 1996), 120.

29. Dallek, *American Style of Foreign Policy*, 31.

30. Ibid., 113–14.

31. "The End of American Isolation," *New Republic*, November 7, 1914, reprinted in *The New Republic Reader*, ed. Dorothy Wickenden (New York: Basic Books, 1994), 27.

32. Cited in Ronald Steel, *Walter Lippmann and the American Century* (Boston: Little, Brown, 1980), 109.

33. Walter Lippmann cited in David Steigerwald, *Wilsonian Idealism in America* (Ithaca, N.Y.: Cornell University Press, 1994), 51.

34. Cited in Robert B. Westbrook, *John Dewey and American Democracy* (Ithaca, N.Y.: Cornell University Press, 1991), 204.

35. Ibid., 205.

36. Randolph Bourne, "The War and the Intellectuals," cited in Westbrook, *John Dewey and American Democracy*, 313.

37. See Arno Mayer, *The Political Origins of the New Diplomacy, 1917–1918* (New Haven: Yale University Press, 1959), 350.

38. Cited in Henry Steele Commager, *Commager on Tocqueville* (Columbia: University of Missouri Press, 1993), 56.

39. Robert C. Hilderbrand, *Power and the People: Executive Management of Public Opinion in Foreign Affairs, 1897–1921* (Chapel Hill: University of North Carolina Press , 1981), 141.

40. Herbert Gutman quoted in Elizabeth McKillen, "Historical Contingency and the Peace Progressives" *Diplomatic History* 20, no.1 (1996): 119.

41. For a thorough discussion of these issues, see Robert David Johnson, *The Peace Progressives and American Foreign Relations* (Cambridge: Harvard University Press, 1995).

42. Bruce D. Porter, *War and the Rise of the State* (New York: Free Press, 1994), 272–74.

43. Barnet, *Rockets' Red Glare*, 158–59.

44. Porter, *War and Rise of the State*, 272–74.

45. See Arno Mayer, *The Political Origins of the New Diplomacy, 1917–1918* (New Haven: Yale University Press, 1959), 357.

46. See Edward Hallett Carr, *The Twenty Years Crisis, 1919–1939* (London: Macmillan, 1940), 50.

47. See Walter Lippmann, *A Preface to Politics* (1913; rpt. Ann Arbor: University of Michigan Press, 1969), and *Drift and Mastery: An Attempt to Diagnose the Current Unrest*, ed. William E. Leuchtenburg (Englewood Cliffs, N.J.: Prentice-Hall, 1961; originally published in 1914).

48. See *New Republic*, May 3, 1922, 286–86.

49. See Walter Lippmann, *A Preface to Morals* (New York: Macmillan, 1929), 278–79.

50. See Lippmann, *Public Opinion*, 228.

51. Ibid., 55.

52. See Walter Lippmann, *Liberty and the News* (New York: Harcourt, Brace and Howe, 1920), 38–41.

53. See Walter Lippmann, *The Phantom Public* (New York: MacMillan, 1924), 13–14.

54. See Lippmann, *Public Opinion*, 164.

55. Ibid., 145–47.

56. Ibid., 197.

57. John Patrick Diggins, "Republicanism and Progressivism," *American Quarterly* 37, no. 4 (1985): 572–98.

58. Lippmann's antidemocratic ethos continued to evolve throughout the next three decades. See, for instance, Walter Lippmann, *Essays in the Public Philosophy* (Boston: Atlantic, Little, Brown, 1955), 26.

59. See Lippmann, *Public Opinion*, 196–97.

60. Ibid., 230.

61. John Dewey, *The Public and Its Problems* (New York: H. Holt, 1927).

62. See William A. Galston, "Salvation through Participation: John Dewey and the Religion of Democracy," *Raritan* 12 (1993): 158. See also Westbrook, *John Dewey and American Democracy*, 310.

63. John Dewey cited in Hilary Putnam, *Renewing Philosophy* (Cambridge: Harvard University Press, 1992), 188–89.

64. See Dewey, *Public and Its Problems*, 368.

65. Ibid., 110.

66. Ibid., 98.

67. Ibid., 122–23.

68. Ibid., 158. See also James W. Carey, *Communication as Culture: Essays on Media and Society* (Boston: Unwin Hyman, 1989), 79.

69. See Dewey, *Public and Its Problems*, 371. See also Christopher Lasch, "The Lost Art of Argument," in *The Revolt of the Elites and the Betrayal of Democracy* (New York: W. W. Norton, 1994), 172.

70. See Dewey, *Public and Its Problems*, 158.

71. The felicitous phraseology belongs to Jay Rosen, *The Impossible Press: American Journalism and the Decline of Public Life* (Ph.D. diss., New York University, 1986), 348. For a useful discussion of the larger issues involved, see James M. Carey, "A Republic If You Can Keep It," in *James Carey: A Critical Reader*, ed. Eve

Stryker Munson and Catherine A. Warren (Minneapolis: University of Minnesota Press, 1997), 220.

72. For the complete story, see Steel, *Walter Lippmann and the American Century*, and Eric Alterman, *Sound and Fury: The Washington Punditocracy and the Collapse of American Politics* (New York: HarperCollins, 1992), chapters 1–3.

73. See Dewey, *Public and Its Problems*, 313.

74. John Dewey cited in Putnam, "A Reconsideration of Deweyan Democracy," 199.

75. To be fair, Dewey did devote himself to the creation of an education system that would inculcate the necessary skills for democratic citizenry in its students. But this too proved overly optimistic.

76. Barnet, *Rockets' Red Glare*, 197–98.

77. See Thomas Ferguson, "From Normalcy to New Deal," *International Organization* 38 (1984): 41–94.

78. See Bill Kauffman, *America First: Its History, Culture and Politics* (Amherst, N.Y.: Prometheus Books, 1995).

79. See Arthur M. Schlesinger Jr., "America and the World, Isolationism Resurgent," (New York: Carnegie Council on Ethics and International Affairs, 1995), 8.

80. See Louis Fisher, *Presidential War Power* (Lawrence : University of Kansas Press, 1995), 63.

81. Richard W. Steele, "The Great Debate: Roosevelt, the Media, and the Coming of the War, 1940–1941," *Journal of American History* 71, no. 1 (1984): 78–79.

82. Cited in Norman L. Hill, *The New Democracy in Foreign Policy Making* (Lincoln: University of Nebraska Press, 1970), 5.

83. Kennan's remarks were delivered extemporaneously to the April 17, 1974, meeting of the Organization of American Historians in Denver and are cited in Warren F. Kimball, *The Juggler: Franklin Roosevelt as Wartime Statesman* (Princeton, N.J.: Princeton University Press, 1991), 18.

84. See Churchill and Roosevelt, *The Complete Correspondence*, vol. 1, ed. Warren Kimball (Princeton, N.J.: Princeton University Press, 1984), 227–31. The document in question is titled "British War Cabinet Minutes, 19 August 1941," CAB6584(41).

85. See William L. Langer and S. Everett Gleason, *The Undeclared War, 1940–1941* (New York: Harper & Bros., 1953), 742–50.

86. Arthur Macy Cox, *The Myths of National Security: The Peril of Secret Government* (Boston: Beacon Press, 1975), 37.

87. This argument is made most forcefully in Robert Dallek, *Franklin D. Roosevelt and American Foreign Policy 1932–1945* (New York: Oxford University Press, 1979), and John Lewis Gaddis, *The United States and the Origins of the Cold War* (New York: Columbia University Press, 1972).

88. In 1937 in *United States v. Belmont*, the Supreme Court ruled that an executive agreement was the equivalent of a treaty and that in certain cases a president's will could replace state law. The president, ruled the court, held "the very delicate, plenary and exclusive power . . . as the sole organ of the federal government in the field of international relations—a field which does not require as a

basis for its exercise an act of Congress." See Walter LaFeber, "The Constitution and Foreign Policy," *Journal of American History* 74, no. 3 (1987): 711.

89. See Barnet , *Rockets' Red Glare*, 211.

90. See Walter LaFeber, *The American Age: United States Foreign Policy at Home and Abroad since 1750* (New York: W. W. Norton and Co., 1989) 382. See also Barnet, *Rockets' Red Glare*, 214; Dallek, *Roosevelt and American Foreign Policy;* and Kimball, *Juggler.*

91. Quoted in LaFeber, *American Age*, 382.

92. Ibid., 386. See also Dallek, *Roosevelt and American Foreign Policy*, 312–13. Roosevelt also frequently exaggerated to the American people their nation's vulnerability. He vastly overstated the number of aircraft the Axis powers possessed as well as their rate of production. In April 1939, he warned U.S. newspaper editors that "the totalitarian nations . . . have 1,500 planes today. They cannot hop directly across our 3,000 miles but they can do it in three hops. . . . It would take planes based at Yucatan, modern bombing planes about an hour and fifty minutes to smash up New Orleans." A year later, addressing the same audience, he repeated the point in much the same terms, though now he claimed that "the European unmentioned country" in question "could put 5,000 bombing planes into Brazil." John A. Thompson, "The Exaggeration of American Vulnerability: The Anatomy of a Tradition," *Diplomatic History* 16, no. 1 (1992): 28.

93. Barnet, *Rockets' Red Glare*, 207.

94. Richard W. Steele, "The Great Debate: Roosevelt, the Media, and the Coming of the War, 1940–1941," *Journal of American History* 71, no. 1 (1984): 71–75.

95. Cited in Small, *Democracy and Diplomacy*, 75–76.

96. Steele, "The Great Debate," 81–85.

97. Cox, *The Myths of National Security:*

98. See Gar Alperovitz, *The Decision to Use the Atomic Bomb and the Architecture of an American Myth* (New York: Alfred A. Knopf, 1995), 614.

99. "Secretary O'Leary Releases Classified Documents on Nuclear Testing, Radiation Releases, Fusion," *DOE This Month* 16, no.12 (December 1994): 3. The true figure may be as high as 130 million pages. See *Secrecy and Government Bulletin* 46 (1995).

100. See Charles A. Beard, "Giddy Minds and Foreign Quarrels: An Estimate of American Foreign Policy," *Harper's*, September 1939, 349–50.

CHAPTER 3

1. For an interesting though possibly overstated argument of this thesis, see David Campbell, *Writing Security: United States Foreign Policy and the Politics of Identity* (Minneapolis: University of Minnesota Press, 1992).

2. See *Foreign Relations of the United States, 1950*, vol. 1 (Washington, D.C.: U.S. Department of State, 1950), 244.

3. See Louis Hartz, *The Liberal Tradition in America: An Interpretation of American Political Thought since the Revolution* (New York: Harcourt, Brace & World, 1955), 5.

4. Cited in Athan Theoharis, *Spying on Americans: Political Surveillance from Hoover to the Huston Plan* (Philadelphia: Temple University Press, 1978), 6.

5. Cited in Harry Howe Ransom, *Can American Democracy Survive the Cold War?* (Garden City: Doubleday, 1963), 12–13.

6. David Wise, *The Politics of Lying: Government Deception, Secrecy and Power* (New York: Random House, 1973), 66.

7. Tim Weiner, "President Moves to Release Classified Documents," *New York Times*, May 5, 1993.

8. See Michael Jay Singer, "United States," in *Administrative Secrecy in Developed Counties*, ed. Donald C. Rowat (New York: Columbia University Press, 1979), 314.

9. See *Nuclear Wastelands*, ed. Arjun Makhijani, Howard Hu, and Katherine Yih (Cambridge: MIT Press, 1995), xxi–xxii, 3.

10. "Atomic Secrets," *New York Times*, editorial page, May 1, 1994.

11. See Thomas G. Paterson, "Thought Control and the Writing of History," in *Freedom at Risk: Secrecy, Censorship and Repression in the 1980s*, ed. Richard O. Curry (Philadelphia: Temple University Press, 1988), 67–68.

12. In October 1997, almost fifty years after its creation, the CIA finally confirmed a spending figure for its overall budget, though it continued to resist any further breakdown. See R. Jeffrey Smith, "Under Pressure, CIA Breaks Overall Figure Out of Fog of Secrecy," *Washington Post*, October 16, 1997, sec.A, page 9.

13. Fisher, *Presidential War Power*, 155.

14. See Theodore Draper, *A Very Thin Line: The Iran Contra Affairs* (New York: Hill and Wang, 1991), 8.

15. Edward R. Pessen, "Appraising American Cold War Policy By Its Means of Implementation," *Reviews in American History* 18 (1990): 453–65.

16. Some actions, such as a ban on assassinations, were undertaken during the Ford administration and remain in effect today. But the CIA still felt empowered to issue assassination manuals to the Contras barely more than a decade later, so the reforms cannot be said to have changed behavior much.

17. John Ranelagh, *The Agency: The Rise and Decline of the CIA* (New York: Simon and Schuster, 1987), 585.

18. See Mark J. Gasirowski, "The 1953 Coup D'etat in Iran," *International Journal of Middle East Studies* 19 (1987): 261–86. See also James A. Bill, *The Eagle and the Lion: The Tragedy of American-Iranian Relations* (New Haven: Yale University Press, 1988).

19. See Tim Weiner, "CIA Destroyed Files on 1953 Coup," *New York Times*, May 19, 1997, sec. A, p. 19.

20. See Stephen Schlesinger and Stephen Kinzer, *Bitter Fruit: The Untold Story of the American Coup in Guatemala* (New York: Doubleday, 1982), 217. See also Richard Immerman, *The CIA in Guatemala: The Foreign Policy of Intervention* (Austin: University of Texas Press, 1982); Piero Gleijeses, *Shattered Hope: The Guatemalan Revolution and the United States, 1944–1954* (Princeton, N.J.: Princeton University Press, 1991); and Nicholas Cullather, *The CIA's Secret History of Its Guatemalan Coup* (Stanford, Calif.: Stanford University Press, 1998).

21. See Theodore Draper, "Is the CIA Necessary?" *New York Review of Books* 45, no. 3 (1997): 18–23. See also *Nation,* July 14, 1997, 3. The lawsuit was brought by Stephen Schlesinger, co-author of *Bitter Fruit.*
22. Richard M. Bissell Jr. with Jonathan E. Lewis and Frances T. Pudlo, *Reflections of a Cold Warrior: From Yalta to the Bay of Pigs* (New Haven: Yale University Press, 1997). 90.
23. Ranelagh, *The Agency,* 333.
24. Agency notification of the Senate Intelligence Committee consisted, according to its then vice chairman, Daniel Moynihan, of "a single sentence in a two-hour Committee meeting and a singularly obscure sentence at that. In no event was the briefing 'full,' 'current,' or 'prior' as required by the Intelligence Oversight Act." See Cynthia J. Arnson, *Crossroads* (New York: Pantheon, 1989), 166.
25. *Documents of American History I,* ed. Henry Steele Commager and Milton Cantor (Englewood Cliffs, N.J.: Prentice Hall, 1988), 176.
26. Cited in Dumas Malone, *Jefferson and His Time* (Boston: Little, Brown, 1962), 176.
27. Cited in Ted Galen Carpenter, *The Captive Press: Foreign Policy Crises and the First Amendment* (Washington, D.C.: Cato Institute, 1995), 17–18.
28. Ibid.
29. Robert K. Murray, *Red Scare: A Study in National Hysteria, 1919–1920* (New York: McGraw Hill, 1955), 12–14.
30. A September 1946 Gallup poll found respondents favoring Henry Wallace's more cooperative approach to Truman's, 78 percent to 16 percent. As late as February 1947, just a month before the announcement of the Truman Doctrine, more than 70 percent of those polled opposed a "Get tough with Russia" policy. See Lawrence S. Wittner, *American Intervention in Greece* (New York: Columbia University Press, 1982), 341.
31. See Richard M. Freeland, *The Truman Doctrine and the Origins of McCarthyism* (New York: New York University Press, 1985), 11.
32. Clark Clifford cited in Barnet, *Rockets' Red Glare,* 280–81.
33. Truman is quoted in Small, *Democracy and Diplomacy,* 82.
34. Cited in Anthan Theoharis, "The Escalation of the Loyalty Program," in *Politics and Policies of the Truman Administration,* ed. Barton J. Bernstein (Chicago: Quadrangle, 1970), 244–45.
35. Ibid., 249–52.
36. Ibid.
37. For details, see Edward R. Pessen, *Losing Our Souls: The American Experience in the Cold War* (Chicago: Ivan R. Dee, 1993). For the CIA's role in these activities, see Angus Mackenzie, *Secrets: The CIA's War at Home* (Berkeley: University of California Press, 1997); Ranelagh, *The Agency;* and Rhodri Jeffreys-Jones, *The CIA and American Democracy* (New Haven: Yale University Press, 1995).
38. See James Hershberg, *James B. Conant: Harvard to Hiroshima and the Making of the Nuclear Age* (New York: Alfred A, Knopf, 1993), 606–37.
39. Cited in David Oshinsky, "The CIO and the Communists," in *The Specter: Original Essays on the Cold War and the Origins of McCarthyism,* ed. William R. Tender (New York: New Viewpoints, 1974), 275.

40. See Ellen W. Schrecker, "Anticommunism," in Foner and Garraty, *Reader's Companion to American History*, 38. See also Stephen J. Whitfield, *The Culture of the Cold War* (Baltimore: Johns Hopkins University Press, 1991), 14–15.

41. Whitfield, *Culture of the Cold War*, 69.

42. Cited in Small, *Democracy and Diplomacy*, 84.

43. Senate Judiciary Committee Subcommittee on Separation of Powers, *Executive Privilege: The Withholding of Information by the Executive*, Hearings, 92d Cong., 1st sess., 1971 (Washington, D.C.: Government Printing Office, 1972), 347.

44. See Eric A. Nordlinger, *Isolationism Reconfigured: American Foreign Policy for a New Century* (Princeton, N.J.: Princeton University Press, 1995), 245.

45. See Hans Kelsen, *The Law of the United Nations* (New York: Praeger, 1951), 755.

46. Robert H. Bork, "Comments on the Articles on the Legality of the United States Action in Cambodia," *American Journal of International Law* 79 (1971): 529.

47. Cited in Bruce Cumings, "When Sparta Is Sparta but Athens Isn't Athens: Democracy and the Korean War," talk delivered during conference of Cold War and classical scholars at the Woodrow Wilson Center, Washington D.C., May 31 to June 2. See also Fisher, *Presidential War Power*, 85–86, and Walter LaFeber, "NATO and the Korean War," *Diplomatic History* 13 (1989): 461–78.

48. Fisher, *Presidential War Power*, 97.

49. Ibid., 102. Arthur Schlesinger Jr., among others, argued the legality of Truman's actions at the time they were undertaken. As would become the custom with nearly all such defenses, Schlesinger hearkened back to Thomas Jefferson's use of the navy against the Barbary pirates, which was not accompanied by a declaration of war. Schlesinger neglected to note, however, that Jefferson explained any such action that went "beyond the line of defense" was, in his view "unauthorized by the Constitution without the sanction of Congress." Congress ultimately enacted ten statutes authorizing Jefferson and Madison to take action in these wars. See Arthur Schlesinger Jr., "Presidential Powers: Taft Statement on Troops Opposed Actions of Past Presidents Cited," *New York Times*, January 9, 1951, and Fisher, *Presidential War Power*, 90.

50. Cited in Small, *Democracy and Diplomacy*, 93.

51. See *The Pentagon Papers* (New York: New York Times, 1971), 287.

52. See Fisher, *Presidential War Power*, 116. See also *Congressional Record*, 110th Cong., 1964. 18399.

53. See John Hart Ely, *War and Responsibility: Constitutional Lessons of Vietnam and Its Aftermath* (Princeton, N.J.: Princeton University Press, 1993), 61. See also Ely's brilliant discussion of the act, 115–38.

54. Cited in Carpenter, *Captive Press*, 42.

55. "Potsdam Censorship Hit," *New York Times*, July 20, 1945.

56. Theodore F. Koop, *Weapon of Silence* (Chicago: University of Chicago Press, 1946), 270.

57. J. Fred MacDonald, *Television and the Red Menace: The Road to Vietnam* (New York: Praeger, 1985), 16–17.

58. See Freeland, *Truman Doctrine*, 137–38.

59. See Jonathan Kwitney, *Endless Enemies: The Making of an Unfriendly World* (New York: Congdon and Weed, 1984), 175–76.

60. See Schlesinger and Kinzer, *Bitter Fruit,* 154.

61. Cited in Carpenter, *Captive Press,* 51.

62. MacDonald, *Television and the Red Menace,* 16–17.

63. Michael Beschloss, *Mayday, Eisenhower, Khruschev, and the U-2 Affair* (New York: Harper and Row, 1986), 234–35.

64. Lester Markel, "The 'Management' of News," *Saturday Review,* February 9, 1963, 51.

65. Cited in Ransom, *Can American Democracy Survive the Cold War?* 242–43.

66. Cited in James D. Aronson, *The Press and the Cold War* (Indianapolis: Bobbs-Merril, 1970), 244.

67. See Lawrence W. Lichty, "Comments on the Influence of Television on Public Opinion," in *Vietnam as History,* ed. Peter Braestrup (Washington, D.C.: Woodrow Wilson Center, 1984), 158. See also Daniel C. Hallin, *The "Uncensored War": The Media and Vietnam* (New York: Oxford University Press, 1986), and William M. Hammond, *The Military and the Media: The U.S. Army in Vietnam* (Washington, D.C.: Center for Military History, United States Army, 1988).

68. Bob Woodward, "Inman Statements Surprise Some Former Confidants in Media." *Washington Post,* January 21, 1994.

69. *Harper's,* the *Nation, Mother Jones,* and others undertook to sue the government to remove this censorship during the war. None of the television networks or national daily newspapers saw fit to join the action.

70. See Marie Gottschalk, "Operation Desert Cloud: The Media and the Gulf War," *World Policy Journal* 9, no. 2 (1992): 454.

71. See John Stuart Mill, *Considerations on Representative Government* (South Bend, Ind.: Gateway Editions, 1962), 34.

72. Sissela Bok, *Lying: Moral Choices in Public and Private Life* (New York: Vintage, 1978, 1989), 139, 150.

73. On the "might have been" question, see chapter 10 of Ellen Schrecker, *Many Are the Crimes: McCarthyism in America* (Boston: Little, Brown, 1998).

74. See Wise, *The Politics of Lying,* 49–50.

75. Ibid., 55.

CHAPTER 4

1. Quoted in Bob Woodward, *The Agenda: Inside the Clinton White House* (New York: Simon and Schuster, 1994), 84.

2. This episode led presidential advisor James Carville to crow that when he died, he wanted to return as the international bond market, because it appeared to have even more power than God.

3. Stanley Hoffmann, "The Crisis of Liberal Internationalism," *Foreign Policy* 98 (1995): 175–76.

4. Thomas Friedman, "Foreign Affairs," *New York Times,* September 29, 1997.

5. Quoted in the *New York Times*, March 15, 1995, sec. A, p. 25.

6. The package included $20 billion from the U.S. currency stabilization fund, a $17.8 billion contribution demanded from the International Monetary Fund, and another $10 million requisitioned from the Bank of International Settlements in Basel by Alan Greenspan. Martin Walker, speaking for almost unanimous elite opinion, called the move "a bold display of leadership in the new strategic arena of global finance in the way that other presidents had acted decisively in the geopolitical causes of the *Cold War*." See Martin Walker, *The President We Deserve: Bill Clinton, His Rise, Falls and Comebacks* (New York: Crown Books, 1996), 301.

7. See Barnaby J. Feder, "Last U.S. TV Maker Will Sell Control to Koreans," *New York Times*, July 18, 1995.

8. Peter Drucker, "Trade Lessons from the World Economy" *Foreign Affairs* 73, no. 1 (1994): 100,

9. Peter Cowhey and Jonathan Aronson, "A New Global Economic Order" *Foreign Affairs* 72, no. 1 (1993): 77.

10. Martin Conroy, "Multinationals in a Changing World Economy: Whither the Nation State?" in Carnoy, Manuel Castells, Stephen S. Cohen, and Fenado Henrique Cardoso, *The New Global Economy in the Information Age*" (University Park, Pa.: Penn. State University Press, 1994), 46.

11. Conroy, "Multinationals in a Changing World Economy," 48.

12. See David Vogel, "The Triumph of Liberal Trade: American Trade Policy in the Post-War Period," presented at The Usefulness of History Conference at the Woodrow Wilson Center, Washington, D.C., December 2, 1994, 16.

13. Bureau of Labor Statistics, 1997 figures, published in the *New York Times*, November 10, 1997, sec. D, p. 1.

14. Quoted in the *Wall Street Journal*, September 25, 1994.

15. During the Vietnam era, the United States government regularly turned a blind eye to heroin smuggling into the country deriving from anticommunist allies in the "Golden Triangle." In the 1980s, it did the same for allies and cronies in Central America, Afghanistan, and Pakistan vis-à-vis their own nefarious narcotic business activities. During the 1990s, the Bush and Clinton administrations deliberately overlooked the involvement of the Mexican government in cocaine smuggling into the United States in order to safeguard the passage of the NAFTA accords. See United States Senate Committee on Foreign Relations Subcommittee on Terrorism, Narcotics and International Operations, "Drugs, Law Enforcement and Foreign Policy" (Washington, D.C.: U.S. Senate, 1988), and Tim Golden, "To Help Keep Mexico Stable, The U.S. Soft-Peddled Drug War," *New York Times*, July 31, 1995.

16. Franklin and Jefferson cited in Eckes, *Opening America's Markets*, 2.

17. Thomas Paine, "Rights of Man," in *Complete Writings of Thomas Paine*, vol. 1, ed. Philip S. Foner (New York, 1945), 359.

18. George Washington cited in Eckes, *Opening America's Markets*, 15.

19. Madison cited in Michael J. Sandel, *Democracy's Discontent*, 139.

20. See Keller, "Trade Policy in Historical Perspective," presented at "The Usefulness of History" Conference at the Woodrow Wilson Center, Washington, D.C., December 2, 1994, 4.

21. Ibid., 6.

22. Theodore Roosevelt cited in Eckes, *Opening America's Markets*, 30.

23. See George M. Fisk, "The Payne-Aldrich Tariff," *Political Science Quarterly* 25 (1910): 35–68. See also Keller, "Trade Policy in Historical Perspective," 15.

24. "Except for the Underwood schedules during World War I, no tariff before or after Smoot-Hawley permitted such a large percentage of US imports, by value, to enter duty free." See Eckes, *Opening America's Markets*, 109.

25. See Keller, "Trade Policy in Historical Perspective," 26–27.

26. See Eckes, *Opening America's Markets*, 24. For the figures on Britain's economic growth between 1870 and 1913, see 52.

27. See Dani Rodrik, *Has Globalization Gone Too Far?* (Washington, D.C.: Institute for International Economics, 1997). See also Jeff Faux, "Hedging the Neoliberal Bet," *Dissent*, Fall 1997, 121.

28. Niskanen cited in John Gerard Ruggie, *Winning the Peace: America and World Order in the New Era* (New York: Columbia University Press, 1996), 122.

29. See David Yoffe, "American Trade Policy: An Obsolete Bargain," in *Can the Government Govern?* Ed, John Chubb and Paul Peterson (Washington, D.C.: Brookings Institution Press, 1989), 117–18.

30. *New York Times*, September 29, 1994, op-ed page.

31. See, for instance, Max Frankel, "And at the fringes, left and right, stand the guardians of an illusory American 'sovereignty,' railing against the new World Trade Organization because it will not give any nation a veto in the resolution of disputes." Quoted from "Beyond the Shroud," *New York Times Magazine*, May 19, 1995, 30. Frankel is the *Times*'s former executive editor.

32. Patrick Buchanan, *Washington Post*, Nov. 7, 1993, sec. C, p. 1.

33. For polling figures, see Walker, *The President We Deserve*, 292.

34. Two important exceptions to this statement are Jeff Faux of the Economic Policy Institute in Washington, D.C., and James Fallows, Washington editor of the *Atlantic Monthly* and later editor-in-chief of *U.S. News and World Report*.

35. Richard W. Stevenson, "Report to Congress Says Nafta Benefits Are Modest, *New York Times*, July 11, 1997, sec. D, p. 1.

36. David R. Obey, Chairman, Staff of the Joint Economic Committee, "Potential Economic Impacts of NAFTA: An Assessment of the Debate," November 1993, 25.

37. See S. M. Lipset and William Schneider, *The Confidence Gap: Business, Labor, and Government in the Public Mind*, rev. ed. (Baltimore: Johns Hopkins University Press, 1987), 17.

38. *New York Times*, Sept. 30, 1994, sec. D, p. 4.

39. In fact, Gary Hufbauer of the pro-NAFTA International Institute for Economics estimated that the United States had lost 225,000 jobs to Mexico owing to the falling cost of labor there following the peso's collapse. See Bob Davis, "Two Years Later, the Promises Used to Sell Nafta Haven't Come True, but Its Foes Were Wrong, Too," *Wall Street Journal*, October 26, 1995, sec. A, p. 24.

40. Martin Walker calls this "NAFTA's dirty little secret. It would benefit the 100 million Americans in a household headed by a college graduate, who were doing very well out of the global economy and the new U.S. export miracle. But

it would not help the 50 million or so in the underclass, and would also threaten the 100 million blue-collar and lower-middle-class white-collar workers in the middle. These were the very people who had elected Bill Clinton. . . ." See Walker, *The President We Deserve*, 294.

41. See Amy Waldman, "Class Not Race," *Washington Monthly*, November 1995, 26; Howard Kurtz, *Washington Post*, Friday, November 19, 1993; and author's interview with senior White House official.

42. *Congressional Record*, November 29, 1994, H11489.

43. Lawrence Tribe quoted in *Washington Post*, October 6, 1994.

44. See Stuart Auerbach and Edward Cody, "Boom Over the Border: U.S. Firms Go to Mexico," *Washington Post*, May 17, 1992. See also Robert A. Bleckner and William E. Spriggs, *Manufacturing Employment in North America* (Washington, D.C.: Economic Policy Institute, 1992), 2.

45. Obey, "Potential Economic Impacts of NAFTA," 23.

46. See Ian Robinson, "Globalization and Democracy," *Dissent*, Summer 1995, 376–77.

47. *Congressional Record*, November 29, 1994, H11489.

48. "Ensuring Equal Treatment for Foreign Taxpayers, Restoring the Balance of Free Trade and Federalism under the GATT and GATS, A Joint Report by the Multistate Tax Commission, and Federation of Tax Administrators," February 10, 1994, 9.

49. A February 1992 GATT panel report illustrates some of the potential dangers to the U.S. federal system. To protect the existence of microbreweries, Minnesota offered them favorable excise tax treatment for their beer, conditioned only on the size of the production facility. No microbrewery located in Canada, where the complaint originated, was denied access to the favorable tax treatment. But employing a simple "beer is beer" standard, the GATT panel swept aside Minnesota's law. This standard negates the ability of states to make rational policy choices even when they have no desire to discriminate. Indeed, higher taxes levied by one state may now be challenged as discriminatory simply because a competitor does business in another state with lower taxes. The decision also ignored the right of a state to adopt different responses to differing local conditions—a right that constitutes the essence of federalism. Moreover, it does so by elevating the terms of GATT over those of the U.S. Constitution. See "Ensuring Equal Treatment for Foreign Taxpayers, "Restoring the Balance of Free Trade and Federalism under the GATT and GATS: A Joint Report by the Multistate Tax Commission, and Federation of Tax Administrators," February 10, 1994, 4.

50. "Testimony of Ralph Nader, On the Uruguay Round Agreements of the General Agreements on Tariffs and Trade, Before the House Small Business Committee," April 26, 1994, 14.

51. Ibid., 11–12.

52. Jeff Gerth and Tim Weiner, "U.S. Food-Safety System Swamped by Booming Global Imports," *New York Times*, September 29, 1997.

53. See Lori Wallach, "Pesticides Contribute to Food Safety Problem," *New York Times*, October 6, 1997, sec. A, p. 26.

54. The WTO structure poses a special threat to California's laws. The nation's most populous state has long been the national leader in developing strong pesticide regulations. Because California provides so much of America's food, weakening its laws reduces the health safety of much of the country. Among the California pesticide protections vulnerable to challenge under WTO rules are bans on the issue of certain pesticides; the Birth Defect Prevention Act and Pesticide Contamination Prevention Act; Proposition 65, which prohibits "knowingly and intentionally" exposing anyone to cancer-causing or toxic chemicals without providing a clear and reasonable warning. See Patti Goldman and Richard Wiles, "Trading Away US Food Safety," *Public Citizen and the Environmental Working Group*, April 1994, 38.

55. See Jeff Gerth, "Where Business Rules: Forging Global Regulations That Pub Industry First," *New York Times*, January 9, 1998, D1.

56. Owing to the powers now accorded the WTO, these laws are currently at risk. In 1991, a three-person panel of GATT experts held that the Marine Mammal Protection Act was a disguised barrier to trade. The act prohibits the importation of fish or fish products that have been caught with nets and that result in dolphin deaths. Such fishing methods have proven fatal to hundreds of thousands of dolphins in the past 20 years. A GATT dispute-settlement panel found that these restrictions violate GATT's prohibitions because they bar tuna imports based not on some product characteristic, but on the process by which the tuna are caught; the United States had not shown that less-trade-restrictive measures, including cooperative international arrangements, were unavailable; and the restrictions are designed to protect a species found outside the territorial United States. See Leesteffy Jenkins, *GATT Briefing Session*, (London: World Society for the Protection of Animals, 1994), 8–9.

57. The *New York Times* did cover this story extensively, however. See, for instance, John H. Cushman Jr., "Trade Organization Rules Against U.S. Effort to Protect Sea Turtles," *New York Times*, April 7, 1998.

58. Jenkins, *GATT Briefing Session*, 8–9.

59. See Ian Robinson, *North American Trade as If Democracy Mattered*, (Washington, D.C.: International Labor Rights Education and Research Fund, 1993), 21.

60. See David E. Sanger, "U.S. Defeated In Its Appeal of Trade Case," *New York Times*, April 30, 1996, sec. D, p. 1.

61. See Alan Tonelson and Lori Wallach, "Overruled by the World Trade Organization," *Washington Post*, weekly edition, May 13–19, 1996, 23.

62. Andrew Kohut and Robert C. Toth, *Trade and the Public*, (Washington, D.C.: Times Mirror Center for the People and the Press, December 13, 1994), 4–5.

63. Ibid.

64. Cited in *Wall Street Journal*, January 19, 1996.

65. *Inside US Trade*, August 16, 1993, 5–6.

66. Paul Blustein, "White House Again Delays Free-Trade Measure as Skittishness Over Issue Mounts," *Washington Post*, September 11, 1997.

67. Kohut and Toth, *Trade and the Public*, 6.

68. Ibid.

69. Bob Dole and Lloyd Bentsen, " 'Fast Track' Issue Deserves Fast Action," *New York Times*, September 17, 1997, op-ed page.
70. Anthony Lewis, "Abroad at Home," November 14, 1997.
71. James K. Glassman, *Washington Post*, November 11, 1997, op-ed page.
72. David Broder, *Washington Post*, November 11, 1997, op-ed page.
73. See "The Fast Track Loss," *Washington Post*, November 11, 1997, and "Courage on Trade," *New York Times*, November 5, 1997.
74. Kohut cited in John F. Harris and Peter Baker, "Clinton Neglected to Sell 'Fast Track' to U.S. Public," *Washington Post*, November 12, 1997.

CHAPTER 5

1. Vaclav Havel, "Address of the President of the Czechoslovak Republic to a Joint Session of the United States Congress," Washington, D.C., February 21, 1990.
2. Michael Oreskes, "American Politics Loses Way as Polls Supplant Leadership," *New York Times*, March 18, 1990.
3. Harwood Group, *Citizens and Politics*, 19.
4. Those expressing "a great deal" of confidence in the executive branch constituted only 12 percent, just half the 1981 figure and less than a third of that in 1966. Eight percent indicated "a great deal of confidence" in Congress, compared to 16 percent in 1981 and 42 percent in 1966. In 1964, 29 percent of those questioned by the Harris poll agreed that the U.S. government was run "for the benefit of a few big interests." By 1980, the number rose to 70 percent. In 1992 it was 80 percent, with another 66 percent believing that " most elected officials don't care what people like me think," up from 47 percent in 1987 and 33 percent in the 1960s. See S. M. Lipset, "Malaise and Resiliency in America," *Journal of Democracy* 6, no. 3 (1995): 5–7.
5. Cited in *New York Times*, August 12, 1995.
6. James S. Fishkin, *Democracy and Deliberation: New Directions for Democratic Reform* (New Haven, Conn.: Yale University Press, 1991), 55.
7. See Alan Brinkley, "The Privatization of Public Discourse," in Alan Brinkley, Nelson W. Polsby, and Kathleen M. Sullivan, *New Federalist Papers: Essays in Defense of the Constitution* (New York: W. W. Norton, 1997, 142.
8. To qualify to win the maximum number of delegates in the Republican presidential primary in New York State, a candidate must collect 1,250 legible signatures in each of the state's thirty-one congressional districts during the month preceding the January 4 filing deadline.
9. According to the Census Bureau, 60.1 percent of Americans with family incomes over $50,000 said they voted in November 1995, up from 59.2 percent in November 1990. By contrast, just 27.1 percent of people with incomes under $15,000 voted, down from 34.3 percent in 1990. Voting among college graduates was up to 63.1 percent from 62.5 percent in 1990. Voting among high school grads dropped from 42.2 percent in 1990 to 40 percent in 1994. Among those

who did not finish elementary school, the numbers dropped from 27.7 percent in 1990 to 23.2 percent in 1994. In 1994, 46.9 percent of whites voted, up from 46.7 in 1990. Blacks reported voting at a rate of 37 percent, down from 39.2 percent in 1990 and 43.2 percent in 1986. Hispanics voted at a rate of 19.1 percent, down from 23.1 percent in 1990 and 24.2 percent in 1986. These figures run well above actual voter turnout. One in five 18- to 24-year-olds voted, a rate that remained consistent. See Paul Taylor, "Behind the Broom of '94, Wealthier, Educated Voters," *Washington Post*, June 8, 1995. See also Benjamin Ginsberg, *The Captive Public: How Mass Opinion Promotes State Power* (New York: Basic Books, 1986).

10. Cited in Fishkin, *Democracy and Deliberation*, 55–56.

11. See Center for Voting and Democracy, *Dubious Democracy and the 1994 Elections*, (Washington D.C.: Center for Voting and Democracy, 1995), 47. See also James S. Fishkin, *The Voice of the People* (New Haven: Yale University Press, 1995), 45. Note that the vote for Clinton was the second-slimmest mandate in U.S. electoral history, though not much worse than Ronald Reagan's 1984 "landslide," which included just 28 percent of eligible voters.

12. Tocqueville, *Democracy in America*, 508.

13. Robert D. Putnam, "Bowling Alone," *Journal of Democracy* 6, no. 1(1995): 66. See also Robert D. Putnam, *Making Democracy Work: Civic Traditions in Modern Italy* (Princeton: Princeton University Press, 1993), and Alan Brinkley, "Liberty and Community," in Brinkley et al., *New Federalist Papers*, 92.

14. Putnam, "Bowling Alone," is the origin of this argument. But Putnam made a far more compelling case for his argument, which included responses to his critics, in "The Strange Death of Civic America," *American Prospect* 24 (1996). The preceding data appears on page 35. Despite the study's many critics, I continue to find Putnam's overall thesis compelling and largely supportable, though it seems obvious that the empirical data supporting it is open to greater interpretation than he originally allowed. For a contrary view, see the Summer 1996 edition of *Public Perspective*, published by the Roper Center for Public Opinion Research at the University of Connecticut. Its findings are summarized in Richard Morin, "So Much for the 'Bowling Alone' Thesis," *Washington Post*, national weekly edition, June 17–23, 1996, 37. See also Ichiro Kawachi, Bruce Kennedy, and Kimberly Lochner, "Long Live Community: Social Capital as Public Health," *American Prospect* 35 (1997): 56–63.

15. Ibid.

16. Ibid, 48. The number of Americans who contribute to the Democratic Party hovers between 100,000 and 500,000. For Republicans, the number is between 750,000 and 1.5 million. Even the Republican figure is less than 1 1/100th of the electorate. See William Greider, Who Will Tell the People: The Betrayal of American Democracy (New York: Simon and Schuster, 1992), 249.

17. The exact figures were $416 million for the Republicans and $221 million for the Democrats. See Helen Dewar, "Petition Drive May Be Last Hope for Campaign Reform," *Washington Post*, April 1, 1998, p. 1.

18. See Fred Wertheimer and Susan Weiss Manes, "Campaign Finance Reform: A Key to Restoring the Health of Our Democracy," *Columbia Law Review* 94, no. 4 (1994): 134–35.

19. See Francis X. Clines, "Election Oversight Unit Barely Treading Water," *New York Times*, November 23, 1997.

20. Roger Tamraz, quoted in *U.S. News and World Report*, September 29, 1997, 20.

21. See Michael K. Frisby, "The Money Man: Peter Knight Helps President in Big Way: Bringing In the Funds: Despite Clinton's Early Talk, His Campaign Manager Plays Old Political Game: Providing Crucial 'Access,' " *Wall Street Journal*, June 18, 1996. Note that in 1961, 365 congressional lobbyists were registered; by 1987, the number had grown to 23,011. At the same time, the number of lawyers registered with the Washington, D.C., Bar Association rose from 12,564 to 46,000. Between 1968 and 1986, the number of corporations with Washington offices grew from 100 to 1,300. Special interests buy favors from congressmen and presidents through political action committees (PACs), devices by which groups such as corporations, professional associations, trade unions, and investment-banking groups can pool their money and give up to $10,000 per election to each House and Senate candidate. Today more than 4,000 PACs of various kinds are registered with the Federal Election Commission; in 1974, when they were sanctioned by law, there were only 500. To those who argue "that special-interest expenditures have no significant influence on public policy," notes Michael Lind, "if all of this money is not buying special favors from congressmen and senators, a great many groups and individuals who are otherwise careful with their resources are acting in a highly irrational manner." See Michael Lind, *The Next American Nation* (New York: Free Press, 1995), 158. See also Richard Morin and Charles R. Babcock, "Out-of-State Donations to Candidates Are on the Rise," *Washington Post*, July 31, 1990.

22. Bill McAllister, "Pressure's Up to $100 Million a Month," *Washington Post*, March 12, 1998, p. 13.

23. Quoted in Oreskes, "American Politics Loses Way."

24. Ed Rollins, speaking at the American Booksellers Association in Chicago, June 16, 1996.

25. Cited in Fishkin, *Democracy and Deliberation*, 6.

26. See David Segal, "Tale of the Bogus Telegrams," *Washington Post*, September 25, 1995, sec. A, p. 1.

27. Cited in Joseph M. Bessette, *The Mild Voice of Reason: Deliberative Democracy and American National Government* (Chicago: University of Chicago Press, 1994), 64.

28. Robert A. Dahl, *A Preface to Democratic Theory* (Chicago: University of Chicago Press, 1956), 131.

29. Matthew Glass, *Citizens Against the MX: Public Languages in the Nuclear Age* (Urbana: University of Illinois Press, 1993), 114.

30. Max Weber, "Science as a Vocation," in Weber, *Essays in Sociology* (New York: Oxford University Press, 1958), 155.

31. Jurgen Habermas, *The Theory of Communicative Action,* vol. 2 of *Lifeworld and System: A Critique of Functionalist Reason* (Boston: Beacon Press, 1987), 351–55. See also the discussion in Glass, *Citizens Against the MX,* 93–99.

32. Habermas explains that "a portion of the public sphere comes into being in every conversation in which private individuals assemble to form a public body. They then behave neither like business or professional people transacting private affairs, nor like members of a constitutional order subject to the legal constraints of a state bureaucracy. Citizens behave as a public body when they confer in an unrestricted fashion—that is, with a guarantee of freedom of assembly and association and the freedom to express and publish their opinions—about matters of general interest. In a large public body this kind of communication requires specific means for transmitting information and influencing those who receive it." See Jurgen Habermas, *The Structural Transformation of the Public Sphere* (Cambridge: MIT Press, 1989), 47.

33. Cited in Jonathan Daniels, *The Man of Independence* (New York: W. B. Lippincott, 1950), 285.

34. Wirthlin Group, *Values and U.S. Foreign Policy* (New York: Carnegie Council on Ethics and International Affairs, 1989).

35. Bob Dole quoted in *New York Times,* February 15, 1996.

36. See Emily R. Rosenberg, "The Cold War and the Discourse of National Security," *Diplomatic History* 17 (1993); and Barton J. Bernstein, "Commentary: The Challenge of 'National Security'—A Skeptical View," *Diplomatic History* 17 (1993).

37. Glass, *Citizens Against the MX,* 102.

38. Antonia Chaynes, "Letter to the Editor," *Salt Lake Tribune,* February 10, 1980.

39. See the essays in Lance W. Bennett and David L. Paletzeds, eds., *Taken by Storm: The Media, Public Opinion, and U.S. Foreign Policy in the Gulf War* (Chicago: University of Chicago Press, 1994). See, in particular, Robert Entman and Benjamin I. Page, "The News Before the Storm," 83–101.

40. Henry Kissinger on *Meet the Press,* August 5, 1990, and Henry Kissinger, *The Washington Post,* August 29, 1990.

41. Barnes and Kondracke, on *The McLaughlin Group,* November 11, 1990.

42. Quoted in Lars-Erik Nelson, March 25, 1991.

43. The conversations between Bush and Powell are reported in Bob Woodward, *The Commanders* (New York: Simon and Schuster, 1991).

44. See Charles Krauthammer, "The Unipolar Moment," *Foreign Affairs: America and the World,* 1990/1991, 23–24. See also "New World Order: What's New? Which World? Whose Orders?" *Economist,* February 23, 1991, 25.

45. Daniel Patrick Moynihan, U.S. Senate, January 10, 1991.

46. Poll numbers cited in David E. Rosenbaum, "Democrats Hope to Avoid Embarrassing Vote on Haiti," *New York Times,* September 14, 1994.

47. Cited in "Word for Word: A President's Ability to Delcare War," *New York Times,* September 30, 1994.

48. Hamilton quoted in Walker, *The President We Deserve,* 263.

49. Cited in Wayne Bert, *The Reluctant Superpower: The United States in Bosnia, 1991–1995* (New York: St. Martin's Press, 1997), 87.

50. Ibid., 84.

51. Eagleburger and the *Times* editorial page are both quoted in Walker, *The President We Deserve*, 276.

52. Russett, *Controlling the Sword*, 87–88.

53. Both Roosevelt and Truman misled the public and their own cabinets about the nature of the U.S.-Soviet agreement at Yalta. Eisenhower deliberately misled the American people about U.S. involvement in American-sponsored coups in Guatemala and Iran and U.S. spy flights over Russia. Kennedy misled the American people about U.S. involvement in efforts to assassinate and overthrow Fidel Castro. Richard Nixon lied about the circumstances that allegedly caused the invasion of Cambodia. Gerald Ford lied in his explanations to the American people about the nature of the Mayaguez incident as well as about the circumstances under which the United States was leaving Vietnam. Jimmy Carter promised to retain control over the Panama Canal treaty during a presidential debate and then reversed himself once in office. Ronald Reagan regularly lied about the nature of U.S. policy in Central America and again when he denied selling weapons to Iran. George Bush lied about his involvement as vice president in the Iran-Contra affair. To my knowledge, Jimmy Carter did not tell any explicit lies as president. See the previous chapter for details. See also John Praddos, *Presidents' Secret Wars* (New York: William Morrow, 1986), and David Wise, *The Politics of Lying: Government Deception, Secrecy and Power* (New York: Vintage, 1973).

54. Cited in Loren Baritz, *Backfire* (New York: Ballatine, 1985), 133.

55. Cited in Small, *Democracy and Diplomacy*, 106.

56. Ibid., xii.

57. See Walter Isaacson, *Kissinger* (New York: Simon and Schuster, 1992), 208–9 and 480–83.

58. When JFK's approval ratings shot up after the Bay of Pigs fiasco, he allegedly commented, "The worse I do, the more popular I get."

59. Russett, *Controlling the Sword*, 25.

60. See Roger Hilsman, *To Move a Nation: The Politics of Foreign Policy in the Administration of John F. Kennedy* (New York: Dell, 1964), 176–80.

61. Russett, *Controlling the Sword*, 49.

62. Ibid., 37–38.

63. For a useful discussion of these issues, see Barry B. Hughes, *The Domestic Context of American Foreign Policy* (San Francisco: W. H. Freeman, 1978), particularly 37–40, and Mueller, *War, Presidents and Public Opinion*, especially chapter 7.

64. See Robert M. Entman and Andrew Rojecki, "Freezing Out the Public: Elite and Media Framing of the U.S. Anti-Nuclear Movement," *Political Communication* 10: (1993): 158.

65. See introduction to this book. See also Daniel Yanklovich and I. M. Destler, eds., *Beyond the Beltway: Engaging the Public in U.S. Foreign Policy* (New York: W. W.

Norton, 1994), and Michael Clough, "Grass-Roots Policymaking: Say Good-Bye to the Wise Men," *Foreign Affairs* 72, no. 1 (1994): especially 9–14.

66. The "vocal minority" quote is from George F. Kennan, *Memoirs, 1925–1950* (Boston: Little, Brown, 1967), 185. The "maladjusted group" quote is cited in David A. Mayers, *George Kennan and the Dilemmas of U.S. Foreign Policy* (New York, 1988), 56. See also George F. Kennan, *Russia Leaves the War* (Princeton: Princeton University Press, 1956), 13.

67. Dahl, *A Preface to Democratic Theory*, 146.

68. See Schlesinger and Kinzer, *Bitter Fruit*. See also Walter LaFeber, *Inevitable Revolutions: The United States in Central America* (New York: W. W. Norton, 1984).

69. See Seymour M. Hersh, *The Price of Power: Kissinger in the Nixon White House* (New York: Summit, 1983), 276, for details.

70. For details, see Kai Bird, *The Chairman: John J. McCloy, the Making of the American Establishment* (New York: Simon and Schuster, 1992), chapter 28.

71. Katherine Q. Seelye, "Arms Contractors to Spend to Promote an Expanded NATO," *New York Times*, March 30, 1998, p. 1.

72. Nathan Glazer, *We Are All Multiculturalists Now* (Cambridge: Harvard University Press, 1997). For a discussion of the implications of the "Minority" conference, see Samuel Huntington, "The Erosion of American National Interests, " *Foreign Affairs* 76, no. 5 (1997): 40.

73. Henry A. Feingold, *A Midrash on American Jewish History* (Albany: State University Press of New York, 1982), 47.

74. Alexander DeConde, *Ethnicity, Race and American Foreign Policy: A History* (Northeastern University Press, 1992), 71. See also Peter Grosse, *Israel in the Mind of America* (New York: Alfred A. Knopf, 1983).

75. See David Wyman, *The Abandonment of the Jews: America and the Holocaust, 1941–1945* (New York: Pantheon, 1984); Michael R. Marrus, *The Unwanted: European Refugees in the Twentieth Century* (New York, 1985); Walter Laquer, *The Terrible Secret* (Boston: Little, Brown, 1980); Bird, *The Chairman*, chapter 10; and Verne W. Newton, *FDR and the Holocaust* (New York: St. Martin's Press, 1996), especially chapters 4, 5, 6, 8, 9, and 10.

76. See John Snetsinger, *Truman, the Jewish Vote and the Creation of Israel* (Stanford: Stanford University Press, 1974), 35, 116. See also Steven L. Spiegel, *The Other Arab-Israeli Conflict: Making America's Middle East Policy from Truman to Reagan* (Chicago: University of Chicago Press, 1985), chapter 2; Aaron Berman, *Nazism, the Jews and American Zionism* (Detroit: Wayne State University Press, 1990); Naomi W. Cohen, *American Jews and the Zionist Idea* (New York: Ktav, 1975); Clark Clifford with Richard Holbrooke, *Counsel to the President* (New York: Random House, 1991), chapter 1; Grosse, *Israel in the Mind of America;* Evan Wilson, *Decision on Palestine* (Stanford: Stanford University Press, 1979); M. J. Cohen, *Truman and Israel* (Berkeley: University of California Press, 1990); and Kenneth R. Bain, *The March to Zion* (College Station: University of Texas Press, 1979).

77. This story is told in some detail in chapter 1 of Clifford, *Counsel to the President,* and from a decidedly different perspective in Townsend Hoopes and Douglas Brinkley, *Driven Patriot: The Life and Times of James Forrestal* (New York: Knopf, 1992).

78. Dulles is quoted in Isaac Alteras, *Eisenhower and Israel: US-Israeli Relations, 1953–1970* (Gainsville: University Press of Florida, 1993), 271. See also Spiegel, *The Other Arab-Israeli Conflict*, 51–54, and Abraham Ben Zvi, *The United States and Israel: The Limits of the Special Relationship* (New York: Columbia University Press, 1993), 43–44, 72.

79. See, in particular, Arthur Hertzberg, *The Jews in America: Four Centuries of an Uneasy Encounter* (New York: Columbia University Press, 1997), 360–61. See also Geoffrey Wheatcroft, *The Controversy of Zion* (New York: Addison Wesley, 1996), 273; Charles Silberman, *A Certain People: American Jews and their Lives Today* (New York: Simon and Schuster, 1985); Bernard Avashai, *The Tragedy of Zionism* (New York: Holmes and Meyer, 1985); Edward Tivnan, *The Lobby: Jewish Political Power and American Foreign Policy* (New York: Simon and Schuster, 1987); and Leonard Fein, *Who Are We: The Inner Life of American Jews* (New York: Harper and Row, 1988).

80. Spiegel, *The Other Arab-Israeli Conflict*, 253.

81. *R N: The Memoirs of Richard Nixon* (New York: Grosset and Dunlap, 1978), 611. See also William Safire, *Before the Fall* (New York: Doubleday, 1975), 574; Hersh, *The Price of Power*, 568; and Isaacson, *Kissinger*, 546–67.

82. The best study of AIPAC's history remains Tivnan, *The Lobby*.

83. Cited in Small, *Democracy and Diplomacy*, 147. See also Tivnan, *The Lobby*.

84. See J. J. Goldberg, *Jewish Power: Inside the American Jewish Establishment* (New York: Addison Wesley, 1996), chapter 8, 36.

85. Former Africa subcommittee chair Howard Wolpe recalls AIPAC's ally Representative Larry Smith demanding that he talk (on the phone) with his contributor, a major AIPAC donor, about his refusal to increase aid to the corrupt Mobutu dictatorship in Zaire. AIPAC was lobbying on behalf of Mobutu as a reward for his willingness to recognize Israel. See Stephen R. Weissman, *A Culture of Deference: Congress's Failure of Leadership in Foreign Policy* (New York: Basic Books, 1995), 91.

86. See Robert S. Greenberger and Laurie Lande, "Progress of Iran Sanctions Measure in Congress Signals Comeback for Pro-Israel Lobbying Group," *Wall Street Journal*, June 18, 1996.

87. See Seymour Martin Lipset and Earl Raab, *Jews and the New American Scene* (Cambridge: Harvard University Press, 1994). See also Philip Weiss, "Letting Go," *New York*, January 29, 1996, 32.

88. See Yossi Shain, "Multicultural Foreign Policy," *Foreign Policy* 100 (1995): 79.

89. Poll data demonstrates that half the Cuban Americans in the United States disagree with the position of the National Cuban American Foundation, which believes we ought to isolate Cuba. See *New York Times*, June 12, 1995.

90. Michael S. Teitelbaum, *Latin Migration North: The Problem for U.S. Foreign Policy* (New York: Council on Foreign Relations, 1985), 34.

91. See Joseph O'Grady, "An Irish Policy Born in the USA," *Foreign Affairs* 75, no. 3 (1996): 2–7.

92. John Jay, "Federalist No. 2," in *The Federalist Papers*, ed. Clinton Rossiter (New York: New American Library, 1961), 9.

93. See George Shultz, *Turmoil and Triumph: My Years as Secretary of State* (New York: Scribner's, 1993), 152. See also Margaret Thatcher, *The Downing Street Years* (New York: HarperCollins, 1993), 170–200.
94. DeConde, *Ethnicity, Race and American Foreign Policy*, 197.
95. Walter Lippmann, *The Phantom Public* (New York: Macmillan, 1935), 77.
96. Weissman, *A Culture of Deference*, 23.
97. Ibid., 2–3.
98. See chapter 3.
99. Small, *Democracy and Diplomacy*, 2.
100. See Robert A. Dahl, *The Tanner Lectures on Human Values* (Cambridge: Cambridge University Press and University of Utah Press, 1989), 67.

CHAPTER 6

1. Thomas Paine, "The Rights of Man, (1791)" in *The Writings of Thomas Paine*, vol. 2, ed. Moncure Daniel Conway (New York: G. P. Putham's Sons, 1967), 388.
2. See Habermas, *Structural Transformation of the Public Sphere*. See also Habermas, *Theory of Communicative Action*.
3. See V. O. Key, *Public Opinion and American Democracy* (New York: Knopf, 1961), and V. O. Key, *The Responsible Electorate* (Cambridge: Harvard University Press, 1966).
4. The data to support this claim is cited in Richard Morin, "Who's In Control? Many Don't Know and Don't Care," *Washington Post*, January 29, 1996.
5. See J. Carey, "A Republic If You Can Keep It," 221.
6. Author's interview.
7. Robert N. Entman, *Democracy Without Citizens: Media and the Decay of American Politics* (New York: Oxford University Press, 1989), 17.
8. See Amy Waldman, "Class Not Race," *Washington Monthly*, November 1995, 26.
9. See Albert R. Karr, "Television News Tunes Out Airwaves-Auction Battle," *Wall Street Journal*, May 1, 1996, sec. B, p. 1.
10. Fowler is quoted in Les Brown, *Les Brown's Encyclopedia of Television*, 3d ed. (Detroit: Visible Ink, 1992).
11. Ben Bagdikian, *The Media Monopoly* (Boston: Beacon Books, 1992), ix–x.
12. ABC's *Good Morning America*, July 31, 1995.
13. Maureen Dowd, "Liberties," August 3, 1995.
14. Cited in *Village Voice*, January 16, 1996, 34.
15. Cited in Todd Gitlin, introduction to *Conglomerates and the Media*, by André Schiffrin, Todd Gitlin, Eric Barnoow, Richard M. Cohen, Gene Roberts, Thomas Schatz, Mark Crispin Miller, David Lieberman, Patricia Aufderhyde, and Thomas Frank (New York: New Press, 1997), 8.
16. Radio transcripts provided to the author by Hightower Radio.
17. The segment ultimately ran once the information was made public in Congress, and hence was no longer subject to libel proceedings.

18. See Eric Alterman, " Ad Copy Rights," *Nation,* November 3, 1997, 6.
19. Quoted in Jenet Conant, "Don't Mess With Steve Brill," *Vanity Fair,* August 1997, 66.
20. Acheson cited in Richard J. Barnet, *Roots of War* (New York: Viking Penguin, 1971), 270.
21. Entman, *Democracy Without Citizens,* 4–5.
22. See George Church, "Fast and Loose with Facts; In the Second Presidential Debate, Accuracy Was No Object." *Time,* November 5, 1984.
23. Entman, *Democracy Without Citizens,* 23–24.
24. For greater detail on this issue, see *TV News Viewership Declines* (Washington, D.C.: Pew Research Center for People and the Press, 1996).
25. Kiky Adato, *The Incredible Shrinking Sound Bite* (Cambridge, Mass.: Joan Shorenstein Barone Center, 1990), 4; cited in Fishkin, *Democracy and Deliberation,* 52.
26. Michael Robinson and Margaret Sheehan, *Over the Wire on TV* (New York: Russell Sage Foundation, 1983), 149; cited in Adato, *Incredible Shrinking Sound Bite,* 62.
27. From 1986 to 1989, for instance, public opinion polls demonstrated increasing concern about drug use in the United States owing to a massive surge in media reporting of the problem. During this same period, however, the percentage of people reporting illegal drug use dropped steadily. See J. Bare, "The War on Drugs: A Case Study in Opinion Formation," *Public Perspective* (November/December, 1990), 29–31.
28. See Seymour M. Hersh, "The Iran-Contra Committees: Did They Protect Reagan?" *New York Times Magazine,* April 29, 1990, 47.
29. See Amy Fried, *Muffled Voices: Oliver North and the Politics of Public Opinion* (New York: Columbia University Press, 1997).
30. See *Time,* July 20, 1987, 14, and *Newsweek,* July 20, 1987, 12.
31. Cited in Fried, *Muffled Voices,* 117.
32. While North's popularity did jump during the days of his testimony in July 1987, this never translated into support for what he had done, or for President Reagan's policies in either Iran or Nicaragua. The number of Americans questioned who considered North a hero ranged from 4 percent in a *Los Angeles Times* poll taken July 10, 1987, which was far fewer than the number who believed that North "could be bought," to 19 percent in an ABC News poll taken the next day. Overall, in four separate polls taken in June and July of 1987, between 68 and 81 percent of Americans questioned disagreed with the appellation "hero" when applied to Oliver North. See Fried, *Muffled Voices,* 84–88, 112–13, and 222–27.
33. The numbers, compiled by the Tyndall Report, appear in Garrick Utley, "The Shrinking of Foreign News," *Foreign Affairs* 76, no. 2 (1997): 2.
34. See *A Content Analysis: International News Coverage Fits Public's Ameri-Centric Mood* (Washington, D.C.: Times Mirror Center for People and the Press, 1995).
35. See *Mixed Messages about Press Freedom on both Sides of the Atlantic* (Washington, D.C.: Times Mirror Center for People and the Press, 1994).
36. Noelle McAfee, Robert Mckenzie, and David Mathews, *Hard Choices* (Dayton, Ohio: Kettering Foundation), 12.

37. *Rush Limbaugh Show,* October 23, 1995.
38. According to Andrew Kohut, director of polling for Times Mirror, "The public, for its part, wants a vastly diminished role for America in the future. It voiced almost as much support for the U.S. playing no leadership role at all, as for the nation being the world's single leader (seven and ten percent respectively.) Among the public who support a shared leadership role, response was almost two to one for a not more active rather than an active role (51% to 27%). There is a broad trend toward isolationism in the public." See *America's Place in the World* (Washington, D.C.: Times Mirror Center for the People and the Press, 1993), 29–30. For an alarmed discussion of this phenomenon, see Arthur Schlessinger Jr., "Back to the Womb? Isolationism's Renewed Threat," *Foreign Affairs* 74, no. 4 (1995): 6.
39. See John Gerhard Ruggie, *Winning the Peace: America and World Order in the New Era* (New York: Columbia University Press, 1996), 95–98.
40. Over and over, as Steven Kull, I. M. Destler, and Clay Ramsay demonstrate in their extensive survey, Congress, the press, and the members of the foreign policy establishment have vastly overestimated the degree of the public's impatience with multilateral intervention and have completely misread the public's desire to ensure that multilateral intervention take precedence over unilateral U.S. military intervention, which remains highly unpopular. See Kull et al., *Foreign Policy Gap,* 179.
41. See Sidney Verba, "The Citizen as Respondent: Sample Surveys and American Democracy: Presidential Address, American Political Science Association, 1995," *The American Political Science Review* 90, no. 1 (1996): 6.
42. See Benjamin Ginsberg, *The Captive Public: How Mass Opinion Promotes State Power* (New York: Basic Books, 1986). 83.
43. Matthews, David, *Politics for People: Finding a Responsible Public Voice* (Urbana: University of Illinois Press,1994), 212.
44. Fishkin, *Democracy and Deliberation,* 83.
45. Fishkin, *Voice of the People,* 86.
46. Page and Shapiro, *The Rational Public,* 367.
47. "Do you think it is frequently, occasionally, or never all right for the President to lie to the American public?"

Frequently	Occasionally	Never
5%	21%	72%

"Do you think there are times when the United States government is justified in lying to the American public?"

Sometimes	Never	Not sure
30%	63%	5%

Sources: Roper Organization, February 6, 1987. *Los Angeles Times,* December 6, 1986.
Lying for Foreign Policy Purposes
"Suppose the Administration in Washington thinks it must lie to the American people in order to achieve a foreign policy goal. Under those circumstances, is it all right for the Administration to lie to the American people, or isn't it?"

All right	Not all right	Depends
18%	72%	7%

Source: CBS News/*New York Times*, October 24,1986.

48. Page and Shapiro, *The Rational Public*, 373.

49. Public opinion about U.S. trade relations with China varies considerably depending on whether the phrase "human rights" is used in the question. In a May 1990 poll, when the phrase was not used a majority supported unfettered trade, less than a year after the crackdown on dissidents in Tiananmen Square. At that time, a *New York Times* survey found 52 percent of Americans would "give the same privileges to China that it gives to other friendly nations," with 37 percent opposed. One year later, in June 1991, a *Washington Post* poll found the same majority support (52% vs. 41%) when the question was only slightly modified ("free trade with China on the same terms the U.S. gives its main trading partners"). In recent years, when the phrase "human rights" was included in the question, opposition to normal trade relations was high for a while but has dropped with time. In December 1993, for example, an NBC poll found that 65 percent of the public said the United States should demand improved human rights policies in China in exchange for keeping its current trade status (with 29% saying good trade relations should be maintained despite disagreements over human rights policies). In May and June of 1994, however, support for demanding improved human rights dropped in two NBC polls using the same question to 51 percent and 50 percent, respectively. A mid-May poll by *Time*/CNN found contradictory sentiment: 60 percent supported a continued policy of requiring human rights progress before China receives preferential treatment on trade policy (vs. 28% for stopping the linking of trade policy to human rights); and 62 percent said U.S. policy should encourage human rights (vs. 29% for establishing a strong trading relationship). See "China and Human Rights" in Kohut and Toth, *Trade and the Public*.

50. See Joan Biskupic, "Has the Court Lost its Appeal?" *Washington Post*, October 12, 1995, sec. A, p. 23.

51. See Michael Dobbs, "Americans Yet to Be Sold On Need for Larger NATO," *Washington Post*, July 3, 1997, sec. A, p. 1.

52. See *America's Place in the World*, vol. 2, 31.

CONCLUSION

1. Author's interview.

2. James Madison quoted in *The Federalist Papers*, ed. Clinton Rossiter (New York: New American Library, 1961), 82. See also Dahl, *A Preface to Democratic Theory*, 11–19.

3. James Madison in *The Federalist Papers*, 84.

4. Alexander Hamilton in *The Federalist Papers*, 432.

5. John Stuart Mill, *On Liberty*, ed. David Spitz (New York: W. W. Norton, 1975), 21.

6. Bessette, *Mild Voice of Reason,*: 34–35.

7. See Robert A. Dahl, "Procedural Democracy," in *Philosophy, Politics and Society*, ed. Peter Laslett and James Fishkin (New Haven: Yale University Press, 1979), 105–7.

8. Habermas, *Structural Transformation of the Public Sphere*, 47. See also Page and Shapiro, *Rational Public*, 363.

9. Madison is quoted from "Federalist No. 68," in *The Federalist Papers*, 89. See also Fishkin, *Voice of the People*, 64–65.

10. See Richard M. Gummere, *The American Colonial Mind and the Classical Tradition* (Cambridge: Harvard University Press, 1963), 45.

11. Conclusion to *Democracy: The Unfinished Journey 508BC to AD 1993*, ed. John Dunn (New York: Oxford University Press, 1992), 241.

12. Dewey cited in Robert Westbrook, "Pragmatism and Democracy: Reconstructing the Logic of John Dewey's Faith," delivered at a conference entitled "The Revival of Pragmatism," Graduate School and University Center, City University of New York, November 4, 1995.

13. Robert A. Dahl, *After the Revolution: Authority in a Good Society* (New Haven: Yale University Press, 1970), 149–50.

14. Robert A. Dahl, *Democracy and Its Critics* (New Haven: Yale University Press, 1989), 340.

15. Andrew Hacker, "Twelve Angry Persons," *New York Review of Books*, September 21, 1995, 46.

16. See Samuel Issacharoff and Richard H. Pildes, "All For One," *The New Republic*, November 18, 1996, 10.

17. See Kevin Phillips, *Arrogant Capital: Washington, Wall Street and the Frustration of American Politics* (Boston: Little, Brown, 1994) 145, 195.

18. Quoted in *Austin American Statesman*, January 22, 1996, sec. A, p. 4.

19. Quoted in *New York Times*, January 22, 1996, sec. A, p. 13.

20. See Dean Acheson, "The American Image Will Take Care of Itself," *New York Times Magazine*, February 28, 1965, 95.

21. Christopher Lasch is quoted in Carey, "A Republic if You Can Keep It," 220.

22. The words belong to James M. Carey. See Carey, "The Press, Public Opinion, and Public Discourse," in *James Carey: A Critical Reader*, ed. Eve Stryker Munson and Catherine A. Warren (Minneapolis: University of Minnesota Press, 1997), 22.

23. Miroslav Nincic, *Democracy and Foreign Policy: The Fallacy of Political Realism* (New York: Columbia University Press, 1992), 107.

24. See E. J. Dionne Jr., *Why Americans Hate Politics* (New York: Simon and Schuster, 1991), 354.

25. Tocqueville, *Democracy in America*, 255.

Appendix

1. The following appendix is based on an extremely circumspect reading of all available public opinion data. I have relied particularly heavily on the interpretations of Benjamin Page and Robert Y. Shapiro, *The Rational Public: Fifty Years of*

Trends in American Policy Preferences (Chicago: University of Chicago Press, 1992); Eugene R. Wittkopf, *Faces of Internationalism: Public Opinion and American Foreign Policy* (Durham, N.C.: Duke University Press, 1990); Bruce Russett, *Controlling the Sword: The Democratic Governance of National Security* (Cambridge: Harvard University Press, 1990); and Richard J. Barnet, *The Rockets' Red Glare: When America Goes to War, The Presidents and the People* (New York: Simon and Schuster, 1990). I spent a great deal of time comparing the past four quadrennial surveys of American "opinion leaders" and the general public conducted by the Chicago Council on Foreign Relations overseen by John E. Rielly. Also helpful were the regular surveys by the Times Mirror Center for the People and the Press (later Pew Research Center for the People and the Press), directed by Andrew Kohut, and the University of Maryland's Program on Public Attitudes polls, directed by Steven Kull and later compiled in Kull et al., *Foreign Policy Gap.*

2. See LaFeber, "The Constitution and Foreign Policy," 696.

3. According to the "values" poll undertaken by the Carnegie Council on Ethics and International Affairs, "74 percent of those polled believed it more important to protect American jobs than to buy a wide variety of imported products at lower prices. 25 percent believed the reverse" (February 1989). "The top priority among all goals went to protecting American jobs, at 80 percent of respondents." See *America's Place in the World.* These numbers are also consistent with those offered in *America's Place in the World, vol. 2,* 15.

4. According to the most recent Chicago Council on Foreign Affairs survey, "Fully 19 percent of the public feels the nation's biggest problem is getting involved in the affairs of other countries. This is up from 6 percent in 1990. The second biggest problem is that too much foreign aid is being sent to other countries. Significant numbers also object to too much military involvement in other countries (6 percent) and to a perceived U.S. role as 'the world's police' (4 percent). There has been a substantial decline for protecting weaker nations against foreign aggression (33 point drop), for promoting and defending human rights in other countries (24-point drop) and for helping to improve the standard of living of lesser-developed countries (19-point drop). See Rielly, *American Public Opinion and U.S. Foreign Policy,* 13–16. At the bottom of the public's foreign policy priorities were 'promoting human rights abroad' (22 percent), fostering democracy overseas (18 percent), and aiding developing countries (18 percent). See *America's Place in the World.* The public, for its part, wants a vastly diminished role for America in the future. It voiced almost as much support for the United States playing no leadership role at all as for the nation being the world's single leader (7 and 10 percent, respectively). Among the public who support a shared leadership role, response was almost two to one for a not more active rather than an active role (51 percent to 27 percent), essentially, the reverse of the Influentials' judgment (*America's Place in the World,* 29). In the 1997 version of this poll, support for a leading role for the United States among the public remained stable relative to 1997 levels while it increased considerably among "influentials," thereby further widening the gap. See *America's Place in the World, vol. 2,"* 27.

5. As recently as November 1995, according to a TIME/CNN poll, 73 percent of U.S. adults believed the country should further reduce its involvement in world politics to concentrate on problems at home. Cited in *Time*, November 27, 1995.

6. Kull et al., *Foreign Policy Gap*, 47.

7. According to one June 1996 poll, support for contributions to UN peacekeeping rises from 57 percent to 82 percent when respondents are asked to imagine an all-volunteer UN army. See Kull et al., *Foreign Policy Gap*, 90.

8. See Arthur Schlesinger Jr., "Back to the Womb," *Foreign Affairs* 74, no. 4 (1995): 6.

9. In a June 1995 University of Maryland poll, when asked "When faced with future problems involving aggression, who should take the lead?," 69 percent of those questioned replied "the United Nations," while just 28 percent responded "the United States." In an April 1995 poll, 66 percent rejected, while only 29 percent embraced, the argument that "when there is a problem in the world that requires the use of military force, it is better for the U.S. to act on its own, rather than working through the UN, because the U.S. can respond more quickly and probably more successfully." See Steven Kull, "What the Public Knows that Washington Doesn't," *Foreign Policy* 101 (1995–96): 105. In 1993, according to the Times Mirror Center for the People and the Press, a favorable attitude toward the United Nations was held by a two-thirds majority of respondents: 14 percent said "very favorable," 53 percent said "mostly favorable." This was appreciably higher than the public rated the U.S. Congress (53 percent "very" and "mostly" favorable), the U.S. court system (43 percent). The poll also found nearly two out of three Americans (62 percent) want the United States to cooperate fully with the international body. See *America's Place in the World*. These numbers slipped in the ensuing four years but remained quite high at 64 percent favorable in the 1997 poll (*America's Place in the World*, vol. 2, 27). Other polls confirmed this view. In 1995, more people told the Chicago Council on Foreign Relations pollsters that it was important to strengthen the UN than to maintain superior U.S. military power(*American Public Opinion and U.S. Foreign Policy*, 16). According to a poll released in March 1995 by the University of Maryland's Program on Public Attitudes in Washington, D.C., the public's attitude toward UN peacekeeping can be summed up as follows. 1. The overwhelming majority of respondents support UN peacekeeping in principle. 2. The majority is ready to support spending substantially more on UN peacekeeping than the United States actually now spends. (However, this attitude may not be readily apparent because the majority imagines that the United States spends much more than it does and feels that this imagined amount is too high.) 3. A plurality is willing to substantially increase the amount they personally spend on taxes in support of UN peacekeeping. 4.The majority feels the United States should pay its UN peacekeeping dues in full.

10. See Kull et al., *Foreign Policy Gap*, 90–93.

11. See Alfred E. Eckes, *Opening America's Market: U.S. Foreign Trade Policy Since 1776* (Chapel Hill: University of North Carolina Press, 1995), 5–12.

12. The protection of American jobs was chosen as *the* most important goal for 85 percent of those Americans polled by the Times Mirror Center for the People and

the Press in November 1993, while the poll's "Influentials" put the goal in the middle of its list of priorities, in sixth place. The public has been consistently and overwhelmingly willing to impose tariffs on foreign goods to protect American jobs: 75 percent favored this option in 1987 (28 percent "strongly") and 77 percent in 1990. This figure was down to a plurality of 48 percent in the 1995 Chicago Council on Foreign Relations survey. (*America's Place in the World*, 22, and *American Public Opinion and U.S. Foreign Policy*, 29). Seventy-eight percent of those questioned in a Gallup poll in February1994 also supported new trade restrictions on Japan. See Andrew Kohut and Robert C. Toth, *Trade and the Public*, 3.

13. See Doron S. Ben-Atar, *The Origins of Jefferson's Commercial Policy and Diplomacy* (New York: St. Martin's Press, 1993), 23.

14. Their concerns are hardly chimerical. American workers have lost literally millions of high-paying manufacturing jobs during the past three decades, while those who have retained their jobs have seen their earnings decline precipitously. U.S. steel-production employment peaked in 1966 with 1,055,500 workers averaging $410 per week in constant 1982 dollars. This was 71 percent more than steelworkers had made twenty years earlier. But a quarter century later, in 1992, the average employed steelworker made less than a steelworker earned twenty years earlier. Over that time, production employment in steel fell 50 percent. In textiles and apparel the pattern was similar. Textile-production employment dropped from 886,000 jobs averaging $261.63 per week in 1973 to 580,800 earning only $246.93 in 1992. Production employment in apparel peaked in 1966 and 1973. It fell 32 percent. Average weekly wages fell 16 percent. Contractions in all three industries cost 1,227,000 jobs. From 1979 to 1991, the United Steelworkers lost 505,000 members; electronics and electrical unions, 178,000; machinist and aerospace workers, 154,000; garment workers, 171,000; clothing and textile workers, 154,000; and oil, chemical and atomic workers, $56,000. From 1985 to 1991, the UAW lost 134,000 members. See Eckes, *Opening America's Market*, 217–19.

15. See Robin Broad and John Cavanagh, "Don't Neglect the Impoverished South," *Foreign Policy* 101 (1996–97), 33.

16. See, for instance, the *U.S. News* poll of 1,000 adults designed by Celinda Lake of Lake Research and Ed Goeas of the Tarrance Group and conducted by Market Facts, TELENATION Survey, November 22–26, 1996.

17. See "The New Political Landscape," (Washington, D.C.: Times Mirror Center for the People and the Press, 1994), 129.

18. See *American Public Opinion and U.S. Foreign Policy*, 39.

19. See Julian L Simon, *Immigration: The Demographic and Economic Facts* (Washington, D.C.: Cato Institution, 1995), 3–7.

20. In a relatively trivial example, until the 1980s it was illegal even for those with proper clearance to speak the name of the National Reconnassance Office, and its existence was not officially acknowledged until 1992. The office accumulated roughly $1.5 billion in a secret bank account. It is funded by money concealed within falsified Pentagon accounts called "the black budget." It spends $6 billion a year.

21. *America's Place in the World*, vol. 2, 28.

22. Cited in William W. Keller, *Arm in Arm: The Political Economy of the Global Arms Trade* (New York: Basic Books, 1995), 12–13.

23. *American Public Opinion and U.S. Foreign Policy*, 17.

24. See John H. Cushman, "Public Backs Tough Steps for a Treaty on Warming," *New York Times*, November 28, 1997, sec. A, p. 36.

25. *America's Place in the World*, 20.

26. Ibid.

27. Cited in Richard Morin, "Who's In Control? Many Don't Know and Don't Care," *Washington Post*, January 29, 1996.

28. University of Maryland, Program on Public Attitudes, poll of 801 randomly selected adult Americans, conducted January 12–15, 1995.

29. In January 1995, 67 percent of respondents agreed with pollsters that "the United States has a moral responsibility toward poor nations to help them develop economically and improve their people's lives." See Steven Kull, "What the Public Knows that Washington Doesn't," 113.

30. *America's Place in the World*, vol 2, 16.

230 Notes to Pages 188–190

INDEX

associations. *See* civic life
Athens (Greece), lotteries in, 171–72
Atlantic Monthly (periodical), 144, 212n. 34
Atomic Energy Act (1946), 75, 79
Atomic Energy Commission, 80
atomic weapons. *See* nuclear weapons
Atwater, Lee, 130

Bagdikian, Ben, 156
Bailey, Thomas A., 23, 88–89, 195n. 3
Baker, James, 9, 144
Balkans, policy on, 135–36, 164. *See also* Albania; Armenia; Bosnia
Baltimore Evening Sun (newspaper), 163
Baltimore Sun (newspaper), 163
Bank of International Settlements, 211n. 6
Barbieri, Paula, 163
Barnes, Fred, 133–34
Barnet, Richard, 24, 31
Bauer, William, 157
Bay of Pigs, 94, 219n. 58
Beard, Charles, 61, 75–76
Belgian Congo, CIA involvement in, 83
Bentham, Jeremy, 7, 171
Benton, William, 70
Bentsen, Lloyd, 123
Bercovitch, Sacvan, 55
Berger, Samuel "Sandy," 1–2
Bessette, Joseph M., 171
Birth Defect Prevention Act, 214n. 54
Bissell, Richard, 83
Bok, Sissela, 96
Borah, William E., 61–62, 70
Bork, Robert, 90
Bosnia: Clinton's policy on, 18–19, 135–36, 164–65; public opinion on, 18–19, 135–36, 164–65; U.S. intervention in, 92, 135
Bourne, Randolph, 59, 61
Bowles, Chester, 70
Brewster, Kingman, Jr., 70
Brill, Steven, 157
Brisbane, Arthur, 49
Broder, David, 123
Bryan, William Jennings, 50–51, 106–7, 111
Brzezinski, Zbigniew, 8–9
Buchanan, Patrick, 108, 110, 124, 180
budget (U.S.): for foreign aid, 189–90; for NATO expansion, 14, 194n. 39; secrecy of, 80. *See also* economy (U.S.); tariffs
Buffalo News (newspaper), 163
Burt, Richard K., 9
Bush, George: Balkans and, 136; campaign of, 159; China relations of, 9, 147; drug smuggling and, 211n. 15; Gulf War and, 92, 133–34; manipulation and cover-ups by, 17–18, 95, 194–95n. 54, 219n. 53; Middle East policy of, 144
business interests: isolationism and, 70; trade agreements and, 121–22. *See also* corporations
Butler, Pierce, 31

Calhoun, John C., 106
California, WTO's structure and, 214n. 54
Cambodia, U.S. intervention in, 92, 95, 138, 166, 219n. 53
Campaign Study Group, 140
Canada: foreign affairs knowledge in, 193n. 31; military enforcement supported by, 1; status of, 31
Capital Cities/ABC, sale of, 156–57
capitalism: disempowerment through, 41; in Reconstruction, 45; republicanism under, 27, 29; support for, 67–68. *See also* commerce; free trade; global capitalism
Carey, James W., 68, 154
Carlyle, Thomas, 67
Carnegie Council on Ethics and International Affairs, 6, 132, 227n. 3
Carr, E. H., 63
Carter, Boake, 74
Carter, Jimmy: campaign of, 219n. 53; Cuba policy of, 150; foreign relations of, 178; Iran and, 140; Iraq and, 2; MX rail system proposed by, 133
Carville, James, 210n. 2
Casey, William, 83, 95
Castro, Fidel, 219n. 53
Catholic Register (periodical), 62
CBS Television: control of, 157, 222n. 17; news coverage by, 3, 160, 161; propaganda and, 74; sale of, 156
CCFR. *See* Chicago Council on Foreign Relations (CCFR)
censorship: in CIA, 81–82; during Cold War, 77, 83–89, 93–95; criticism of, 79–80; media's role in, 65–66; voluntary, 92–95; during war, 62–63, 84–89
Censorship Board, 62–63
Center for Political Studies (U. of Michigan), 160
Centers for Disease Control and Prevention, 118–19
Central America: drug smuggling and, 211n. 15; protest movement and, 138; public misled on, 219n. 53; U.S. expansionism in, 45. *See also* El Salvador; Guatemala; Nicaragua; Panama
Central Intelligence Agency (CIA): activities of, 80–83, 93–94, 208n. 24; budget of, 82, 207n. 12; censorship oath in, 81–82; creation of, 80; restrictions on, 207n. 16; restructuring of, 187–88; U-2 incident and, 97
Central Intelligence Group, 80
Chase Manhattan company, 140
Chaynes, Antonia, 133
Chicago Council on Foreign Relations (CCFR): on elite vs. mass opinion, 16; on foreign involvements, 227n. 4; on foreign policy opinions, 226–27n. 1, 228n. 9; on immigration, 186; on job protection, 228–29n. 12; on NAFTA, 17; on weapons sales, 188
Chicago Tribune, 50
Chicago World's Fair (1893), 46, 48
Chile, CIA involvement in, 83, 140

China: food imported from, 118; public opinion on, 225n. 50; U.S. relations with, 9, 147; workers' wages in, 105
"China lobby," 147
Chinese Americans, influence of, 147
Christianity, influence of, 58–59. *See also* Protestantism; Puritanism
Church, Frank, 150
Churchill, Winston, 71, 92–93
CIA. *See* Central Intelligence Agency (CIA)
"Citizen Genet" (Genet, Edmond-Charles-Édouard), 31–32
citizens: apathy of, 179–80; approaches to, 11–12; education for, 3–4, 12–13, 26, 33, 64, 176–77; elitist attitudes toward, 3, 6–13, 25–26, 65–69, 89, 136, 158–59, 166–67; vs. experts, 131–32, 148–49; government distrusted by, 112; information sources for, 159–67; media and, 128–29, 153; political manipulation of, 18, 194–95n. 54; questions raised by, 2–3; responsibilities of, 125–26; values of, 14–19, 181–82, 227n. 3. *See also* civic life; leaders; public opinion; voting
citizenship, definitions of, 40
civic life: associations' role in, 127–28; commitment to, 24–25; decline of, 153–54
Civil Service Commission, 86–87
Civil War: censorship during, 84; governmental effects of, 45–49; precursor to, 106; rights during, 45
Clancy, Tom, 1
Clark, Dick, 150
Clark, George Rogers, 37
Clay, Henry, 37–38
Clean Air Act, 120
Clifford, Clark, 86
Clinton, DeWitt, 37–38
Clinton, William J.: Bosnia policy of, 18–19, 135–36, 164–65; campaign of, 103, 129; cover-up by, 18; drug smuggling and, 211n. 15; on ecology, 189; economy and, 102–3; election of, 127, 216n. 11; free trade and, 105, 110–14, 118, 121–23; Haiti and, 92, 134–35, 147, 164–65; Iran and, 144; Irish question and, 146; on Mexican situation, 104; on national "town meeting," 1, 3–4; opposition to, 110; popularity of, 122–23, 167; on UN army, 183; on weapons sales, 188
Clough, Michael, 12
CNN: ads on, 157; on China relations, 225n. 50; merger of, 156; national "town meeting" broadcast by, 1–4
Cobb, Frank, 61
Codex Alimentarius Commission, 119
Cohen, Bernard C., 24
Cohen, William, 1–2
Cohn, Roy, 87–88
COINTELPRO, activities of, 87–88
Colby, William, 82
Cold War: cause of, 8; censorship during, 77, 83–89, 93–95; decision making during, 4; democracy during, 77–79, 86–89, 96–97;

effects of, 96–97, 101–2; end of, 14; ethnicity during, 141; irony of, 91; legacy of, 133–34; media's role in, 93–95; presidential power in, 89–92; public opinion on, 85–86
Commentary (periodical), 144
commerce: as basis for expansionism, 39, 44, 46; vs. democracy, 32–33; foreign policy's purpose as, 30; Spanish American War and, 50. *See also* capitalism; corporations; economy (U.S.); free trade; trade policy
Committee of Public Information, 62–63
Committee on the Present Danger, 138
Committee to Defend America by Aiding the Allies, 73
Common Sense (Paine), 24, 28
communications industry: control of, 156–58; power of, 155–56. *See also* journalism; media
Communism: fear of, 86, 87–88, 96–97; media as counter to, 93–95; role of, 78
Communist Party, 87–88, 93, 96
Conant, James B., 73
Congressional Budget Office, 114–15
Congress of Industrial Organizations (CIO), 87–88
consumers, 108, 153–55
containment policy, 77–78, 85–86, 208n. 30
"Contract with America," 110
corporations: D.C. offices of, 217n. 21; globalization of, 104; power of, 139–40, 142–43. *See also* communications industry; multinational corporations; transnational corporations (TNCs); *specific companies*
corporatism, in American identity, 77–78
Council on Foreign Relations, 12, 139, 141, 148
Court of International Trade (CIT), 108
Creek Indians, 33
Creel, George, 63
Crèvecoeur, Hector St. John de, 14
Crisis of Democracy, The (Huntington), 9–10
Croly, Herbert, 58–59, 61, 77
Crosby, Ned, 172–73
Cuba: CIA involvement in, 83, 219n. 53; intervention in, 16; Soviet troops in, 150. *See also* Bay of Pigs; Spanish American War
Cuban Americans, influence of, 145, 221n. 89
Cuban Missile Crisis, 137
Cyprus, U.S. policy on, 146

Dahl, Robert A.: on citizen panels on policy, 173; on democracy, 4n; on elections, 131, 139; on "pseudo-democratization," 151
Daily Worker (newspaper), 93
Dallek, Robert, 59
D'Amato, Alphonse, 126
Darrow, Clarence, 111
Davis, Elmer, 74
Debs, Eugene V., 62
Declaration of Independence, 55
DeConde, Alexander, 148
Dellinger, Walter E., III, 135
democracy: abroad vs. at home, 60–61; blamed for results of foreign policy, 63–64; as cause

democracy (*continued*)
of Cold War, 8; vs. commerce, 32–33; debate over, 64–69, 154, 204n. 58; definition of, 4n, 6, 10, 61, 131; degeneration of, 125–31; disillusionment with, 52–53, 63–64; vs. expertise, 131–32; foreign policy held outside of, 5–11; as ideal, 125, 152, 163; in interwar years, 69–74; jury system applied to, 172–80; majority vs. minority in, 131, 139–40, 170, 175–76; mass direct type of, 168–69; media's role in, 49–51; passion vs. reason in, 170–71. *See also* republicanism
Democratic Party: campaign money raised by, 128–29, 216nn. 16–17; on free trade and tariffs, 106–7, 123–24; secrecy policies and, 91; on tariffs and trade, 45, 110–11
democratization: failure of, 151; of foreign policy, 4–5, 14, 18–19, 62, 168–69
Destler, I. M., 224n. 40
Dewey, John: on democracy, 64, 67–69, 128, 131, 153–55, 168, 171–72; on education, 205n. 75; on foreign policy establishment, 15; on imperialism, 60–61; on individualism, 41; influences on, 26; on Lippmann, 10, 64, 153
Dewey, Thomas, 142
Diggins, John Patrick, 58, 64–65, 66
Dingell, John, 113
Dionne, E. J., 179
Disney Company, 156–57
Dole, Bob, 103, 105, 123, 132, 183
dolphins, preservation of, 119
domestic policy: vs. foreign policy, 4–5, 14–15, 102–5, 124, 181; influences on, 86; public opinion on, 126, 215n. 4
Dominican Republic, U.S. intervention in, 53, 83, 135
Dorgan, Byron, 113
draft, 45
Draper, Theodore, 82
Drucker, Peter, 104
drugs: NAFTA and, 17–18; public opinion on, 223n. 27; smuggling of, 211n. 15
Du Bois, W. E. B., 96
Dulles, Allen, 93–94
Dulles, John Foster: on Guatemalan coup, 82; on Indonesian coup, 82; on Jewish influence, 143
DuPont Corporation, 70

Eagleburger, Lawrence, 136
ecology. *See* environmental preservation
Economic Policy Institute, 212n. 34
Economist (periodical), 153
economy (U.S.): in election debates, 88; globalization's impact on, 102–5; government's role in, 112; public perception of, 109–10; stock markets and, 46, 102–4, 156–57. *See also* budget (U.S.); capitalism; commerce; free trade; trade policy
education: for citizens, 3–4, 12–13, 26, 33, 64, 176–77; Dewey's role in, 205n. 75; rationale for, 26; voting participation and, 215–16n. 9
Egypt, Israeli invasion of, 142–43

Eisenhower, Dwight D.: on Communism, 88; on Israel, 142–43; manipulation by, 97, 219n. 53; secrecy policies of, 79, 82–83, 87
Eisner, Michael D., 156–57
elections: campaign finances in, 129–31, 155, 169; campaigns for, 128–31, 136–37, 160; economy and, 103; function of, 4, 131, 139; manipulation of, 126, 144; military intervention linked to, 137; participation in, 130–31, 171–72; television coverage of, 160; trade agreements and, 121–22. *See also* voting
electoral college, function of, 171–72
Elizabeth (Queen of England), 148
El Salvador: human rights in, 162; labor reform in, 185; Reagan's use of, 149
Ely, John Hart, 31, 92
Emergency Peace Campaign, 72
England. *See* Great Britain
Entman, Robert M., 138, 154, 159, 162
environmental preservation: concerns for, 4, 101–2; GATT as challenge to, 119–20, 214n. 56; sustainable global type of, 189
Erlanger, Steven, 194n. 39
Espionage Act (1917), 62, 85
ethnicity: foreign policy influence and, 140–49; voting participation and, 215–16n. 9. *See also* Jews
Europe: anti-Semitism in, 142; elections in, 79; rejection of, 30–31, 70, 197n. 32; voting participation in, 126–27. *See also* France; Germany; Great Britain; Greece; Ireland; Italy; Russia; Soviet Union (USSR); Spain
European Union, trade with Iran and, 144
Executive Order 8381 (FDR), 72
Executive Order 12333 (Reagan), 87
Executive Order 12356 (Reagan), 80
expansionism: as destiny, 41–43; as exploitation, 50–51, 200n. 96; frontier thesis and, 46–48; Jefferson's concept of, 34–37, 44; means of, 44, 46, 182; Monroe Doctrine as, 38–39; rationale for, 53–58. *See also* free trade; imperialism

Fairness Doctrine, abolished, 156
Fallows, James, 212n. 34
Fascell, Dante, 150
Faux, Jeff, 212n. 34
Fazio, Vince, 116
FDA (Food and Drug Administration), 118
FDR. *See* Roosevelt, Franklin D. (FDR)
Federal Bureau of Investigation (FBI), 85–88
Federal Communications Act (1934), 93
Federal Election Commission, 128–29, 217n. 21
Federal Employees Program, 86–87
federal government: Civil War's impact on, 45–49; debate over, 25; lying by, 166–67, 224–25n. 48; pre-Civil War characteristics of, 44–45; WTO as challenge to, 116–17, 213n. 49
Federal Humane Slaughter Act, 120
Federalists: categorization of, 196n. 22; on definition of America, 28; goals of, 25, 27, 31; on navy expansion, 30

Great Britain: foreign affairs knowledge in, 193n. 31; media in, 153; military enforcement supported by, 1; Monroe Doctrine and, 38; trade policy of, 109; U.S. relations with, 31–32, 72, 73, 148; virtual representation in, 27–28; voting participation in, 126; in War of 1812, 37–38

Greece: lotteries in ancient, 171–72; support for, 146

Greek Americans, influence of, 146

Greenfield, Meg, 113

Greenspan, Alan, 103, 211n. 6

Greer (U.S. destroyer), 73

Grenada, U.S. intervention in, 9, 92, 135

Grossman, Lawrence K., 157

Gruson, Sidney, 93–94

Guatemala: CIA involvement in, 82–83, 94, 140, 219n. 53; food imported from, 118

Guinier, Lani, 175

Gulf War, 92, 95, 133–34

Gunther, Marc, 157

Gutman, Herbert, 61

Haass, Richard N., 9

Habermas, Jürgen, 131–32, 153, 154, 171–72, 218n. 32

Hacker, Andrew, 173–74

Haiti: customs duties in, 200n. 94; slave rebellion in, 36; U.S. intervention in, 53, 92, 134–35; U.S. policy on, 147, 164–65

Hamilton, Alexander: on electoral candidates, 171; goals of, 25, 51; influences on, 55; newspaper founded by, 42; on passion vs. reason, 170–71; on representation, 66, 169; on Revolution, 29–30; strategies of, 35; on tariffs, 106; on war powers, 31. *See also* Federalists

Hamilton, Lee, 135

Harbury, Jennifer, 83

Hard Copy (TV program), 153

Harper's (periodical), 210n. 69

Harris poll, on domestic politics, 126, 215n. 4

Hartz, Louis, 78

Harvard University, restrictions on, 87–88

Havel, Vaclav, 125, 172

Hay, John, 47–48

Haymarket Square Riot (1886), 57–58

Hearst, William Randolph, 49

Hegel, G. W. F., 44

Heritage Foundation, 138

Hersh, Seymour M., 161

Hightower, Jim, 157

"Hightower Radio" (radio program), 157

Hilsman, Roger, 137

Hiss, Alger, 89

Hitler, Adolf, 142

Hoffmann, Stanley, 103

Hofstadter, Richard, 200n. 96

Hollings, Ernest, 122

Holmes, Oliver Wendell, 85

Holocaust, 142, 145

Hoover, J. Edgar, 87–88

Hoover Institution (Stanford U.), 138

House, Col. Edward M., 53

House Foreign Relations Committee, 135

Houston Post (newspaper), 163

How to Spot a Communist (pamphlet), 96

Hufbauer, Gary, 212n. 39

human rights policy: enforcement of, 2–3; public opinion on, 225n. 50, 227n. 4; reporting on, 162

Huntington, Samuel, 9–10

Hussein, Saddam, 1–2

Hutcheson, Francis, 196n. 22

Hutchins, Robert, 70

IBM Corporation, 105

"imagined community," in revolutionary America, 37, 199n. 64

immigration: expansionism and, 42; fears of, 16, 56–58, 59; legislation on, 64, 146; NAFTA and, 111–12; strategy for controlling, 186–87

imperialism: growth of, 50–51; rationale for, 60–61. *See also* expansionism

income tax, 45

Indian Arts and Crafts Board, 79

Indians. *See* Native Americans

individualism, concept of, 41, 46–48

Indonesia: CIA involvement in, 83; labor reform in, 186

industrialization, political impact of, 41

Influence of Sea Power on History, The (Mahan), 45–46

Inman, Bobby, 95

International Campaign to Ban Landmines, 148

internationalism, free trade component in, 108

International Labor Organization, 185

International Monetary Fund, 104, 114, 211n. 6

International Socialist Review (periodical), 62

International Trade Administration (ITA), 108

International Trade Commission (ITC), 108

Interstate Commerce Commission, 107

IRA (Irish Republican Army), 146

Iran: CIA involvement in, 82–83, 93–94, 219n. 53; Shah's overthrow in, 140; trade with, 144; weapons sales to, 17, 95, 159, 161, 219n. 53, 223n. 32

Iraq: in Gulf War, 133–34; motives of, 95; possible attack on (1998), 1–4

Ireland, status of, 62, 146

Irish Americans, influence of, 146

Irish Republican Army (IRA), 146

isolationism: effect of, 72, 96; rejection of, 71; strategies of, 70–71; support for, 70, 164–65, 224n. 38

Israel: founding of, 142; invasion by, 142–43; media used by, 145; recognition of, 221n. 85; support for, 143–45; U.S. policy on, 141–42

ITA (International Trade Administration), 108

Italy: civic life in, 127; foreign affairs knowledge in, 193n. 31; workers' wages in, 105

ITC (International Trade Commission), 108

ITT World Communications, 93, 140

Jackson, Andrew, 40
Jackson, Jesse, 110
James, Philip, 119
James, William, 50
Japan: attack by, 70–71; attitudes toward, 16;
    elections in, 79; League of Nations and, 63;
    protectorate over Korea, 53; workers' wages
    in, 105
Jay, John, 32–33, 147–48
Jefferson, Thomas: on European influence, 70;
    foreign policy of, 33–37, 44, 51; on free trade,
    105, 184–85; navy used by, 209n. 49; opposi-
    tion to, 46, 58; on Revolution, 29; on right to
    property, 34–36; vision of, 66, 169; on war,
    30–31. See also anti-Federalists
Jefferson Center for New Democratic
    Processes, 172–73
Jeffersonians. See anti-Federalists
Jews: advantages of, 144–45; genocide of, 142,
    145; influence of, 140–44, 151
jobs, as foreign policy issue, 15, 16, 18. See also
    workers
Johnson, Hiram W., 70
Johnson, Lyndon B., 72–73, 91–92, 136, 138
journalism: changing context of, 112–13; on
    corruption, 95; new form of coverage in, 69;
    paradox of, 154–55; propaganda and, 73–74;
    restrictions on, 84–89, 93; shortcomings of,
    65–66; untruth in, 158–62. See also censorship;
    media; newspapers
Journal of Democracy, 5
Judd, Charles, 131
judiciary, depoliticization of, 169
jury system, as blueprint for alternative, 172–80

Kalb, Bernard, 193n. 25
Kaltenborn, H. V., 74
Kansas, voting in, 126
Kantor, Mickey, 116, 118, 119
Kaptur, Marci, 113–14
Keeter, Scott, 130
Kennan, George F., 7–8, 26, 71, 78, 139
Kennedy, John F., 94, 97, 136, 137, 219n. 53,
    219n. 58
Kentucky, nullification resolution in, 84
Kettering Foundation, 13, 126, 165
Key, V. O., 153
Khrushchev, Nikita, 97
Kirkland, Lance, 112
Kissinger, Henry: on environment, 102; on Gulf
    War, 133; influences on, 10; on public opin-
    ion, 136–37; Rhodesia and, 147; terminology
    of, 46, 149; Vietnam War and, 17
Kodak Camera company, 45
Koestler, Arthur, 163
Kohut, Andrew, 224n. 38, 226–27n. 1
Kondracke, Morton, 134
Koop, Theodore F., 93
Korea: information censored on, 94; Japanese
    protectorate over, 53; U.S. intervention in,
    90–91, 96–97. See also South Korea
Kramnick, Isaac, 196n. 22

Kraslow, David, 97
Krauthammer, Charles, 134, 145
Kull, Steven, 224n. 40, 226–27n. 1

labor movement: in Cold War, 96; NAFTA and,
    112; revival of, 122–23. See also workers
LaFeber, Walter, 5, 42, 181
LaFollette, Robert, 61–62
Lamumba, Patrice, 83
Langer, William, 87
Laos, secret war in, 79, 83
Lasch, Christopher, 177
Latin America, U.S. intervention in, 53–54, 79,
    140. See also Chile; Cuba; Dominican Repub-
    lic; El Salvador; Guatemala; Haiti; Mexico;
    Nicaragua; Panama
lawyers, number of, 217n. 21
leaders: function of, 170; support for, 137; trust
    in, 97, 126, 215n. 4
League of Nations, 63–64, 202n. 10
League of United Latin American Citizens, 146
Lebanon, U.S. intervention in, 92
Levi, Edward, 87
Levi Strauss Corporation, 186
Lewis, Anthony, 123
LG Electronics, 104
liberal republicanism: Adams on, 39–40;
    applied to foreign policy, 182–90; concept of,
    27–29, 181–82; racism in, 56
liberty, concept of, 26–27, 34–35
Limbaugh, Rush, 153, 163–64
Lincoln, Abraham, 43, 45, 58
Lind, Michael, 217n. 21
Lindbergh, Charles, 73
Lippmann, Walter: on access to information,
    172, 177; on democracy, 64–69, 75–76, 204n.
    58; on governance by experts, 149, 173; influ-
    ences on, 26; on media, 153; on
    progressivism, 60, 61; on public opinion, 7–8,
    10, 77, 153
Lipset, Seymour Martin, 145
Lloyd-LaFollette Act (1913), 83
lobbyists: impact of, 13; military contractors as,
    140; NGOs' relation with, 149; registration of,
    217n. 21; strategies of, 130–31; trade agree-
    ments and, 109, 122
Locke, John, 7, 26–27, 64, 105, 192n. 14
Lodge, Henry Cabot, 63, 82
Los Angeles Times (newspaper): downsizing by,
    163; free trade debate and, 112–13; on Iran-
    Contra scandal, 161, 223n. 32
Louisiana Purchase, 33–37, 44, 51
Louisville Courier-Journal, 58
Love, Kenneth, 93
Loyalty Review Board, 86–87
Luce, Henry, 73, 74
Ludlow, Louis, 71
Ludwig (King of Bavaria), 57
luxury, republican fear of, 28–29

McCarran Act (1950), 87
McCarthy, Joseph, 87–88, 89, 159

McCloy, John J., 140
McHenry, Donald, 8, 192n. 21
Machiavelli, Niccolo, 25, 27, 64
McKinley, William: assassination of, 57; campaign of, 106–7; on expansionism, 48; on Philippines, 55; Spanish American War and, 49–50
McMahon/Atomic Energy Act (1946), 75, 79
Madison, James: attitudes of, 7, 66; on common people, 25–26; on expansionism, 36; on free trade, 106; on minority rights, 131; power of, 209n. 49; on representation, 28, 149, 169–70; on republicanism, 29, 196n. 22; on war, 30–31; in War of 1812, 37–38, 44
Mahan, Alfred Thayer, 45–48
Maine (battleship), 49–50, 200–201n. 102, 201n. 6
Malvinas/Falklands War, 148
Mandela, Nelson, 172
Manhattan Project, 75
Manifest Destiny, 42, 50–51. *See also* expansionism
Mansfield, Mike, 81
Marine Mammal Protection Act, 214n. 56
Markel, Lester, 94
Marshall Plan, 85–86
Martineau, Harriet, 40
mass direct democracy, 168–69
Masses, The (periodical), 62
Matthews, David, 165
Mayaguez incident, 219n. 53
media: campaigns conducted through, 128–30; censorship and, 65–66; Cold War and, 93–95; control of, 156–58; declining foreign-news coverage in, 162; democracy and, 49–51; downsizing in, 162–63; economic interests of, 155–56; Fairness Doctrine abolished in, 156; on free trade, 108–13, 121–22; role of, 9, 49–51, 68, 152–55, 156–57; shortcomings of, 13–14, 153–54, 160–61, 162–64; sources for, 158–59; Spanish American War and, 49–51; untruth in, 158–62; variety of, 153; workings of, 149. *See also* censorship; journalism; television
Melville, Herman, 43, 55
Metro-Goldwyn-Mayer (MGM), 74
Mexican Americans, influence of, 145–46
Mexican War, 42–44
Mexico: DEA officers killed in, 17–18; drug smuggling and, 211n. 15; economy of, 104, 211n. 6; food imported from, 118; foreign affairs knowledge of, 193n. 31; trade agreements and, 111–12, 114–15, 121–22, 212n. 39; U.S. annexation of, 41–42, 51; U.S. intervention in, 53, 54, 59–60; U.S. manufacturing in, 115. *See also* Mexican War
MGM (Metro-Goldwyn-Mayer), 74
Miami Herald (newspaper), 163
microbreweries, GATT's impact on, 213n. 49
Middle East policy, influences on, 140, 142–47. *See also* Iran; Iraq; Israel; Persian Gulf War; Saudi Arabia
Migratory Bird Conservation Commission, 79

military intervention: as last resort, 182–84; opposition to, 181, 224n. 40; as "police action," 135, 178; public opinion on, 16–17, 137–38, 194n. 49; support for, 137–38; timing of, 137. *See also* war; weapons sales
Mill, James, 7
Mill, John Stuart, 33, 95, 171
Miller, Perry, 54–55
Miller, Robert, 94
ministers/ambassadors, limited number of, 30, 197n. 32
Minneapolis Star-Tribune (newspaper), 155
Minnesota, GATT's impact on, 213n. 49
Mitterrand, François, 102
Mobil Corporation, 110
Mobutu Sese Seko, 221n. 85
modernization, Christianity as precondition for, 48
Monroe, James, 36, 38–39, 44
Monroe Doctrine, 38–39, 200n. 94
Montesquieu, Baron de La Brède et de (Charles-Louis de Secondat), 105
Montgomery bus boycott, 87
Montreal Protocol, 189
Morgan, John Pierpont, 49
Morganthau, Hans, 10–11
Mossedeq, Mohammed, 82
Mother Jones (periodical), 210n. 69
Motion Picture Committee Cooperating for National Defense, 74
movie industry, government use of, 73–74
Moynihan, Daniel P., 134, 208n. 24
Muhlenberg, Frederick, 32
multiculturalism, 12, 140–42
multinational corporations, development of, 45
Murdoch, Rupert, 144
Murphy, Thomas S., 156
Murray, Philip, 88
Murrow, Edward R., 74

NAACP (National Association for the Advancement of Colored People), 87
Nader, Ralph, 6, 110, 152
NAFTA (North American Free Trade Agreement): attitudes toward, 16, 17–18; debate over, 110–13, 146; drug smuggling and, 211n. 15; effects of, 109, 115, 120–24, 212–13n. 40; food safety laws and, 118–19; goals of, 114–15; labor reform and, 185; media coverage of, 13–14; passage of, 112–13; support for, 121–22
Napoleon I (Napoleon Bonaparte), 36
National Association for the Advancement of Colored People (NAACP), 87
National Association of Arab Americans, 145
National Association of Manufacturers, 50
National Council of La Raza, 146
National Cuban American Foundation, 145, 221n. 89
National Issues Convention (1996), 8, 14–15, 176
National Issues Forum, 13, 14–16

Pew Foundation (*continued*)
mass vs. elite opinion, 16–17; on NAFTA, 123–24
Pforzheimer, Walter, 80
Philippines: killings in, 55; U.S. annexation of, 48, 50
Phillips, Kevin, 176
Phocion, 40. *See also* Adams, John Quincy
policy: citizens' knowledge of, 11; development of, 130–31; "foreign" vs. "domestic," 4–5, 14–15, 102–5, 124, 181; "gray areas" in, 176; jury system applied to, 173; media sources on, 158–59. *See also* domestic policy; foreign policy
political action committees (PACs), 129, 217n. 21
politics: attitudes toward, 126, 128, 215n. 4; as career, 40–41; of foreign policy, 139–40, 149–51; in interwar years, 69–74; money's role in, 174–75; Populist movement and, 57–58; progressivism in, 56, 58–63; stable values of, 181–82, 227n. 3; strategies in, 6, 18, 149–50, 194–95n. 54; terminology in, 55–56
Polk, James K., 42–44, 200n. 87
polling, methodology of, 165–66. *See also* public opinion
polyarchy, definition of, 4n
Populist movement, 57–58, 106–7
Porter, Bruce, 63
Portillo, Lopez, 145–46
Potsdam conference, 93
Powell, Gen. Colin, 134
Powers, Francis Gary, 97
presidents: Constitution subverted by, 36, 37; cover-ups by, 17–18; executive agreements made by, 205–6n. 88; lying by, 224–25n. 48; manipulation by, 136–37; power of, 31, 34, 52–53, 168–69, 177–78; responsibilities of, 8–9; strategies of, 125–26, 149, 151; treaty negotiations by, 32–33, 122–24; war-making power of, 42–44, 71–72, 89–92, 133–35, 182. *See also specific presidents*
preventive detention, 87
Program on Public Attitudes (U. of Maryland), 190, 226–27n. 1, 228n. 9, 230n. 28
progressivism: characteristics of, 52–53, 56, 59; free trade in, 107; isolationism and, 70; League of Nations and, 63–64; political impact of, 56, 58–63
Promise of American Life (Croly), 58–59
propaganda, 73–74, 94
property, right to, 34–36, 46–47
Proposition 65 (Calif.), 214n. 54
Protestantism: expansionism and, 41–42, 48–49; liberty and, 27; Revolution and, 29–30. *See also* Puritanism
Public and Its Problems, The (Dewey), 67
public health: GATT as challenge to, 118–20, 214n. 54; secrecy's impact on, 80
public opinion: on Balkans, 135–36, 164; blamed for results of foreign policy, 63–64; on China, 225n. 50; on Cold War, 85–86; on

covert action, 187–88; data on, 24, 164–67; definition of, 23, 65, 165–66; deliberative poll of, 172–73; dismissed by foreign policy experts, 3, 6–11, 177; on domestic policy, 126, 215n. 4; on drugs, 223n. 27; on ecology, 189; on foreign aid, 189–90; on foreign involvements, 182–84, 227n. 4, 228n. 5; on foreign policy impact, 14–16; on free trade, 109–10, 121–23, 184–86; on human rights policy, 225n. 50, 227n. 4; on immigration, 186–87; influences on, 63, 65, 71–74; on Iran-Contra scandal, 161–62, 223n. 32; on isolationism, 70, 164–65, 224n. 38; on lying, 224–25n. 48; on military intervention, 16–17, 137–38, 194n. 49; on NATO, 9, 167; on peace, 182–84; on possible attack on Iraq (1998), 1–4; on protecting jobs, 228–29n. 12; shortcomings of, 6, 16, 18; stability of, 13, 181–82; utilization of, 171, 226–27n. 1; on Vietnam War, 15–16, 87, 138; on weapons sales, 188. *See also* citizens; civic life
Public Opinion (Lippmann), 10, 64, 173
public sphere: concept of, 132, 218n. 32; creation of deliberative, 172–80
"public's right to know," 154
Pulitzer, Joseph, 49
Pullman, George Mortimer, 49
Puritanism, effects of, 54–55
Putnam, Robert, 127–28, 216n. 14
Puttnam, Hilary, 69

Raab, Earl, 145
Rabin, Yitzhak, 145
"race suicide," 57
racism: in early Republic, 37; immigration and, 56–57; in liberal republicanism, 56; Mexican War and, 42; Spanish American War and, 50
raison d'état (Kissinger), 46
Ramsay, Clay, 224n. 40
Rather, Dan, 3, 161
Rawls, John, 156
RCA Global, 93
Reagan, Ronald: communications companies and, 155–56; election of, 216n. 11; foreign relations of, 178–79; on free trade, 109; Grenada invasion and, 9, 92, 135; influences on, 29–30, 55; manipulation by, 87, 194–95n. 54, 219n. 53; protest movement and, 138; secrecy policies of, 80, 83; strategies of, 149; weapons sales by, 17, 143, 159, 223n. 32
Realpolitik, use of term, 200n. 92
regulation, development of, 44–45
Religious Congress (1893), 48
republicanism: as alternative to direct democracy, 168–69; concept of, 25–27, 179, 195n. 11; decline of, 40–42, 51; elements of, 28–29, 64, 70; jury system applied to, 172–80; passion vs. reason in, 170–71; representation in, 28, 169–70; war feared in, 34, 37, 43
Republican Party: campaign money raised by, 128–29, 216nn. 16–17; "Contract with America" of, 110; secrecy policies and, 79, 91; talk

radio and, 164; on tariffs and trade, 45, 106–8, 110–11, 124

Revolution (American): common people in, 24; European politics rejected after, 29–31; foreign policy after, 24–25; "imagined community" in, 37, 199n. 64; peace treaty for, 31

Rhodesia, U.S. policy on, 147

Rielly, John E., 226–27n. 1

rights: context for exercising, 124; foreign policy excluded from, 7–8; of government, 97; majority vs. minority, 131, 139–40, 170, 175–76; under NAFTA, 115; public's, to know, 154; secrecy's impact on, 79–80; during war, 45, 52, 62–63, 71–72; of workers, 184–86. *See also* free speech; property

Robinson, Michael, 160

Robinson, Randall, 147

Rockefeller, David, 140

Rockefeller, John D., 49

Rockefeller, Nelson, 82

Rodrik, Dani, 109

Rojecki, Andrew, 138

Rollins, Ed, 130

Roosevelt, Franklin D. (FDR): censorship by, 92–93; election of, 70, 71, 72–73; FBI investigations and, 86–87; foreign policy of, 17, 52, 70–75; frontier thesis and, 48; Holocaust and, 142; manipulation by, 73–74, 206n. 92, 219n. 53; secrecy policies of, 72–75, 78, 89, 91

Roosevelt, Theodore (TR): foreign policy of, 52, 53–54, 59; influences on, 47, 59, 142; on lynching, 57; on public opinion, 53; on tariffs, 107; on war, 50–51, 54

Rorty, Richard, 168

Rosenberg, Emily R., 132

Rosenthal, A. M., 145

Rousseau, Jean-Jacques, 7, 174

Rowe, James T., 86

Rusk, Dean, 89, 94

Russett, Bruce, 136, 137

Russia: anti-Semitism in, 141–42; expansionism of, 38; knowledge about, 167; U.S. intervention in, 53. *See also* Soviet Union (USSR)

Russian Research Center (Harvard University), 8

Russo-Japanese War, 59, 141–42

Rwanda, genocide in, 135, 165

safety laws, GATT as challenge to, 117–19

Safire, William, 145, 149

Salt Lake City Tribune, 133

Saltonstall, Leverett, 81

Sandel, Michael, 27, 41

San Francisco Commonwealth Club, 48

Santo Domingo, custom houses in, 53

Sarnoff, David, 94

Saturday Evening Post (periodical), 63

Saudi Arabia: dissidents tortured by, 2; military support for, 16, 194n. 49; weapons sales to, 143

Schenck v. United States, 85

Schiff, Jacob H., 141

Schlesinger, Arthur, Jr., 10, 209n. 49

Schlesinger, Stephen, 208n. 21

Schmidt, Helmut, 178–79

Schrecker, Ellen W., 96

Schwarzkopf, Gen. Norman, 134

scope of conflict, use of term, 13

Sears, labor policy of, 186

sea turtles, preservation of, 119–20

Sea Turtles Act, 120

secretary of state, power/role of, 53

Sedition Act (1798), 33, 84

Sedition Act (1918), 62, 84–85

self-government: concept of, 25–26; inadequacy of, 40–41; rationale for, 26–27, 67. *See also* democracy; republicanism

Senate Armed Services Committee, 81

Senate Foreign Relations Committee, 135, 150

Senate Intelligence Committee, 208n. 24

Senate Munitions Committee, 72

"Seven Sisters" (oil companies), 142–43

Shapiro, Robert Y., 13, 166

Shaw, Bernard, "Bernie", 3

Sheehan, Margaret, 160

Shields, Mark, 113

Al-Shiraa (Lebanese weekly), 159

shrimp, imports of, 119–20

Simpson, O. J., 163, 174

Singer Sewing Machine company, 45

Sinn Fein, negotiations with, 146

60 Minutes (TV program), 157, 222n. 17

Small, Melvin, 23, 42

Smith, Adam, 105

Smith, Larry, 221n. 85

Smith, William French, 87

Smith Act (1940), 88

Smoot-Hawley Tariff (1931), 107–8, 110, 212n. 24

social class, voting participation and, 126–27, 215–16n. 9

social contract, concept of, 27

social sciences, reform through, 56, 67–68

society, productive class vs. state in, 34–35. *See also* civic life

Somalia, soldiers in, 164, 183

South Africa: protest movement and, 138; U.S. policy on, 147

South America: CIA involvement in, 83, 140; food imported from, 118; U.S. interests in, 39, 45; U.S. intervention in, 60. *See also* Malvinas/Falklands War

South Carolina, "Tariff of Abominations" and, 106

Southern Christian Leadership Coalition, 87

South Korea: military support for, 16, 194n. 49; workers' wages in, 105

sovereignty, vs. free trade, 110–11

Soviet Union (USSR): blamed for Cold War, 8; duplicity of, 89; expansionism of, 78; Korean situation and, 90–91; as military threat, 88–89; revolution in, 102; troop deployment by, 150. *See also* Cold War; Russia

Spain: foreign affairs knowledge in, 193n. 31; Louisiana Purchase and, 36; negotiations with, 39; Spanish American War and, 50–51

Spanish American War: effects of, 48, 59; expansionism in, 49–51; *Maine* incident in, 49–50, 200–201n. 102, 201n. 6
Spartacist League, 2
special-interest groups: influence of, 138–39; system for countering, 172–80. *See also* antiwar movement; corporations; lobbyists; political action committees (PACs)
spectator theory of knowledge, 68
Springer, Jerry, 153
Sri Lanka, labor reform in, 185–86
Stafford, Gen. Thomas, 133
Stalin, Joseph, 8, 88, 92–93
Standard Oil Company, 45, 70
Stanford University, Hoover Institution, 138
Stanton, Edward, 84
state: definition of, 44; vs. productive class, 34–35
state government: food safety laws and, 118; WTO as challenge to, 116–17, 213n. 49, 214n. 54. *See also specific states*
Steel, Ronald, 200n. 92
Stephanson, Anders, 51
Stevenson, Adlai, 88
stock markets, 46, 102–4, 156–57
Stuart, R. Douglas, Jr., 70
suffrage. *See* voting
Sukarno, Achmed, 82–83
Sulzberger, Arthur, 93–94
Sweeney, John, 122
Swing, Raymond, 74

Taft, Robert A., 90
Taft, William Howard, 107, 142, 201n. 1
Talbott, Strobe, 9
talk radio, 163–64
Talleyrand-Périgord, Charles-Maurice de, 36
Tamraz, Roger, 129
Tariff Commission, 107
"Tariff of Abominations," 106
tariffs: attitudes toward, 16, 106; effects of, 109, 184–85; in Reconstruction, 45; significance of, 106–7; superceded by quotas, 108
Taussig, Frank, 109
taxes: GATT's impact on, 117; on income, 45; on microbreweries, 213n. 49
Taylor, Gen. Maxwell, 9, 193n. 25
technology, support for, 67–68. *See also* media
Teeley, Peter, 159
television: effects of, 128; interests of, 155–56; manufacturers of, 104; news coverage by, 160, 162–63. *See also specific networks*
Tet Offensive, 94–95
Texas, annexation of, 41–42
Thailand, food imported from, 118
Thomas, Norman, 70
Tiananmen Square (China), 9, 147, 225n. 50
Time (periodical): on China relations, 225n. 50; influence on, 145; on Iran-Contra scandal, 161; on national "town meeting," 3
Times Mirror: on Balkans, 135–36; on foreign policy opinions, 226–27n. 1, 228n. 5, 228n. 9;

on free trade, 121–22; on job protection, 228–29n. 12; on mass vs. elite opinion, 16–17
Time Warner company, 156–57
Tocqueville, Alexis de: on aristocracy vs. democracy, 127, 179–80; on foreign policy, 5; on individualism, 40–41; on media and democracy, 49; on presidential power, 42; on war, 61
Today (TV program), 157
Tonkin Gulf incident (1964), 73, 91, 138
TR. *See* Roosevelt, Theodore (TR)
Trade Agreements Act (1934), 108
trade policy: debates over, 110–14; emphasis on, 140; implications of accords, 4, 18; influences on, 102–5, 144; in poll questions, 225n. 50. *See also* capitalism; commerce; free trade; tariffs
Trading with the Enemy Act, 85
TransAfrica (organization), 147
transnational corporations (TNCs), 104–5, 111, 122
treason, fears of, 83–84
treaties (general), 32–33, 114, 122–24
Treaty of Ghent, 41
Treaty of Guadeloupe Hidalgo, 200n. 87
Treaty of Versailles, 63–64
Tribe, Lawrence, 114
Trilateral Commission, 9–10
Trotskyites (Spartacist League), 2
Truman, Harry S.: atom bomb and, 75; beliefs of, 132; censorship by, 93; containment policy of, 77–78, 85–86, 208n. 30; domestic policies of, 86; election of, 86–87, 208n. 30; free trade and, 114; Israel supported by, 142; on Korean situation, 90–91, 96; manipulation by, 219n. 53; secrecy policies of, 78–80; on Soviet Union, 89
Truman Doctrine (containment policy), 77–78, 85–86, 208n. 30
Trump, Donald, 153
tuna, imports of, 214n. 56
Turkey: bombing by, 2; U.S. policy on, 146
Turner, Frederick Jackson, 46–48

UAW (United Auto Workers), 229n. 14
Ulam, Adam, 8
Underwood Tariff (1913), 107, 212n. 24
Union Carbide Company, 70
United Auto Workers (UAW), 229n. 14
United Fruit Company, 139, 140
United Kingdom. *See* Great Britain; Ireland
United Nations: inspections by, 1; peace enforced by, 182–84, 228n. 7, 228n. 9; public expectations of, 18–19; treaty for, 114; U.S. debts to, 164
UN Center on Transnational Corporations, 104
UN Security Council, 90–91
United Parcel Service (UPS), 122
United States: debate over self-definition of, 28; elite vs. mass values in, 15–16; growth of, 38; idealization of, 61, 75–76; possible attack by, 1–4. *See also* U.S. Congress; U.S. Constitution

U.S. Air Force, 133
U.S. Commerce Department, 108
U.S. Congress: Balkans and, 135–36; on campaign finance system, 129–31; CIA and, 81–83; citizens' distance from, 40–41; on foreign aid, 190; Founders' intent for, 169–71; Gulf War and, 134; Haiti and, 134–35; jury system compared to, 174, 176, 177–78; Korean situation and, 90–91; Mexican War and, 42–43; nuclear freeze by, 138; power of, 150–51, 169, 177–78; on secrecy, 79; Spanish American War and, 50; tariffs used by, 106–8; trade agreements and, 113–14, 122–24; treaty approval process in, 114; trust in, 215n. 4; Vietnam War and, 91–92; war powers of, 71, 170. *See also* various committees under House and Senate
U.S. Constitution: GATT provisions and, 117; interpretations of, 72, 168–71; Louisiana Purchase and, 36, 44; vs. secrecy, 77–81; subversion of, 36, 37, 44, 51; on treaties, 32; on war, 30–31, 43, 74–75, 89–90, 135, 209n. 49. *See also* rights
U.S. Department of Energy, 75
U.S. Justice Department, 86–88
U.S. Navy: deployment of, 53, 72; growth of, 30, 45–47
U.S. News and World Report (periodical), 144, 212n. 34
U.S. Post Office, 62, 84–85
U.S. Public Health Service, 80
U.S. State Department: attitudes in, 142, 158–59; informer in, 83; recruitment by, 12
U.S. Supreme Court: on CIA censorship oath, 81; on executive agreements, 205–6n. 88; on money and speech, 169
United States v. Belmont, 205–6n. 88
U.S. War Department: confidential papers of, 62, 72; habeus corpus and, 45
United Steelworkers, 229n. 14
University of Maryland, Program on Public Attitudes, 190, 226–27n. 1, 228n. 9, 230n. 28
University of Michigan, Center for Political Studies, 160
uranium miners, exposure of, 80
USSR. *See* Soviet Union (USSR)
USTR (Office of the U.S. Trade Representative), 108
U-2 incident, 97, 219n. 53

Vance, Cyrus, 11–12
Verba, Sidney, 6, 165
Vietnam War: drug smuggling during, 211n. 15; elections during, 4; expansion of, 17; impact of, 11–12; media during, 94–95; peace talks on, 137; presidential power in, 91–92; protest movement's impact on, 138; public misled on, 219n. 53; public opinion on, 15–16, 87, 138
Village Voice (periodical), 156–57
Virginia: land ownership in, 34; nullification resolution in, 84

virtual representation: effects of, 41–42, 57, 121; repudiation of, 27–28
voting: declining interest in, 59, 126–27, 130–31, 154, 215–16n. 9; eligibility for, 40, 195n. 7; foreign policy and, 24; influences on, 65–66, 175; proportional type of, 175–76. *See also* citizens; elections

Walker, Martin, 211n. 6, 212–13n. 40
Walker, Robert J., 41–42
Wallace, Henry, 86, 208n. 30
Wall Street Journal (newspaper): on fast-track negotiations, 123; on free trade, 110; on telecommunications bill, 155; on trade with Iran, 144
war: censorship during, 62–63, 84–89; congressional powers of, 71, 171; Constitution on, 30–31, 43, 74–75, 89–90, 135, 209n. 49; presidential power of, 42–44, 71–72, 89–92, 133–35, 182; public demand for, 49–50; rationale for, 50–51; repudiation of, 34, 37, 43, 53, 70, 72–73, 181; rights during, 45, 52, 62–63, 71–72; secrecy in, 78–79. *See also* Civil War; Malvinas / Falklands War; Mexican War; Persian Gulf War; Revolution (American); Spanish American War; War of 1812; World War I; World War II
Warhol, Andy, 153
Warner Brothers, 74, 157
War of 1812, 37–38, 44
War Powers Act (1973), 92
Warren, James, 26
Washington, D.C., Bar Association, 217n. 21
Washington, George: on commerce, 105; on European politics, 30; on expansionism, 39; foreign relations under, 31–33; on missionary impulse, 55; Wilson's use of, 54, 202n. 10
Washington Post Company, 155
Washington Post (newspaper): on China relations, 225n. 50; on fast-track negotiations, 123; free trade and, 110, 113; influences on, 145, 155; poll by, 165
Watergate affair, 159
Waters, John P., 17
Watterson, Henry, 58
Wealth of Nations, The (Smith), 105
weapons sales: to Iran, 17, 95, 159, 161, 219n. 53, 223n. 32; rationale for, 140; reduction of, 188; to Saudi Arabia, 143
Weber, Max, 131
Weekly Standard (periodical), 144
Weekly Star (periodical), 153
Weil, Martin, 146–47
Weinberger, Caspar, 148
Weissman, Stephan, 150
Welch, John, 157
Western Union International, 93
Westinghouse Electric Corporation, 156
Weymouth, Lally, 145
White, Walter, 96
White, William Allen, 73
Whitman, Walt, 43